MW01000876

IGNITING THE INTERNET

IGNITING THE INTERNET

Youth and Activism in Postauthoritarian South Korea

Jiyeon Kang

University of Hawai'i Press
Honolulu

© 2016 University of Hawai'i Press
All rights reserved
Printed in the United States of America
21 20 19 18 17 16   6 5 4 3 2 1

Library of Congress Cataloging-in-Publication Data
Names: Kang, Jiyeon, author.
Title: Igniting the Internet : youth and activism in
   postauthoritarian South Korea / Jiyeon Kang.
Description: Honolulu : University of Hawai'i Press,
[2016] | Includes bibliographical references and index.
Identifiers: LCCN 2015045227 |
ISBN 9780824856564 hardcover : alk. paper
Subjects: LCSH: Internet and youth—Political aspects—
Korea (South) | Youth—Political activity—Korea (South) |
Political participation—Technological innovations—
Korea (South) | Information technology—
Political aspects—Korea (South)
Classification: LCC HQ799.2.I58 K36 2016 |
DDC 320.40835/095195—dc23
LC record available at http://lccn.loc.gov/2015045227

*Publication of this volume has been assisted by a grant
from the Association for Asian Studies.*

University of Hawai'i Press books are printed on acid-free
paper and meet the guidelines for permanence and durability
of the Council on Library Resources.

Contents

Acknowledgments

When I first encountered the online phenomenon in 2002 that later became the topic of this book, I did not imagine that it would stay with me for over ten years—or that I would receive this much support from so many around me and from those I met during the research process itself.

About half of this book is based on research I conducted as a graduate student at the University of Illinois at Urbana–Champaign. Cara Finnegan was an ideal mentor for such an unorthodox rhetoric dissertation. She read numerous revisions of my draft, encouraged me to find my own research questions and answers, and showed me unconditional trust even when I did not trust myself. The "organic approach" that she taught me defines me as a scholar, and I intend to pass it on, along with the unconditional support I received from her. The late Nancy Abelmann opened a very important path to ethnography, to Korean studies, and to a special mentor and friend. It was my privilege to work with and learn from her, and to spend time with her, discussing research, ideas, and life, sometimes just strolling around her neighborhood. I will miss her immensely. Through Peggy Miller I came to appreciate the power of narrative and learned the importance of warmth and care toward the people I study. I also extend my warmest thanks to Stephen Hartnett, James Hay, and Michelle Koven for their input in the earliest stage of this project.

At the University of Iowa, I received invaluable intellectual and institutional support from many wonderful colleagues. The Center for Asian and Pacific Studies supported my fieldtrip to Korea in 2012–2013. The Department of Communication Studies also sponsored fieldwork and conference trips, and created an ideal environment for completing my project. In particular, I appreciate Jeff Bennett, Joy Hayes, Jae-On Kim, Kembrew McLeod, John Durham Peters, Stephen Vlastos, and Isaac West for their insights and generosity.

The many students, activists, and journalists who volunteered for interviews also deserve recognition. It's disappointing that their names cannot be identified here, but I'm enormously grateful for their generosity and openness in sharing their lives. Listening to their (sometimes deeply personal) stories was a privileged and humbling experience. I just hope that this book captures even a glimpse of how complex, hardworking, honest, and thoughtful they were, in all different ways. I was able to meet many of them only through the valuable help of a number of people. Chul-kyu Kim and Hae-jin Lee generously let me contact participants whom they met in the streets during the heat of the 2008 protests. Joo-hyung Kim, Ok-tae Kim, Beom-jun Lee, Sojin Park, and many others helped me directly recruit interviewees.

I feel extremely blessed to have met many peers and colleagues whom I can also call friends. They reminded me that while academe can be lonely at times, it also allows you to find a supportive community and delight in the brilliance and generosity of your friends. Melissa Anne-Marie Curley, Natalie Fixmer-Oraiz, Andy High, Rachel McLaren, and Jenna Supp-Montgomerie are the regulars of our weekly "writing party," where much of the original writing for this book occurred. This Friday-morning group also deserves credit for producing the title of the book. Many others inspired and encouraged me at various stages of completing the project: Songmi An, Steve Choe, Hyun Eun Choi, Vanessa Fixmer-Oraiz, Mary High, Yu Kyung Kang, Yumi Nishi, Alyssa Park, Matthew Jeremy Ritchie, Chiaki Sakai, David Supp-Montgomerie, Laura Stengrim, Darrel Wanzer-Serrano, and Hyaesin Yoon.

Parts of chapters 2 and 4 were published in *Communication and Critical/Cultural Studies* and in the *Journal of Korean Studies.* It was through then-CCCS editor John Sloop's efforts that I received outstanding feedback for both my Korean content and the cultural studies side. Guest editors Nancy Abelmann and Jesook Song's feedback was crucial for not only chapter 4 but the entire ethnographic part of the book. Earlier versions of the chapters were presented at conferences and workshops, and feedback from these was formative of many ideas and arguments included in the final text. Robert Oppenheim and MeeRa Lee offered valuable feedback at the Association for Asian Studies Conference. Saeyoung Park and Nick Harkness's co-organized conference *Politics of Public Space* in 2011 introduced this project to Korean studies scholars from various disciplines, most notably Jae Jung Seo and Hyung Il Pai. The 2012 *Rising Stars in Korean Studies* conference by David Kang at the University of Southern California offered a rare opportunity to meet with leading scholars in the field. Myungkoo Kang and the Seoul National University Institute of Communication Research forum in 2012, and the Social Science Research Council Korean

Studies Junior Faculty Workshop in 2013 were instrumental in conceptualizing this project as a book in Korean studies. At its revision stage, I received crucial feedback from the *Media and Contemporary Korea* workshop organized by Olga Fedorenko at New York University and the Rhetoric colloquium at the University of Wisconsin–Madison.

I am also grateful to Stephanie Chun at the University of Hawai'i Press for her critical help throughout the process. Sam Collins and an anonymous reviewer offered valuable feedback that was crucial in guiding me through the final stages of my revisions. The publication of this book is supported by the First Book Subvention Program of the Association for Asian Studies and the College of Liberal Arts and Humanities at the University of Iowa.

Most important, the boundless support from my family has been solid ground I could always stand on without doubt. Myung-yeon, Jung-heon, Si-eun, and Si-hyung were heartwarming cheerleaders from Taiwan. The love, understanding, and prayer of my parents Hoig Kang and Joung-sun Park sustained me daily even when I lived on the other side of the Pacific Ocean; I dedicate this book to them.

Note to Readers

This book uses the McCune–Reischauer Romanization system to transliterate Korean words and names. For personal names, the family name comes first, followed by a space and the given name, except for names that already have an established transliteration in other ways (for instance, Syngman Rhee instead of Yi Sŭng-man). For works by Korean authors in English, the author's name is written as it appears in the original publication.

This book adheres to ethnographic conventions to protect informant confidentiality. For that reason, the names of my interviewees are pseudonyms—when a pseudonym first appears, it is marked with an asterisk to denote this. An exception is the authors of online messages published in a publicly accessible online forum or mass-media report. For these, I have used the existing usernames because they are already public. The names of places throughout this book are all real.

Introduction

Igniting the Internet and the New Dynamics of Popular Politics

For South Korea—one of the world's most highly connected societies—the transformative influence of the Internet on political participation began early in the twenty-first century. In 2002 the country's vibrant cyberspace transformed a vehicular accident involving two U.S. service members into a national furor that forced Koreans to reexamine the fifty-year relationship between the United States and South Korea. In response to the accident, the country's technologically savvy youth used the Internet to organize protests that grew into nightly gatherings at city centers nationwide. Internet-born, youth-driven mass protest has since become a familiar and effective repertoire for activism in South Korea, even as the rest of the world struggles to find its feet with this emerging model of political involvement.

The first protest began as a response to the deaths of two thirteen-year-old girls, Sin Hyo-sun and Sim Mi-sŏn, in a suburb of Seoul on June 13, 2002. The driver of a sixty-ton U.S. Army bridge carrier failed to notice the girls at the shoulder of a narrow local road, and the vehicle crushed them. At the time—in the midst of the World Cup soccer tournament cohosted by South Korea and Japan—news of the accident barely traveled beyond the neighborhood. South Koreans were immersed in a sense of elation at hosting an international spectacle: evidence of the country's transformation from client state to producer of global culture. As the national squad defeated seemingly insuperable teams to reach the semifinals, young Koreans organized themselves online and poured into the streets dressed in the red of their team's uniforms. The municipal government of Seoul saw an opportunity to showcase the country's grassroots dynamism and decided to allow crowds to congregate in the city center. Watching the games on huge outdoor

1

screens and collectively cheering for their players in this newly opened space, South Koreans experienced a sense of both national pride and catharsis.

However, when the tournament ended in July and excitement slowly abated, Hyo-sun and Mi-sŏn's deaths belatedly saddled South Koreans with a very different sense of national identity. Photographs of the young victims crushed under the treads of a U.S. military vehicle were released online, seizing the attention of Internet users with the graphic brutality of the images. Conveyed with the pictures was the news that South Korea did not have jurisdiction over the case because of the Status of Forces Agreement (SOFA), a bilateral accord governing the legal rights of the 37,000 resident U.S. troops (28,500 as of 2014).[1] American troops had been stationed in South Korea since the end of the Korean War (1950–1953), and the 101 separate military installations throughout the country were a well-established part of the South Korean landscape.[2] The news that a military vehicle had crushed two children walking in their own neighborhood spread rapidly and awakened Internet users to the ramifications of the presence of the U.S. military. On Web sites formerly dedicated to the World Cup, the girls' deaths emerged as a different but equally intense symbol of the country's stature: a client state still suffering from the remnants of the Cold War era. South Korea's technologically savvy youths circulated the story and image widely, along with photographs of the girls and heartfelt messages dedicated to the deceased "friends and sisters."

The Internet phenomenon turned into a national cause célèbre in November when the U.S. military court in Seoul found Sergeants Fernando Nino and Mark Walker, the commander and the driver of the vehicle, respectively, not guilty of negligent homicide. The two were then free to leave the country. For the mourning South Koreans, that no one was held responsible for the deaths was unreasonable. After the verdicts, the Internet exploded with impassioned commemorations, letters to the deceased, and incendiary remarks targeted at the two soldiers, at the U.S. military presence in South Korea, and at the South Korean government itself.[3] One Internet user's heartfelt open letter and proposal for a candlelight vigil to commemorate the girls went viral. On the evening of November 30, 2002, more than ten thousand Internet users responded to the call and filled downtown Seoul, the epicenter of the World Cup street celebrations (see figure 1). The letter continued to circulate even after the date of the original gathering, accompanied by participant accounts of poignant, cathartic experiences at the vigil. Similar vigils soon became nightly events held in city centers nationwide,

Fig. 1   A candlelight vigil in downtown Seoul in December 2002 © Dong-a Ilbo.

and peaceful gatherings with speeches and performances by volunteers within the crowd established a familiar repertoire for the gatherings.

Politicians and the media were confounded by the outpouring of animosity toward South Korea's closest ally, and by the unprecedented mass participation of teenagers. Some critics situated the vigils within South Korea's robust social movement tradition, which opposed both the authoritarian regimes and America's willingness to overlook their repressive actions and was instrumental to democratization in 1987. The language of the 2002 vigils evoked these anti-American rallies because the new protesters also criticized the U.S.–South Korean alliance, with slogans such as "Retrial of the GIs at a Korean Court" and "Withdraw U.S. troops from Korea."[4] However, other critics concluded that the teenagers at these vigils were merely resurrecting the nationalistic and festive gatherings of the recent World Cup.[5]

By 2013 the teenage participants of the original 2002 vigils had long since reached adulthood and moved on to college and careers, but using the Internet to mobilize the public for peaceful candlelight protests nonetheless continued. In 2004 South Koreans turned out to protest the conservative party's impeachment of President Roh Moo-hyun; in 2005 high school students demonstrated against hairstyle regulation and educational reform;

and in 2006 candlelight rallies supported controversial stem cell researcher Hwang Woo-suk during his fraud scandal. In 2008 junior high and high school students initiated "candlelight festivals" when President Lee Myung-bak proposed the resumption of American beef importation despite widespread concern about mad cow disease, and they established the "candle girl" as an iconic figure of protest. In 2010 college students' demands for reduced tuition fees garnered support from a broad range of protesters that included both their parents' generation and high school students; and in the summer of 2013 South Koreans assembled with candles to condemn the Korean National Intelligence Service's alleged involvement in the 2012 presidential election. Despite their varied goals, these protests often had a significant impact on politics and culture. The 2002 protests, for example, directly influenced the December presidential election: liberal candidate Roh Moo-hyun had been considered too radical for mainstream Koreans, but during the surging criticism of the U.S.–Korean relationship he was seen as an assertive leader who would stand against American influence, and was elected (see chapter 3). In 2008 the candlelight protests led to multiple apologies from President Lee Myung-bak and the resignation of eight cabinet members (see chapter 5).

In this book I examine the consolidation of Internet-born, youth-driven activism in the first decade of the new millennium to answer two questions repeatedly asked about the candlelight protests: What is the nature of these Internet-born mass gatherings? and Who are the young Koreans in the streets? I argue that by "igniting the Internet," these protests demonstrated that online communities had become a new social space with distinct communicative dynamics for expressing opinions, forging alliances, and making judgments without conforming to established political discourse of any stripe. Internet users circulate and recirculate the news of an event that captivates them, and the shared captivation subjects the event and its potential causes to public scrutiny, even when existing legal and political frameworks would condone it.

By 2008 these candlelight protests had consolidated into a recognizable protest repertoire, resulting in significant political implications that transcended any immediate institutional changes. This new repertoire made dissent easy, established teenagers as active political participants, and fashioned new political sensibilities liberated from authoritarian-era preconceptions and limits. The *cultural ignition process,* a larger cultural process that takes place through captivation, shifts focus from the power of technology to the alliance formed through it, from individual actions to collective experiences, and from existing political fault lines to vernacular political judgments.

I personally felt both intrigued by and uneasy about the mass presence of teenagers at these new protests. Teenagers offering irreverent parodies and chanting anti-American slogans was certainly a novel phenomenon. Watching the World Cup street celebrations and the subsequent candlelight vigils from my expatriate vantage point in the Midwest United States, I was reminded of my childhood in the mid-1980s, when young students (myself included) were taught patriotism and even mobilized in mass gatherings to celebrate national achievements. At the time, criticism of the Korean government or of the United States was confined to self-identified activists, who still occasionally waged large-scale protests and clashed with police into the mid-1990s (when I attended a university in Seoul). With those memories in mind, I saw the young Koreans flooding the Internet and the streets in 2002 as a peculiar combination of patriotism and activism.

In examining this rise and consolidation of candlelight protest in South Korea, I elaborate on the role of *captivation* to explain the cultural ignition process on the Internet.[6] Captivation as a social and cultural practice thrives on technological innovation because users can share, via hyperlinks, the messages, images, and sounds that fascinate them. Participants in this process are not necessarily intentional political actors; however, online captivation with an issue does suggest the existence of nascent vernacular knowledge and judgment, although without conformance to existing political norms. For example, captivation with a conspiracy theory suggests that the public cares about an issue at hand but institutional politics has failed to offer a reasonable account for it.[7] As chapters 2 and 5 respectively show, young Internet users' captivation with the two girls' deaths or with mad cow disease indicates the users' vernacular judgments that the terms of the U.S. military presence and the free trade agreements were problematic. This explains the cultural ignition process, in which a new agenda surfaces online, rapidly forms a collective that shares attention to the agenda, and affects the dynamics of public communication in a manner distinct from existing politics.

The ten-year study in this book focuses particularly on the inaugural protests in 2002 and on another wave at the maturation of the protest repertoire in 2008. A multimodal approach, analyzing Internet discourses, mainstream media discourses, and interviews with young participants, highlights the spectrum of technological, political, and cultural forces at work. Internet discourses capture the momentary passion and intensity of collective captivation, while mainstream media demonstrate the existing political perspectives through which the public has understood these newly emerging youth movements. The participants' retrospective narratives in interviews conducted between 2006 and 2012 illuminate the long-term influence of online activism that remains with individuals well after the moment has passed. The analysis here also offers an account of the political subjectivity of contemporary South Korean youth, who were born from the mid-1980s to the mid-1990s and therefore never experienced the earlier ideological warfare between authoritarianism and democratization.

In hindsight, the South Korean protests were a precocious case of popular politics emerging on the Internet. This highly connected nation matured into the social media age well ahead of the global curve and so encountered the social consequences of online connectivity before the rest of the modern world. The ten-year progression in this study therefore offers a unique historical perspective for understanding the evolution of Internet politics. When South Korea was already a decade into its now-familiar Internet-born protest repertoire, the rest of the world was only beginning to see similar forms of activism. In 2010 the YouTube video of a Tunisian fruit vendor's self-immolation to protest the actions of a municipal inspector traversed national boundaries and conveyed both anger and mobilization strategies to neighboring countries. Over the following two years, mass mobilizations summoned by social media brought down a number of repressive regimes in the Arab world, efforts that quickly gained labels such as "Twitter uprising" or "Facebook revolution." In North America, the call by Canadian magazine *Adbusters* to "Occupy Wall Street" for a day circulated well beyond its intended audience or duration and drew millions to a long-term campout in the heart of New York City, through which young protesters subjected the practices of Wall Street to public scrutiny—actions that then spread worldwide. In Israel, Greece, Spain, and the UK, frustrated youths experiencing precarious working conditions challenged neoliberal economic policies and held their governments accountable for high unemployment and holes in the social safety net.[8]

Of course, the administrative reactions to these protests were very different, ranging from eviction orders and pepper spray to death at the hands of autocratic regimes. However, like their predecessors in South Korea, participants in these protests were disproportionately urban, educated, middle-class youths who used the Internet to document their frustration, or captivation, with corrupt politicians, with growing inequality in society, and with police violence.

Pundits and activists around the world have argued the nature, significance, and potential consequences of these protests, but such debates typically amount to a variation of the same question: Will social media revolutionize politics? Scholars and commentators—from *Foreign Policy* magazine to the *International Socialist Review* to *New Scientist*—posed the question with excitement and hope, and many enthusiastically endorsed the central role of the Internet in social change in the Arab world and beyond.[9] However, in response, skeptics dismissed the value of this new activism. Malcolm Gladwell argued that social media fosters only the kind of activism that requires little devotion and negligible risk, while effecting significant social change instead requires a strong cadre of committed, articulate supporters.[10] In the two years after the Arab Spring, pundits watched while these "revolutions" either remained unfinished or were actively repressed by a police state or fundamentalist leaders. The first wave of these Internet-born youth protests ebbed, resulting in mixed consequences for each country's domestic and international politics.

There was certainly ample evidence to undermine any initial optimism. The first people to seize the potential of the Internet were neofascists on USENET newsgroups before the World Wide Web era. White supremacists, skinheads, and neo-Nazis continue to find homes in cyberspace.[11] In Japan, *netto uyoku* ("right-wingers on the net") are known for making incendiary and disparaging remarks targeted at China and Korea from behind the veil of online anonymity.[12] The South Korean online community *Ilbe* draws younger users who use humor to express undiluted right-wing nationalism, racism, and misogyny. And, while some take advantage of the Internet to find a home for their extremism, a majority of users are content with "slacktivism"—a portmanteau of *slacker* and *activism* that refers to easy feel-good practices of "liking" or retweeting progressive content without commitment to the cause.[13]

These examples evoke both the best and the worst of popular politics. The Internet is an antielitist and vibrant social space in which anyone can contribute to public discussion without being expelled for style or substance, or compelled to conform to dominant norms.[14] However, participants often do not bother to engage with one another, and the complexity of social issues is effaced while sensational and simplistic discourses circulate faster and wider.

That said, such a bifurcated assessment stems from gauging the Internet's political potential only by its utility in established politics: the Internet is rendered merely an additional tool for existing political causes in disseminating information and mobilizing citizens, or as a faithful (or distorted) simulation of existing political discussion. This approach fails to grasp the intimate texture of interactions on the Internet, which reformulates the processes of sharing information, forging alliances, and making judgments.

Captivation: A New Modality of Politics

By investigating captivation—exploring the question of what grabs an Internet user's attention among competing discourses and makes that user further circulate the material—I propose a new popular cultural dynamic on the Internet through which shared yet underarticulated public sentiments can be voiced without translation into the language of established politics. On the Internet, sensational images, news, and even conspiracy theories captivate users and spread faster and more broadly than traditionally researched reports. A seemingly isolated incident can draw major attention, leading to temporary gatherings ranging from flash mobs to the South Korean candlelight protests at hand to campouts in city centers under the banner of "Occupy." Such volatility can have uncertain results: the attention often lacks a well-defined agenda, passes quickly, and is unlikely to fashion transformed citizens. However, this captivation and the consequent temporary but impassioned collective action is not merely the pathology of the Internet but a modality through which "social actors engage others publicly."[15]

Captivation is an inherently public process that invites others to share in an experience. On the Internet, a user's attention is valuable currency, and personal and emotional stories and images compete for public notice. In the era of the printing press, only certain parties had the power to access and produce knowledge. With the Internet, however, the production of information is easier and its dissemination faster, and information from both mainstream media and alternative sources is available.[16] In this environment, the challenge for both producer and user is navigating the *overabundance* of information and multisensory stimuli. In such an information-rich world, attention is a scarce resource.[17] This is an "attention economy," as rhetorical scholar Richard Lanham posits, in which producers compete for the user's gaze, and what the user "looks *at*" becomes as important as (or more important than) what he or she "looks through."[18]

Captivation is therefore a consequence of both the architecture of the Internet and the user's attention, and so cannot be reduced to a function of either. The user's captivation determines the value of information and constitutes an interpretive community. The Internet is a system of hypertexts, a corpus not organized linearly but connected through hyperlinks. Users who navigate through competing words, images, and sounds experience captivation: they concentrate their attention on a text, release it, and then move to the next. This trajectory of attention creates connections among texts and so composes a narrative in its own right.[19]

Furthermore, captivation increases exponentially as the number of people who pay attention to and circulate a text grows. By being captivated, a user becomes the center of a new network whose circulation expands its reach to further audiences. When chronologically organized, an online post can be buried below hundreds of others within a matter of days, or even hours or minutes; however, the number of linked connections—an important element of Google's search-prioritization algorithms, for example— makes a message visible by placing it at the top of search results. Similarly, on most social media platforms such as Twitter, Reddit, or Facebook, the message with the most recent response is automatically moved to the top of the list. An Internet user's captivation circulates the message, determining its visibility for other viewers and inviting them to the interpretive community around it.[20] The scope of the resulting community is not confined by geographic proximity, and thus exceeds the boundaries of the nation-state. Even opponents can be co-opted as significant contributors across political distance, because criticisms and attacks make an issue more salient.[21]

In the context of politics and culture, captivation has long been suspect. Plato was wary of weak-willed citizens lured by sophists' eloquent rhetoric, Kant saw charm and emotion tainting the judgment of beauty, and Max Weber was concerned that charismatic leaders would captivate the public to the detriment of critical reasoning.[22] Frankfurt School critics were similarly troubled by commodities and mass media that offer an illusion or false satisfaction and so make citizens docile.[23] Guy Debord warned against captivation by spectacle that mesmerizes citizens and supplants genuine social activity.[24] More recently, the term *viral*—used to refer to information that replicates widely online—has implicitly situated the public as unknowing hosts infected by information.[25] This anxiety over captivation arises from understanding it as a psychological process happening between the viewer and a mesmerizing object—an image, person, or event—and equating it with the concealment or mystification of the true nature of things.[26]

However, captivation is not mere concealment: it reveals nascent and vernacular social knowledge that is shared within a collective but not readily legible to the larger public. Captivation therefore requires a cultural explanation. Why do only certain images—like the aftermath of the accident that killed Hyo-sun and Mi-sŏn—go viral and induce protest, while other gruesome and shocking pictures make only faint ripples in the ever-changing surface of the attention economy? Anthropologist Alfred Gell concludes that this is related to the contextual knowledge of viewers—an object captivates when viewers are aware that an origination process exists but they cannot easily comprehend or rehearse it.[27] Captivation with an object thus depends not only on the viewer's imagination being stimulated by the image but also on the viewer's contextual knowledge being sufficient to recognize the significance of the object. Viewers of the images of the girls shared "access to the essential elements needed to make the conceptual leaps and connections," which made the images a prominent symbol of national identity in 2002.[28]

Because captivation points to the unarticulated yet potent larger forces that brought the object into being, it alludes to shared knowledge, values, and judgment at a specific juncture. In their *No Caption Needed*, rhetorical scholars Robert Hariman and John Lucaites show that an image becomes "iconic"—not needing a caption—when it "can effectively tap into the tacit knowledge held by the audience . . . and activate deep structures of belief that guide social interaction and civic judgment and then apply them to the particular case."[29] For instance, the shared suffering from poverty in the Great Depression and the repression of emotion during WWII respectively made the photographs "Migrant Mother" and "V-J Day in Times Square" iconic images of America.[30]

In this book I investigate the junctures at which certain texts, images, and figures have captured public attention online and become conveyers of understanding and judgment where no explanation is needed. These processes offer a glimpse of what Raymond Williams calls *emergent forms,* practices and relationships that are shared but not yet visible, or what Kent Ono and John Sloop call *vernacular discourse,* discourses and passions that confirm a marginalized group's identity and account for its experiences but are not recognizable to the universal public.[31] In 2002 Koreans were captivated by the two girls' deaths because they couldn't understand why South Korea—a seemingly proud producer of global culture, as evidenced during the World Cup—had no voice in the subsequent investigation and trial. The stark contrast between national images during the World Cup and those in the aftermath of the trials absorbed the attention of South Koreans and catalyzed an eruption of online conversation about the seemingly unreasonable, or simply obsolete, terms of the U.S. military presence in South Korea.

This is certainly not to say that captivation itself is a new communicative dynamic generated by the Internet. Captivation has always existed as a background process in constituting a collective and communicating its shared worldview. Michael Warner famously theorized, "A public is constituted through mere attention," arguing that a public is created not by an institutional framework but by attention to a discourse.[32] Like Gell's captivated viewer, a potential member becomes part of a public with sufficient knowledge to recognize the significance of a text, or at least with an active "willingness to process a passing appeal."[33] Dilip Gaonkar and Elizabeth Provinelli further suggest a shift in the examination of captivation, from a question of whether it happens to how it is reconfigured in the public culture of an era.[34] For example, in Benedict Anderson's *Imagined Communities,* captivation with national events reported via newspapers enabled readers to imagine conationals who shared the same language and interests as members of the newly established nation-state. In Jürgen Habermas's account of the modern public sphere, captivation with unique human individuality portrayed in novels and letters enabled readers to recognize both their independence and the commonality shared with other citizens, preparing them to come together to form a public.[35]

What we see today is the salience of multisensory, personal, and affective discursive forms on the Internet. Furthermore, the scope and tempo of captivation has increased to an extent that effects qualitative changes to political culture in several ways. First, multisensory forms are as important as text (perhaps more) for interpersonal and civic communication online: communicative media now include photos, YouTube videos, memes, and selfies (with *selfie* being the Oxford Dictionary word of the year for 2013).[36] Digital memes—popular images or video clips of "parody, pastiche, mash-ups"—convey commentaries on politics or larger social norms, ranging from satire of a politician's words to the humorous depiction of flawed masculinity.[37] The picture of Hyo-sun and Mi-sŏn's bodies in 2002 and a video clip of downed and faltering cattle in 2008 were representations of the public's emerging dissent—over the handling of a tragic event, and over the government's disregard for public concern about mad cow disease. As Hariman and

Lucaites put it, images are an "ideal medium of activating tacit social knowledge" because they invite viewers to identify and judge the substrate and because they evoke emotional experiences associated with them.[38]

Second, captivations with the personal, the multisensory, and the affective are closely associated with the redrawing of public-private boundaries in the social media setting. Social media scholars Alice Marwick and danah boyd call this phenomenon "context collapse"—the flattening of multiple audiences into one. A message intended for one's family could be viewed by colleagues or by the entire public and induce unexpected consequences, ranging from the creation of a YouTube celebrity to a scandal.[39] Furthermore, personal mobile media present users with a new capacity to "skip back and forth across those [private–public] boundaries at will," and so afford a space for "political play."[40] Practices typically observed in social networking sites and online games, such as voicing emotions, expressing artistic abilities, and breaking taboos, can traverse the public-private boundaries and contribute to "the breakdown of traditional authority and control."[41] As I discuss in chapter 1, irreverent jokes and parodies of dominant cultural norms were popular themes in South Korean online communities dedicated to humor, photography, and celebrity. After the acquittal of Sergeants Nino and Walker in 2002, these existing communities and habitual practices were instrumental in generating and spreading news of the tragedy, parodies of the not-guilty verdicts, and criticism of the U.S.–Korea relationship. In the redrawing of public-private boundaries, "*affective* interpersonal responses" and "*effective* civic responses" take place simultaneously.[42]

Third, captivation on the Internet also affects the formation of collectives. Alliance through captivation does not require shared identity or other sustained categories of commonality; instead it is temporary and ad hoc, lasting only while people with different motivations converge on a platform. The notion of captivation builds from current models that attempt a cultural explanation for Internet collective action beyond the physiological model of "viral" or "contagion." For instance, perceived social rewards (what Clay Shirky calls "plausible promises") enable concerted action without a coordinator. A user decides to edit a *Wikipedia* entry out of boredom, to show off his or her knowledge, or with a sense of contributing to the knowledge of humankind. By offering a platform for these multiple rewards, *Wikipedia* attracts collaborators without an established coordinator and so constantly renews itself.[43] The gift economy, modeled after the canonical anthropological account of society, is another possible explanation.[44] Henry Jenkins,

Sam Ford, and Joshua Green argue that the spread of images and videos is a function of engaged viewers who desire to share their objects of emotional investment.[45] In his ethnography of the South Korean online community *DC Inside,* Yi Kil-ho similarly argues that sharing talent in producing images and video without compensation sustains and renews the community.[46] Finally, yet others find the personal pursuit of belonging as constitutive of collectives online. New media scholar Zizi Papacharissi concludes that the Internet provides an "affective-rational hybrid environment" in which people look for the sense of participation or the feeling of being connected.[47] Lance Bennett and Alexandra Segerberg find that a collective is formed online through a constellation of personal motivations of users to express themselves or to recommend a cause to others "by sharing their personal participation stories, photos, and videos."[48]

A number of scholars view this temporary alliance of heterogeneous motives as the degeneration of participatory politics. For instance, social movement scholar Sidney Tarrow argues that Bennett and Segerberg valorize the personalization of political action and wrongfully validate the separation of individuals from the "integrative structures of society . . . such as class identification, church, party, union, and traditional family."[49] He is only one of many who voice concerns that Internet politics lacks the interpersonal ties to build meaningful collective identities and instead leads to fragmentation, consolidation of disagreement, and increased extremism.[50] Similarly, labels such as "individualistic social experimentation"[51] and "networked individualism"[52] imply that members of such temporary alliances are far from ideal citizens concerned with the public good.

Even though this criticism aptly describes individuals, it is important to also notice the particular collective dynamics that cannot be reduced to the sum of individuals. For instance, some critics defined Occupy Wall Street as a frivolous youthful rebellion by citing the absence of a coherent agenda and the participation of heterogeneous groups. However, what captivated young Americans was a plausible plan to go to Wall Street and express the underarticulated yet shared grievances that job prospects were dire, the gap between rich and poor was growing faster than before, and politicians were more responsive to corporate interests than to constituents. The flash mob, which first emerged in 2003, exemplifies this new form of Internet-born ad hoc network. The flash mob is an assembly at a prearranged time and place for coordinated action, ranging from frivolous pillow fights to political protests such as the 2012 demonstrations in France against a derogatory caricature of the Prophet Mohammad.[53] These gatherings do not result from shared identity or interest but are based instead on captivation with the cause or even with the form of the mob itself.[54] The temporary alliance calls for suspending models that presuppose an intentional actor and instead attending to the political *effect* generated by the combination of Internet architecture and captivated user.[55] In reflecting on the role of social media in the Occupy movement, *Time* magazine noted, "Deciding what you don't want is a lot easier than deciding and implementing what you do want."[56] Social media might not be optimal tools for deliberation; however, they *are* sites where agendas captivate users and spontaneously circulate to form a potent collective.

When it goes beyond the boundaries of deliberative politics, captivation also places mainstream politics under such intense scrutiny that even a minor incident can undermine public trust and political legitimacy. Political scandals certainly occurred before the new media age, swaying politics with disclosures of wrongdoing; however, the Internet era now allows diverse individuals and groups to participate in *producing* such incidents. Furthermore, "every nook and cranny of power" is subject to public exposure.[57] All it takes to turn classified information into a catalyst for scandal is one additional link. WikiLeaks, for example, added just one node to a corpus of documents and transformed the nature of the text from classified to public, contrary to the original authors' intentions. Furthermore, because the Internet lacks a center, once information is released there, it is nearly impossible for anyone to control its circulation. This gives rise to what Manuel Castells calls "scandal politics," in which any established power is subject to continual challenge to its legitimacy.[58] The Internet does not necessarily produce informed and critical citizens, but scandal politics can quickly turn users into an attentive and critical public in particular instances. Online politics is defined not by established procedures or agendas but by inventive and radical forms that exceed the bounds of existing institutions and rules.

Youth Internet Activism in South Korea's New Democracy

The effect generated by the politics of captivation is contingent, drawing from collective experience, underarticulated sentiment, and vernacular judgment within a particular historical context. In South Korea, scholars and media have variously celebrated—and warned against—the candlelight protests as indicative of a new generation of youth activists, of new Internet politics, or of disillusionment with representative politics. In analyzing the politics of captivation, my intention is not to add a fourth category to such debates but to reconsider how these elements work together at particular junctures and to address the confusion caused by valorizing one factor over the others.

In the aftermaths of the 2002 and 2008 candlelight protests, confusion between youths as individuals and the youth as a collective resulted in conflicting accounts of protest participants. In their attempts to find "anti-American attitude" at the protests, a number of scholars concluded that the young participants in the 2002 vigils were critical of the United States and thus constituted a new generation of "political force" distinct from the predominantly pro-American older generation.[59] However, as chapter 5 describes, by 2008 (when they were well into their twenties) many former protesters had become conservative college students who would "give in to the hollow promise [by Lee Myung-bak] to 'Save the Economy' . . . and accept contract positions made by eliminating their fathers' secure fulltime positions."[60] Similarly, chapter 6 shows that the teenagers who occupied city centers in 2008 had by 2013 become tired young people worried about their precarious futures.

As such, I am wary of generational categories that implicitly conclude that these young protesters are altogether different from the older generation. "Generation" became a buzzword for scholars, press, and marketers to (at least attempt to) explain the teenagers of the candlelight protests.[61] In 2002 when young Koreans gathered by the hundreds of thousands in city centers for the World Cup and for candlelight vigils, new generational designations immediately appeared—for example "Generation W" to refer to the World Cup, or "Generation P," a mouthful of praise to refer to a generation that "brings about *paradigm-shift* through *passion* and *power* in active *participation* in various societal issues."[62] Similarly, after the 2008 festivals, "Candlelight generation" became a household term to refer to the youth as a new political subject.[63] Even though these generational categories have journalistic value in capturing the intensity of new phenomena, they are often implicitly based on "adult paranoia about young people" that youth threaten stability.[64] Members of the "candlelight generation" objected to such categories in 2010, disputing the implicit conclusion that the older generation couldn't understand modern youth and arguing that the appeal of these labels came from older Koreans' projection of hope that this new generation might be agents for the country's progress.[65]

Confusion also stems from the fact that the Internet is a space shaped by typically tech-savvy and young users. While some attributed the political fallout of the protests to the youth themselves (as either individuals or a collective), others saw these changes as a consequence of the Internet, which offered progressive perspectives and alternative forums outside mainstream media and institutional politics.[66] These elements were either welcome or suspect, depending on the critic's perspective. For instance, *Sisa Journal* (the Korean equivalent to *Time* magazine) named "the netizen" as "Person of the Year" for 2002, celebrating the Internet for giving rise to a new kind of spontaneous citizen.[67] Similarly, progressive political scientists saw in the 2008 protest Koreans' distrust of institutional politics and desire to represent directly their own interests.[68] Meanwhile, it is noteworthy that a number of progressive pundits who enthusiastically endorsed the 2008 beef protests had turned into critics by early 2009, lamenting that the candlelight protests were a moment of "spectacle" driven by the fears of middle-class consumers but failing to create enduring alliances with other disenfranchised groups.[69]

Ultimately, these attempts at isolating a critical ingredient to explain the candlelight protests subsided over the ten-year progression of the protest repertoire, as Internet-born activism became established as a process of temporary alliance with no guarantee of transformed citizens or of a democratic Internet politics. My analysis in this book therefore attends more to new types of collective practices online, in the streets, and in personal lives than to the individual political leanings of participants.

However, we cannot exclude the possibility that citizens will become transformed politically as a *result* of these repeated practices. Because of the precarious division between North and South Korea, criticism of the government or of the U.S. military presence in South Korea had generally been taken as sympathy toward North Korea—which often led to persecution. Speaking or acting in public without first considering the ideological ramifications was foolish at best and dangerous at worst. However, the recurring candlelight protests since 2002 have allowed South Korean youth to "feel at ease" with occupying city centers, and to view the expression of dissenting voices as both possible and desirable.[70] The youths who promulgated the candlelight protests were inadvertent political actors—the first to *live* South Korea's new democracy, with fewer preconceptions and limits—and represented a significant departure from those who *fought* for that democracy. The emergence of new "habits" and the accompanying disappearance of obsolete ones suggests the formation of a new political subject.[71]

Objects and Methods of Analysis

In *Igniting the Internet,* I combine three objects of inquiry: the sociocultural context of youth in the first decade of the twenty-first century, online discourses surrounding the various candlelight protests (2002–2013), and retrospective narratives by participants conducted three to four years after each major protest (2006–2012). The historical trajectory of the youths at these protests (born between the mid-1980s and mid-1990s) informs the social, cultural, and technological factors that shaped their worldviews, as well as their capacity to express these views.

In particular, I analyze discussion boards that exemplified the emergence, dissemination, and consummation of the 2002 and 2008 protests. For online communities, I begin with one focal point in each year: for 2002 it is *Ko Sin Hyo-sun Sim Mi-sŏn Yang Ch'umo Moim* (Commemorative Group for Sin Hyo-sun and Sim Mi-sŏn, hereafter *Moim*), and for 2008 it is *Ch'otpul Sonyŏŭi K'oria* (Candle Girls' Korea). The selection of these online communities and my subsequent analytical methods developed out of necessity, but with several important considerations for the architecture of the Internet.[72]

First, these two communities are representative of dozens of forums dedicated to the protests on Daum.net (the largest online portal in South Korea, providing individuals and groups with free online space) and of hundreds of similar communities online. Further, both show the progression of discourse from the beginning. *Moim* opened on June 27, 2002, two weeks after the deaths of Hyo-sun and Mi-sŏn—making it one of the earliest forums dedicated to the two girls, and also one of the largest, with between seven thousand and eight thousand members in 2002. *Candle Girls' Korea* opened on May 17, 2008, only a few days after the initial candlelight festival.

Second, these two communities operated without the leadership of social movement organizations. In 2002, alternative newspapers and Web sites affiliated with activist organizations initially served as the most active forums: *Oh My News,* a liberal online newspaper; the Pan-Korean Community for Two Girls Killed by a U.S. Armored Vehicle (PKC), a civic organization established by radical activists after the court-martial verdicts; and *Voice of the People,* an online news site affiliated with the radical nationalist movement.[73] Discussions on these Web sites unfolded primarily in specific sections devoted to reactions to news reports and op-eds. However, in user-created forums like *Moim,* participants initiated and developed discussions among themselves. In 2008, the challenge was that there were *too many* user-created forums, communities, and channels. *Agora*—a large, open discussion board established as a part of Daum.net in 2004—was the center of details, rumors, and updates from the street protests. By this time, online streaming Web sites, such as Afreeca TV (established in 2006), served as a prominent venue through which individuals (called "broadcast jockeys") offered live coverage of and commentary about the candlelight protests. Additionally, online communities dedicated to other causes became hotbeds for information circulation and mobilization. For instance, *82 Cook, Ssangko, Soul Dresser, Lemon Terrace,* and similar women's online communities dedicated to cooking and recipes, beauty, fashion, and interior design were loci of prominent, independent subgroups during the candlelight protests, such as the "high heel brigade" or the "baby stroller brigade."[74]

Third, although the dispersed nature of Internet discourse makes it impossible to examine all messages and posts regarding the vigils, an online community nonetheless serves as a node and sifting mechanism for research. Posts on a group's page contain hyperlinks to prominent messages, images, and communities regarding the protests. In particular, popular discourses are repeatedly copy-pasted or hyperlinked, an indication of the perceived significance of a discourse for users. *Moim* and *Candle Girls' Korea* served as a filter for both their members and for me in my research. The reposted messages, and especially those that inspired responses or appeared in multiple places on the forum, highlight the intensity of attention these messages received. At the peak of the 2002 protests, more than ten thousand images and messages were posted daily on the major forums, which experienced freezes and loss of data from the high traffic. *Moim* and *Candle Girls' Korea* therefore illustrate nicely how the grassroots discussions progressed from the earliest days.

While these Internet communities captured the "in-the-moment" passion and intensity of the collective discourse, retrospective narratives of protest participants also illuminate the *long-term* influence of the protest experience on individuals. I conducted interviews in 2006, 2011, and 2012 with sixty young Koreans (thirty in 2006, and thirty in 2011–2012) between the ages of eighteen and twenty-seven, recruited through *Moim* and *Candle Girls' Korea* and through college campuses in Seoul and its vicinity. Among them, about half were nonparticipants who remembered the protests; I interviewed them because reasons for nonparticipation are important for understanding the perception of the candlelight protests within South Korea's broader movement tradition. Furthermore, a number of self-identified "non-participants" had in fact attended the protests—going there to practice photography, casually joining when they accidentally encountered an event, or finding themselves suddenly surrounded by peaceful marchers. This unintended or casual participation is itself a unique feature of Internet-born activism, distinct from traditional activism in which ignorance of the cause and of the state's likely reaction would lead to significant danger.

I met with these young people individually or in groups of two to seven over an average of two hours, using prepared questions about initial impressions of the girls' deaths or of the beef importation issue, and about the meaning of the protests to the interviewees personally and more broadly to South Korean society. I asked direct questions only at the beginning and then let respondents proceed and even digress—the topics and ideas they associated with the vigils were as important as their direct impressions. From these interviews I obtained 650 pages of transcripts in Korean, the relevant parts of which I translated into English. The retrospective narratives from the interviews revealed how (or simply whether) the temporary experiences of these young people remained with them after the protest movements concluded.

In analyzing the narratives, I draw on what William Labov theorized as a *narrated* event versus a *narrative* event. A narrated event refers to an event within a person's story; in my interviews, it refers specifically to past participation as described and evaluated directly by the interviewees. A narrative event refers to the actual event of storytelling. In this book, I draw on how interviewees remember and make sense of their past experiences at the moment of the interview.[75] As Stanton Wortham describes, narrating the past actively reconstructs the past event and the self from a vantage point in the present, and so constructs the present identity as a continuation, maturation, or departure from the past self.[76] In analyzing retrospective narratives, particular methodological tools came from Richard Bauman and Charles Briggs's concepts of contextualization, decontextualization, and re-contextualization, which attend to how narratives relocate a past event into a different historical, social, and cultural context and thus transform the nature of the event.[77]

All of that said, I should be clear about a significant limitation of the analysis presented in this book: I am not attempting to write the complete and definitive accounting of the candlelight protests. My focus on youth participants does not capture the crowds at the protests in their entirety. Heterogeneous groups co-existed, including anti-American activists, members of labor unions, progressive college students, concerned mothers, and casual visitors. The candlelight protests were "many individual stories being shared in ways that establish a common protest network" rather than "many people sharing a common story."[78]

Outline of the Book

This book consists of six chapters and is divided into two parts. Part I, "The Rise of Internet-Born Youth Activism," analyzes the appearance of the candlelight vigils in 2002 and the influence of these protests on mainstream politics during the presidential election in December of that year. This section ends with the recollections of youths four years later about the then-new format of the candlelight protest. Part II, "The Maturation of Internet Politics and Postauthoritarian Youth," examines the online and street performances of the 2008 protests—a period that saw the maturation of the Internet-born street protest as a movement repertoire—and then analyzes young participants' memories from the protests as recalled in 2011 and 2012. These two parts together describe the rise and consolidation of new idioms and practices of political action and their relationships to authoritarian remnants and to postauthoritarian political culture and practices in formation.

In the first chapter I introduce the life experiences of South Korea's urban youth (born between the mid-1980s and mid-1990s), who were the primary Internet users and participants in the candlelight protests of 2002 to 2013. "South Korean Youth in the New Millennium" situates them in South Korea's historical trajectory, with particular attention to the political legacies of the authoritarian period and to social, economic, and cultural changes in the postauthoritarian era.

Part I begins with chapter 2, "The Birth of the Internet Youth Protest," which examines the progression of the inaugural youth activism of 2002—namely, the candlelight vigils (*ch'otpul chiphoe*). Here I analyze the process through which the tragedy of the two girls' deaths captivated the attention of young Koreans on the Internet, symbolizing the perception of an obsolete and violent U.S. military presence in South Korea and instigating the street protests that became the first candlelight vigils.

I then explore the confluence of the vigils and the sixteenth presidential election on December 19, 2002, in chapter 3, "The Internet in Mainstream

Politics." Liberal candidate Roh Moo-hyun achieved a dramatic victory, and young Koreans attuned to the vigils projected onto Roh their hope for an ideal leader assertive against the United States and responsive to the people. On the basis of this election, I reflect on this convergence between the politics of captivation and mainstream politics.

Based on my ethnographic interviews in 2006, chapter 4, "Remembering the Vigils," explores how young people remembered the protests of 2002 (both in the streets and online) four years later. The intensity of emotion and corporeal experiences prominent in my interviewees' recollections suggests that the format of the candlelight protest was a significant departure from South Korea's ideologically charged social movement tradition.

Part II then examines the period from 2008 to 2012, by which time the genre of Internet-born candlelight protest functioned as a de facto standard for youth activism. Chapter 5, "Internet Activism Transforming Street Politics," analyzes both the online discourses and the street performances of the 2008 candlelight festivals (*ch'otpul munhwaje*). The manifestation in the streets of irreverent subversion and parody, which had previously been contained largely to the safe and anonymous online space, suggests new democratic sensibilities liberated from authoritarian preconceptions and limits.

Based on my 2011 and 2012 interviews with young people who participated in the more recent candlelight protests since 2008, chapter 6, "Youth at the End of the Candlelight Decade," shows how these young Koreans, now in their late teens and early twenties, still retained memories of direct and impassioned participation in politics. Despite having to navigate an increasingly competitive environment, they continued to believe in the potential of critical citizens to monitor and protest the exercise of political power.

In the conclusion I trace, in broad strokes, how the issues illuminated by South Korea's youth activism in the candlelight protests continue to emerge in various countries and on the global stage. I discuss the interplay of local historical context, structural variations across different cultures and societies, and the role of chance in the cultural ignition process, and I speculate about the future of Internet-born youth activism.

CHAPTER 1

South Korean Youth in the New Millennium
Faint Memories of Authoritarianism, New Opportunities for Political Participation

Chi-yun* was in eleventh grade in 2008 when she learned that South Korea would resume the importation of American beef despite widespread concern over bovine spongiform encephalopathy, commonly called "mad cow disease." She was tipped to the change in policy after frequenting Internet communities dedicated to celebrity news and humor, where she saw a sudden outburst of messages condemning the government's decision and then reports from candlelight protests across South Korea. She was curious about what had drawn such a large number of people to participate, so she attended a protest at Kwanghwamun Square in Seoul. As a college student three years later, she told me, "Somehow a picture of me with a big smile ended up on the main page of an Internet news site. It was from a candlelight festival, where people were performing, singing, dancing, and marching while chanting Article 1 of the Constitution, 'The Republic of Korea is a democracy.' It was a festive environment. . . . I went to the protest every weekend."[1]

Her picture on the Web site portrayed Chi-yun as a veritable "candle girl," the face of the 2008 protests, and her story exemplifies how youth politics in South Korea had changed by the first decade of the twenty-first century: dissenters no longer weighed the repercussions of criticizing the government and instead made their feelings plain by participating in candlelight protests. The protests over U.S. beef importation were only the most recent in a series of Internet-born youth movements that had mass media, politicians, and activists asking how seemingly depoliticized young Koreans had come to fiercely criticize the government—and even to openly denounce the United States, their country's closest ally.

What the head-scratchers failed to realize was that this question sim-ply did not apply to the Korean "millennials," born between the mid-1980s and mid-1990s and raised *after* the authoritarian era. The South Korean youths I encountered while researching this book were the first "digital na-tives," who grew up using the language of computers and the Internet.[2] Like millennials in other countries, they were familiar with getting news from the Internet; they were also comfortable with expressing their thoughts and with finding like-minded people on social media. As a product of the par-ticular context in South Korea, these young people shared distinct political and cultural experiences. They were the country's first generation to *live* democracy rather than to fight for it—even if they were not entirely liber-ated from authoritarian legacies in the educational system, in compulsory military service, and even in the traditions of the democratization move-ment itself.

Chi-yun and her fellow teenage participants at the candlelight protests represent a new type of political actor that emerged with the Internet-born protests of the early 2000s: young Koreans able to participate in national politics with fewer preconceptions about and limits on what they might achieve. However, by "political actor" I don't necessarily mean a self-identified intentional actor. Youth participants like Chi-yun did not al-ways join the protests with the formal intention of undermining the government; nevertheless, their unreserved expression of grievances ef-fectively scrutinized the ideological underpinnings of government deci-sion making and envisioned democratic participation beyond the bounds of existing institutional procedures.

The chronological narrative I offer in this chapter has two purposes. One is to document the cultural, political, and economic changes experienced by young South Koreans that prepared them to participate in Internet-born street protests: the legacies of the authoritarian era, the postauthoritarian reforms and economic changes in the 1990s, and the development of Inter-net culture. The other is to critically reflect on "youth" as a social construct closely intertwined with both national and political identity. Since the early twentieth century, high school and college students had been imagined as agents of modernization and resistance against colonial and authoritarian rule.[3] They were objects of education for competing political visions.

Kwanghwamun Square, where candlelight protesters have gathered since 2002, captures how youth were imagined and mobilized in important junctures of contemporary Korean history. The space served as a theater for the national sovereignty and sacredness promoted by the regimes that followed the Korean War (1950–1953). Nearly 2.5 hectares large (about 6.2 acres), Kwanghwamun is surrounded by palaces from the Chosŏn dynasty dating from the fourteenth century, national government buildings, a national theater, and the U.S. Embassy; it evokes a narrative that South Korea is the only legitimate state on the Korean peninsula and the U.S. is an important patron against the Communist North. It is no coincidence that until the 1980s this ideologically charged space was barred from use by ordinary citizens and was therefore a prime target of protesters who contested the regimes' legitimacy. Even after democracy came to South Korea, these experiences with students remained as an interpretive lens through which scholars and critics viewed the youth collective at Kwanghwamun and other city centers. Yet, as I will show, young Koreans at these protests experienced a sociopolitical environment distinct from the political subjectivity experienced by the youth of the previous era.

Youth in the Colonial and Authoritarian Eras: Conveyors of the Nation's Political Ideals

As a social construct, Korean youth occupied an important space in the trajectory of Korean modernization and progress as the imagined conveyors of the nation's political ideals. The "young person" (*ch'ŏngnyŏn* or *sonyŏn*) was given particular significance in the early twentieth century when Korea was building a modern nation-state. As the country struggled to cope with Western and Japanese imperial powers, young men were considered agents to "depart from the past and achieve the future."[4] According to literary scholar Dafna Zur, the *sonyŏn* was imagined as a modern subject, departing from a backward country to revive national glory; furthermore, the "Great Korea" to be achieved was symbolized as youthful.[5]

In the 1910s, Korean students studying abroad in the United States and Japan brought a new modern knowledge back to their homeland. In this period, the student with at least some high school education became a particular youth subject and was considered a prime agent of the country's advancement.[6] During Japanese rule (1910–1945) and the subsequent authoritarian regimes, the student youth as a collective were given the identity of resisting injustice and confronting the leadership for the future of the nation. For instance, in the 1919 March First Movement against the Japanese, elite high school students made up a majority of those who poured into the streets to stand up against colonial rule.

After the Japanese occupation ended and the Korean peninsula became a frontline for Cold War ideological confrontation, youth were considered crucial agents who would fulfill the competing political ideals held by either the authoritarian regimes or the oppositional movement. Although the division of Korea was intended as a temporary measure to facilitate the surrender of Japanese troops on the peninsula, external political pressures maintained the divide. The Soviet Union backed Kim Il-sung as leader of the Democratic People's Republic of Korea, while the United States championed Syngman Rhee (1948–1960) as president of the recently established Republic of Korea. Both North and South Korea claimed to be the sole legitimate polity on the Korean peninsula, each calling the other a client state of the aligned superpower. Until the Soviet bloc collapsed and South Korea achieved indisputable economic supremacy over the North in the 1990s, each regime's legitimacy was something to be vigorously confirmed and contested. Moreover, South Korea's authoritarian leaders—who seized power through a sequence of military coups—had to shore up their legitimacy in the face of the democratization movement. For decades, these leaders invoked national security and prosperity to legitimize authoritarian control. President Rhee justified repressive actions during his three terms in the name of protecting the country from the Communist threat and of pursuing reunification. After Rhee stepped down, Park Chung Hee (1961–1979) seized power through a coup and continued to justify authoritarianism in the name of national security and prosperity, as did Chun Doo-hwan (1980–1988) after seizing power in the vacuum created by Park's 1979 assassination.

Amidst this ideological contestation, youth occupied an important position as both foot soldiers for and symbols of competing visions. In the aftermath of the fraudulent presidential election of 1960 (which Syngman Rhee won by the impossibly wide margin of 64 percent), high school and college students were the first to organize protests. The discovery of the mutilated body of Kim Chu-yŏl—a high school student who had participated in the antigovernment protests—catalyzed national anger, and students nationwide took to the streets in demonstrations that at their peak drew participants even from junior high and elementary school. What would later be called the April Revolution of 1960 led to Rhee's resignation and exile in the United States. This was the first significant grassroots popular movement since the Korean War and served as the "prototype of South Korean radical movement," leading to further protests against colonial legacies, authoritarian regimes, and the North-South division.[7] With the April Revolution, students established themselves as influential actors in Korean politics, challenging the status quo.

Park Chung Hee, who seized control in the resulting power vacuum, channeled this youth energy into his national development project while aggressively oppressing any oppositional student efforts. Park believed that strict ideological education combined with martial training would instill in students the values of anticommunism and patriotism, creating productive citizens for the project of state-driven industrialization and modernization. During his almost twenty years in power, he implemented a number of projects to sew these beliefs into the fabric of South Korean society. The "Charter for National Education" of 1968 begins with "We are born with the historic mission of national resurrection and prosperity" and stresses that "the love of the state and nation based on anti-communism and the democratic spirit is the way of our life." Until 1994 this charter was printed on the first page of every textbook from elementary to high school, and students would memorize it. In addition, Park established a pledge of allegiance and required that ceremonies held by governments, schools, and even private corporations begin with reciting the pledge in front of the flag and playing the national anthem.[8] Under Park's ideological education, the patriotic and potent youth of the April Revolution were called to become docile and productive instruments of modernization.[9]

The official history curriculum and rituals established during Park's two-decade rule continued well after the authoritarian governments had fallen. Until 2003, South Korea's sole history textbook still emphasized the glories of the premodern kingdoms in order to instill national unity and patriotism while downplaying contemporary history (which was saturated with coups d'état and violence by the state).[10] The successive authoritarian governments emphasized that the Communist bloc had been responsible for dividing the Korean peninsula, for ravaging the country during the Korean War, and for threatening South Korea's liberal democracy. The government also painted the United States as the liberator of Korea from Japanese rule, and as a military and economic patron throughout the Korean War and postwar reconstruction.[11] It is no coincidence that until the 1980s Kwanghwamun Square was an arena both for demonstrating the country's military preparedness against North Korea and for celebrating the national heroes who brought recognition to South Korea in international sports and science competitions. For instance, figure 2 shows a division of South Korean

Fig. 2   A division of South Korean soldiers marching before their dispatch to Vietnam on October 1, 1965 © Dong-a Ilbo.

soldiers marching into Kwanghwamun before being dispatched to Vietnam in 1965 to fight alongside the American military.

While the successive government regimes reinforced state nationalism, students nonetheless established themselves as voices for democracy and social justice, producing alternative visions for the nation. In 1965 college students led protests against the Park Chung Hee government's proposal to normalize diplomatic ties with Japan without receiving an apology for violence during colonial rule. In the 1970s college students forged alliances with organized workers to protest inhumane conditions and the suppression of trade unions. These students and dissident intellectuals produced and developed a counternarrative to Park's ideological education: that of *minjung*—literally, "the common people," those who were "politically oppressed . . . and economically exploited" in the developmental state.[12] The *minjung* were imagined as normative agents for social change and "potential antidotes to the brutal pace and deleterious side effects of development."[13] College students had time, knowledge, and student councils and societies, all of which were prominent resources relative to workplaces and other sectors of society. As historian Namhee Lee documents, students "constituted, organized, and articulated" the "projected visions and potentialities" of the *minjung* movement by turning their universities into centers of social agitation, and became revolutionaries fighting against authoritarian rule.[14]

In subsequent 1980s democratization efforts, two iconic memories defined the youth of that era as a generation of activists: the Kwangju massacre of 1980 and the mass uprising of 1987. In 1980, when then-general Chun Doo-hwan attempted to take the presidency through an indirect election after seizing power in a coup, hundreds of thousands of citizens mobilized nationwide to demand a direct election and democratic freedoms. Chun targeted protesters in Kwangju, a city of 720,000, for reasons that remain unclear. He blamed the uprising on Communist agitation, a familiar justification for suppressing antigovernment movements in postwar Korea. The Korean Special Forces, nominally under the Combined U.S. Forces Command, were dispatched to Kwangju; the military isolated the city and killed hundreds of civilians in what would later be characterized as a massacre.[15] Despite the Chun regime's strict control of the press, news of the massacre and stories of the citizens' resistance spread to activists and college students through underground publications.

For activists in the 1980s, Kwangju was the embodiment of the illegitimacy of the Chun government and of the U.S. policy to tolerate it in order to stabilize South Korea during the Cold War. Historian Bruce Cumings describes the Kwangju event as a defining point for a generation of South Koreans, much like the Vietnam War was for baby boomers in the United States.[16] The memory of Kwangju also defined college as a bastion of the democratization movement, as writer Yi Ŏ-yŏng recounts: "Tear gas and the scent of lilac are vivid memories for the democratization generation. When the lilac flower blooms on campus in the spring, student protests tend to hit their peak. Since the Kwangju uprising of May 1980, spring on college campuses began and ended with protests. In the 1980s, college students agonized whether to resist or escape into the scent of lilacs mixed with tear gas."[17]

In 1987 the torture and death of university student Park Chong-ch'ŏl during an interrogation was an impetus for spreading the democratization movement to a broader spectrum of college students and white-collar workers. Then, the day before scheduled nationwide protests on June 10, university student Lee Han-yŏl was killed by a tear gas grenade during a street protest. The two deaths transformed the June 10 protest into a prolonged nationwide demonstration. Millions occupied city centers, eventually forcing Chun to agree to a direct presidential election on June 29. The 1987 protests were a watershed event in the overthrow of the authoritarian regime and marked a coming-of-age for the so-called democratization generation, who remained politically active even after the transition to democracy.

During the 1980s democracy movement demonstrators repeatedly attempted to enter Kwanghwamun Square and the nearby U.S. Embassy to rebuke South Korea's authoritarian government and the United States for condoning human-rights violations. These incidents resulted in increased security for Kwanghwamun, and, before democratization in 1987, protesters succeeded in entering the square only four times. Those who were caught were sentenced to one to two years in jail.[18] However, on July 9, 1987, Lee Han-yŏl's funeral procession passed directly through City Hall Plaza to Kwanghwamun, which had filled with a crowd of more than one million people (see figure 3). The crowds in this space marked the significant achievements of the 1987 democratization movement. However, Lee's funeral was also a reminder of the steep social and physical costs, even martyrdom, of achieving this change.

Fig. 3   The funeral march for Lee Han-yŏl in downtown Seoul on July 9, 1987
© Koh Myoung-jin.

These efforts played a historic role in overturning authoritarianism and building a vibrant civil society in the 1990s, what anthropologist Jesook Song calls "as much an epistemological change as an organizational change."[19] From the radical movement tradition emerged a distinct student subject that still exerts influence on contemporary politics. "Generation 386" was originally coined in the 1990s, referring to people in their thirties (hence the 3) who went to college in the eighties (the 8) and were born in the sixties (the 6). In the 1990s, student participants of the 1980s democratization movement entered mainstream politics, established influential nongovernmental entities, organized the first labor party, and elected progressive politicians to the National Assembly.[20] Even though these Koreans were in their forties and fifties by the 2000s, Generation 386 remains a household term referring to the powerful cohort, which still retained "its symbolic value" as progressive agents of democratization until the Roh Moo-hyun administration (2003–2008).[21]

The student-youth of South Korea's authoritarian era left legacies that persisted well beyond their time as protesters, and this rich history of ideological contention established interpretative frameworks that persisted into the twenty-first century. The four-decade contest between authoritarianism and the democratization movement had created strong associations among criticism of the government, anti-Americanism, and sympathy toward North Korea—qualities that typically resulted in oppression by the government. This period also created normative ideas about the political role of Korean youth and what it means to be a political actor. The radical movement tradition reminded South Koreans that criticizing the government could mean physical and social sacrifice. In a divisive ideological environment, the space outside the binary of the status quo and the opposition is small. In South Korea, a young citizen had to decide whether to be an activist or a conformist; dissent demanded devotion, and was accompanied by social cost. Taking action without first considering the ideological or social ramifications was foolish at best and dangerous at worst.

Youth in a Postauthoritarian and Neoliberal Era: The Changing Currency of Dissent

Although the Korean peninsula remained perhaps the final locus of the Cold War, the ideological paradigms that had dominated the 1980s slowly crumbled after democratization. The pillars of South Korean ideological contestation—anticommunism, alliance with the United States, and national security—gradually became less relevant. As a result, many topics were no longer taboo, including sympathy toward North Korea, criticism of the United States, and denunciation of the government, which opened possibilities for political participation with fewer preconceptions and limits. At the same time, college students faced growing competitive pressure after the 1997–1998 financial crisis. As they increasingly withdrew from the political front, high school students became more active in voicing their political views.

In the 1990s South Korea's civilian governments (led by former antigovernment activists) reappraised the nation's authoritarian past and introduced progressive perspectives to the official educational curriculum. Under the Kim Young-sam government (1993–1998), former presidents Chun Doo-hwan and Roh Tae-woo (1988–1993) were brought to criminal court for conspiracy and insurrection in connection with the 1979 coup, and for the 1980 killings of protesters in Kwangju. With the trial came an official rewriting of contemporary history, including redefining the 1980 Kwangju uprising: it was no longer a riot, but a "democratization movement."[22]

This change was further accompanied by a reevaluation of allies and enemies in light of extreme North Korean poverty, the 1997 financial crisis, and the American War on Terror. Since the mid-1990s, a series of reports about famine and destitution ravaging North Korea allowed Koreans in the South to view those in the North as poverty-stricken brethren rather than a threat to national security. In June of 2000 President Kim Dae-jung (1998–2003) made a historic visit to P'yŏngyang, the first such presidential visit since the division of the peninsula in 1948; it stirred romantic dreams of reconciliation. South Koreans were captivated by reunions of divided families and the opening to tourism of North Korea's Kŭmgang Mountain. As political scientist Chalmers Johnson notes, the reunions and the tours had effects similar to those of Richard Nixon's 1972 visit to Beijing, which captivated Americans and shifted the Cold War stalemate. South Koreans saw the North–South summit as the "start of the end of the Cold War" on the Korean peninsula.[23]

At the same time, South Koreans' long-held belief in American benevolence began to fade. When the 1997 Asian financial meltdown brought South Korea to the verge of bankruptcy, the Kim Young-sam government turned to the International Monetary Fund (IMF)—which South Koreans deemed to be controlled by the United States—for an emergency bridge loan. The resulting $57 billion loan came with "IMF conditionality" that South

Korea agree to restructure the nation's economy. The Clinton administration used the crisis to open Korean financial and commodities markets to foreign investors.[24] This caused South Koreans to doubt U.S. sponsorship of Korean economic growth and led many to view the United States as a global competitor attempting to "subjugate" the South Korean economy.[25]

A few years later, in 2002, President George W. Bush declared North Korea to be part of the "axis of evil," against which the United States could employ preventive military—including nuclear—measures. Bush escalating the possibility of a peninsular crisis in this way further soured South Korean attitudes toward the United States.[26] Shortly after the "axis of evil" statement, 53.7 percent of South Koreans "disliked" the United States according to a Gallup poll, compared with only 15 percent in its 1994 survey. The generational difference was noteworthy: only 23.1 percent of respondents in their twenties and 21.2 percent in their thirties had a positive view of the United States, while 40.9 percent of respondents in their forties and 50 percent of those in their fifties and older viewed the United States in a positive light.[27]

However, the seemingly jarring anti-Americanism after the "axis of evil" statement was not caused by the statement itself, rather it was a manifestation of South Koreans' gradually changing political milieu. As political scientist Katharine Moon explains, when Korea suffered from war and poverty in the 1950s and 1960s, American material generosity—from weaponry to gifts for local orphanages—was instrumental in rebuilding social capital and was gratefully accepted. But, as South Korea achieved rapid development and entered postindustrial society in the 1990s, the country no longer needed this generosity. Furthermore, with the end of the Cold War, the political legitimacy of U.S. forces as the "bulwark of the free world" no longer stood.[28] The growing criticism of the United States was a consequence of the growth of South Korea's civil society, accompanied by a weakening of the ideological binary that had dominated the authoritarian era. The changes in the 1990s had altered the currency of dissent. Criticism of the Korean government or of the United States was no longer associated with radicalism.

With this political liberalization, the exponential growth of consumer culture and aggressive economic restructuring gradually transformed the status of college students from being at the vanguard of social change to becoming cultural consumers, and eventually to becoming a precarious labor resource in a competitive market. In this recently democratized civil

society, new political parties, trade unions, and civic organizations addressed
tensions in areas of environment, labor, peace, education, and gender.[29]
The student movement declined in its influence, and its targets diffused
in the absence of the authoritarian government. With democratization
came the rise of personal desires for individual expression and fulfillment
beyond collectivistic demands. This new demand, combined with rapid
economic development and political liberalization, led to a striking expansion of cultural industry and consumerism.[30] The labels "Generation X"
and "New Generation" (*sinsedae*) were widely used to distinguish the new
youth from the politically charged youth of the democratization era. These
terms marked social changes—for example, that Koreans in their twenties
were no longer more progressive than older Koreans, and that political identity did not project college students as a collective. Some scholars view this
change as consumerism and cynicism replacing the "romantic passion" of
the 1980s, while others see the liberation of youth culture from the bounds
of ideological burden.[31]

Additionally, the period of IMF involvement (1997–1998) ushered in
new anxieties over high unemployment, loss of lifetime positions, and global
competition, radically changing the culture of the university.[32] The Korean
won devalued by 40 percent, which raised production costs for some of
Korea's chief industries and led to bankruptcies. Between 1996 and 1998,
the overall unemployment rate rose from only 2.6 percent to a record high
of 7.6 percent, and unemployment for Koreans between the ages of fifteen
and twenty-four rose from 6.1 to 15.9 percent.[33] In 1997–1998, the average
urban household income declined by 14.4 percent, and the number of
households below the poverty line increased from 4 to 12 percent.[34] Until
the mid-1990s a degree from a reputable university had guaranteed a decent
job, which allowed students to concentrate on activism during their first few
years without worrying about the future. However, during the IMF era university graduates had to compete with experienced workers for jobs.[35]

Even though Korea recovered from the financial crisis, youth unemployment remained twice the overall unemployment rate (8.3 percent, compared with overall unemployment of 4.2 percent as of 2012).[36] Even when a
new graduate landed a job, it was likely to be a contract or freelance position. As more and more youths sought university education as a means to
secure employment, the college entrance rate among high school graduates
rose from 60 percent in 1997 to 84 percent in 2008, further devaluing the

university diploma.[37] The opening of financial markets and influx of foreign corporations added a particular anxiety and pressure for college students and employees alike to equip themselves for global competitiveness—including acquiring English competency and a cosmopolitan sensibility, as well as honing their creativity.[38] English proficiency tests became a staple requirement for job applicants, and even for graduation from some universities. South Korea soon became the largest market for these exams, representing 18.5 percent of worldwide testing in 2006 (in a country with only 0.8 percent of the global population).[39]

The generational categories popularized during this period, such as "Generation IMF" and "Generation 880-thousand won," indicate that Korean youth was largely imagined as a precarious subject under global neoliberal reforms. "Generation IMF" was widely used to refer to the first group of college students to experience the new job market beginning in 1997. Economist Kim Se-gyun argues that this generation is liberal when it comes to cultural issues but conservative regarding economic concerns, and they generally supported Lee Myung-bak's proposal to boost the economy in the 2007 presidential election.[40] That year, the term "Generation 880-thousand won" (*88 manwon sedae*)—coined by a best-selling book of the same name—was used to describe the current fragmented youth and their bifurcated condition in neoliberal Korea. The total of 880,000 won, roughly eight hundred U.S. dollars, was the monthly income one could earn through a minimum-wage temporary position—which a Korean in his or her twenties entering the market was likely to land in. This was also the price of the new "Prada" phone, a collaboration between the Italian luxury brand and a Korean cell-phone manufacturer. The term "Generation 880-thousand won" therefore captured the intensifying division between young Koreans who merely got by and those who inherited economic advantages.[41]

The youth imagined with these labels were no longer a political subject for Korea's particular national ideal, but simply a local variant of the global youth left adrift amid neoliberal changes. As literary critic So Yŏng-hyŏn aptly notes, it became hard for young Koreans to imagine a future or progress. Faced with competition for survival, conceiving of a common generational identity or solidarity became impossible. For them, the status quo was not something to resist but a goal to achieve.[42] We see similar generational characteristics in other countries. Japan's "Lost Generation" grew up during that country's recession in the 1990s and settled for odd jobs or part-time work, without opportunities for the higher-paying, salaried jobs that their predecessors enjoyed. Italy's "Generation Thousand Euro" (*Mileuristi*) was similarly comprised of young postgraduate employees who subsisted on monthly pay of one thousand euros (about 1,300 U.S. dollars at the time). Following the financial crisis of 2007–2008, a variety of comparable categories also emerged: "Generation 700 Euro" in Greece, "*Mileurista*" in Spain, and "*Génération Précaire*" in France.[43]

Yet, while Koreans in their twenties were detaching from politics, teenagers increasingly gained access to the progressive knowledge and critical-thinking skills that had previously been available only to concerned university students. In 2003, during the Roh Moo-hyun presidency, modern and contemporary Korean history (since the 1860s) was added to the high school curriculum. Now students had access to multiple editions of history textbooks, ranging from those that continued to parrot the regime's narrative to a revisionist history that critically appraised the authoritarian governments and U.S. patronage. The continuing effort to reappraise contemporary history culminated in the Truth and Reconciliation Commission of 2005, which examined the period from Japanese rule in 1910 up until 1992. Along with the official changes, the Korean Teachers and Educational Workers Union (KTU), which was formed in 1989 by democratization activists and legalized in 1996, further brought critical-thinking skills into the classroom.[44] For example, the KTU developed and shared curricula about the status of U.S. forces in Korea after the deaths of Hyo-sun and Mi-sŏn in 2002, about the international antiwar and peace movements in reaction to the U.S. military campaign in Iraq, and about the politics of economic globalization associated with the Asia-Pacific Economic Cooperation summit in Korea in 2005.[45]

Youths who participated in or observed the 2002 and 2008 protests recalled discussions in high school that introduced them to critical-thinking skills and a progressive worldview. For Myŏng*, then a high school student living in a city two hours from Seoul, the 2002 candlelight vigils were a privilege allowed to only a handful of elite students at her school: "We all had to stay in school until late in the evening to prepare for the college entrance exam. However, a few top students were 'dispatched' to the vigils. Teachers told them, 'You need to go and experience the protests, because the topic can be on the critical essay exam.'"[46] Since 1993 the government has allowed universities to administer their own exams in addition to the standardized college entrance exam, and elite schools adopted critical essay exams. Kŏn-ho* was in ninth grade when he participated in the 2008 beef protests, and by that time critical thinking and essay preparation had become part of the official curriculum. He recalled, "The 2008 candlelight protests were a big issue in my social studies class. We debated the topic. And, you know, the critical essay exam was an important part of university admissions at that time. . . . As these exams ask your opinion on current events, my classes incorporated a lot of current issues and newspapers."[47] Bin-na*, another participant in the 2008 protest, recalled a similar experience in her high school: "We had mock trials quite often and debated whether an action was right or wrong. . . . In junior high my homeroom teacher was greatly interested in social issues. He showed us a documentary about the Kwangju democratization movement and encouraged us to think about it. I also wrote lots of critical essays."[48]

It is against this backdrop that the candlelight protests can be best understood. Teenagers at the protests were not only direct descendants of the 1980s radical movement tradition but new types of social actors who flourished after the achievement of democratization. They had little experience with ideological confrontation or the social costs associated with dissent; instead, critical perspectives once held only by student activists were now readily available through standard educational curricula. As a result, these teenagers were able to participate in Internet politics, and later in street protests, with fewer preconceptions and limits than their predecessors.

Youth on the Internet: The Convergence of Play and Politics

The young Koreans at the candlelight protests had already been actively using the Internet for entertainment purposes by early 2002, supported by broad access to high-speed connections and the early development of online games and communities. With access to alternative news sources and discussion forums, Korean youth had been developing their own modes of commentary characterized by vibrant debate and irreverent parody. These online practices produced the 2002 vigils as a convergence of playful participation and traditional politics, and they continued to evolve with the consolidation of the candlelight vigil into an established protest repertoire.

At the time, the active online presence for South Korea's youth was unique even among modern industrialized nations. This highly connected society of forty-seven million matured into the social media age well ahead of the global curve. While the nation was recovering from the 1997–1998 financial crisis, the government implemented initiatives to support the new media industry with the slogan, "Korea will lead in the information age, although it lagged behind in globalization."[49] Growth and competition among telecommunication companies led to price reductions and a corresponding increase in demand for services. The monthly cost of home broadband decreased from forty U.S. dollars in 1999 to only thirty dollars by 2003.[50] In 2002 57.4 percent of all Koreans had a high-speed Internet connection, the highest broadband penetration rate in the world at the time, and still the highest as of 2012 at 98 percent (while the rate in the United States during the same period grew from 12 to 76 percent).[51]

Based on this infrastructure, a robust online culture established itself relatively early in the Internet age, with homegrown content and communities. South Korea's two major portal services, Daum.net and Naver.com, launched in 1997 and 1999. Offering free e-mail accounts and, later, free space for online communities, they quickly replaced English-based services such as Yahoo! and AltaVista. In 2002 90 percent of all Korean Internet users regularly logged onto Daum, making it one of the most visited Internet portals in the world.[52] Similarly, South Korean social networking site Cyworld has grown exponentially since 2002—well ahead of both Myspace (launched in 2003) and Facebook (in 2005)—and it had twenty-five million users by 2011.[53] Online games, following the enormous popularity of StarCraft since 1998, also contributed to the vibrant Internet culture among young Koreans.[54] According to a 2003 report on online gaming among Korean youth, more than 70 percent of Koreans between ages thirteen and twenty-four played games on the Internet. Even more notable is that more than 40 percent of Korean youths were also members of an online community dedicated to games, 30 percent had attended offline meetings of that community, and more than 50 percent reported making friends through online games.[55] Clearly, Korean cyberspace was not merely a tool for offline relationships and agendas; by the end of the 1990s it was already a hub of new relationships based on shared interests.

Furthermore, three prominent online phenomena in the early 2000s suggest that the Internet had become a locus of vernacular politics: alternative news sources, parody sites like *DC Inside,* and discussion forums such as *Agora.* First, in 2001 and 2002 online news sites *Pressian* and *Oh My News* launched, serving as hubs for progressive news and commentary. These and other similar news outlets instantly attracted already active Internet users with live updates on critical events, progressive op-eds, and investigative reporting into issues not covered by the mainstream press. *Oh My News* additionally published news and editorials from "citizen reporters" (volunteer

contributors whose number had reached 75,000 by 2013), offering live updates and alternative perspectives on important issues even before mainstream press covered them.[56] The day before the presidential election in
2002, with progressive Roh Moo-hyun and conservative Lee Hoi-chang
locked in a close race, *Oh My News* received six million visitors and 190 million page views—surpassing any mainstream media outlet.[57]

Second, parody and satire sites had been increasing in popularity among
young liberal users since the late 1990s, establishing parody as the signature
style of Internet culture. *Ttanji Ilbo,* an online parody of the conservative
Chosun Ilbo, launched in 1998. Literally meaning "knocking the opponent
to the ground," *Ttanji Ilbo* took a sarcastic view of the conservative media
with wry humor and manipulated images.[58] Meanwhile, *DC Inside* began
as a community dedicated to digital cameras ("DC") and photography in
1999. Much like the American 4chan or Japan's 2channel, *DC Inside* evolved
from a community for sharing photos and Photoshopped images into one
for cultural and political commentary using images and irreverent parody.
As anthropologist Yi Kil-ho notes, *DC Inside* was responsible for producing
many of the popular jokes, neologisms, and images that have gone viral on
the Internet—and for trolling, including provoking others with inflammatory messages or disclosing the identity of anonymous users. Out of *DC Inside* grew *Ilbe,* an online community known for its extremely conservative
perspective, derogatory remarks about political foes, and hateful content
about women and minorities.[59]

Third, *Agora,* an open online forum on Daum.net (now South Korea's
largest portal service), emerged in 2004 as a primary space for discussion
about political and social issues.[60] Named after the ancient Greek word for
"marketplace," *Agora* became a veritable online public square where concerned Internet users gathered to share information and opinions on emerging issues before mainstream news covered them. For instance, when the
government decided to resume importation of American beef in 2008, *Agora* became the center of information and debate about mad cow disease (as
detailed in chapter 5). Scientific reports circulating on *Agora* drew as many
as fifty-two million page views, with two million visitors daily during the
heat of the 2008 protests.[61]

These three types of community—alternative media, parody sites, and
discussion forums—served as crucibles both for the subversion of mainstream politics and for online protest: it wasn't always easy to tell the difference between frivolous play and political criticism on the Internet. With

this infrastructure in place, the South Korean online community could disseminate, respond to, and even mobilize against events in a way never seen before.

Early in 2002 this newly expanding online space facilitated an important precursor to the youth-driven protests taken up in this book. Anti-American sentiment erupted when U.S. president George W. Bush announced his plan to visit South Korea in February, shortly after his "axis of evil" statement. The news rallied many South Korean peace activists and progressive politicians. Civic groups released statements criticizing Bush's bellicose rhetoric; they described the United States as a barrier to inter-Korea peace efforts and reframed Bush's visit as an attempt to sell fighter aircraft and other weapons to South Korea.[62] Although street protests were confined largely to activists, Internet users—already wary of Bush's plan for the Korean peninsula—were sympathetic to the activists' arguments, discussing and recirculating them online.

Popular anti-American sentiment (*panmi*) then erupted unexpectedly when Internet users seized upon a controversial verdict at an international sporting match. On February 21, two days after Bush arrived in Seoul, South Korean short-track speed skater Kim Tong-sŏng was disqualified during the Salt Lake City Winter Olympics after finishing first in the 1,500-meter final. Rival Apolo Anton Ohno of the United States was instead awarded the gold. South Korean Internet users immediately accused Ohno of exaggerating the contact that disqualified Kim, and quickly concluded that the gold medal had been stolen. Their anger intensified when Jay Leno, host of NBC's *Tonight Show*, defended the referee's decision and made an inflammatory joke: "The Korean player was angry enough to have kicked *and* eaten his dog when he returned home."[63] Leno's remark spread rapidly among South Koreans on the Internet.

More than a hundred new communities appeared online devoted to self-proclaimed anti-Americanism. Internet users organized online protests and sent more than sixteen thousand angry e-mails to the U.S. Olympic Committee, shutting down the organization's Web site. Koreans also participated in an online poll conducted by NBC about the ruling, resulting in a 96 percent response that the Olympic ruling was unfair.[64] As the online protests progressed, a number of parody images and songs went viral, typically originating from *DC Inside.* For instance, a "Lord of the Cheating" poster superimposed Ohno's face onto the film poster for *The Lord of the Rings.* The original text, "The one who has the ring rules them all," became

"The one who cheats rules the game." Tongue-in-cheek credit lines identify as "producers" both Ohno and the judges who disqualified Kim.

The public outcry against what was considered an unfair home advantage for Ohno made anti-Americanism a pop-culture phenomenon.[65] "Fuckin' U.S.A.," a parody of Beach Boys hit "Surfin' U.S.A.," went viral. It begins with the Salt Lake City Olympics, then targets U.S. foreign policy for South Korea:

> Did you see the short track race? . . .
> You stole the Gold Medal.
> You always get what you want by force. . . . Did you hear what Bush said?
> He threatened North Korea and intervenes in South Korean politics.
> You're a bully.

At the same time, the most sought-after audio file on the Web was "Paper Plane," a fictional comedic conversation between Kim Dae-jung and George Bush in which the latter pressures Kim to purchase F-15 fighters. In addition to circulating these files, Internet users organized a boycott of U.S. products, including Coca-Cola, Hollywood films, and U.S. restaurant chains, while opposing the government's plan to purchase the jet fighters.[66] This online parody and subversion of mainstream politics that proliferated around 2002 didn't simply mirror or even derive directly from existing politics. Instead, the well-developed online culture and postauthoritarian upbringing of modern Korean youth provided the sociocultural backdrop against which they were able to express shared emotion, produce irreverent parody, and dismiss taboos—something that cultural critics Paik Wook-in and Ho-young Lee argue had been possible only in personal settings during the authoritarian era.[67] By the time of Hyo-sun and Mi-sŏn's deaths in June, South Korea's younger generation was ready to revive the popular "anti-American" slogans of early 2002 and organize another collective action.

The emergence of South Korea's postauthoritarian youth activism was a slow and uneven process. Even though authoritarian rule officially ended in 1987, early in the twenty-first century young people still heard its echoes when they enlisted in the military, attended school, or listened to their parents. However, changes in South Korean politics and culture since the 1990s gradually erased the remnants of authoritarianism as well as the sense of sacrifice and fear associated with dissent, and weakened the taboo of criticizing the government or the United States. Given these changes, it's difficult to conclude that modern South Korean students who participated in Internet and street protests were direct successors to the anti-American activists of the democratization era. These teenagers were much less bound by the need for ideological legitimacy that had tempered political action by the previous generation; the online protests surrounding the 2002 Winter Olympics and Bush's War on Terror had left young people with a vibrant online space in which to express both nationalism and their newfound skepticism of U.S. peacekeeping efforts on the Korean peninsula. Furthermore, the irreverent criticism did not allow for an easy distinction between serious dissent and play. This convergence suggests the appearance of a new mode of political participation marked by little fear of dissent, yearning for national respect in accord with Korea's recent economic and political development, lessening of the anxiety associated with political participation, and use of the Internet as a vibrant space for grassroots discourse.

PART I

THE RISE OF INTERNET-BORN YOUTH ACTIVISM

CHAPTER 2

The Birth of the Internet Youth Protest
The 2002 Candlelight Vigils

Immediately after the deaths of Hyo-sun and Mi-sŏn in Yangju on June 13, 2002, local residents and activists held protests in front of Camp Casey, where the armored vehicle that hit the girls was based. The protesters were angered by the deployment of convoys through narrow village roads during the day and distributed petitions demanding a thorough investigation of the accident. They were joined by activists who had long criticized the U.S. role in the division of Korea. However, most South Koreans were still celebrating their team's victories in the World Cup, which held the country transfixed, and paid no attention to the incident or the protests that followed. Nonetheless, the patriotism and festivities of the World Cup contributed to belatedly igniting the Internet with the girls' deaths nearly five months later, when U.S. courts-martial found the operators of the vehicle not guilty of negligent homicide.

Here, I examine this critical period between June and December 2002, when the deaths of Hyo-sun and Mi-sŏn became a national tragedy and symbol of South Korea's position under the thumb of U.S. patronage. I argue in this chapter that the girls' deaths captivated young Koreans because they felt that the terms of the U.S. presence—established in the 1950s amid the ruins of the Korean War (1950–1953)—did not reflect South Korea's present stature. In the period between the accident and the inception of the vigils, young Internet users circulated their objects of captivation, ranging from photographs of the girls to parodies of the verdicts to the call for a rally, and composed emotional narratives to share their intense anger and to mobilize for protest against the acquittals. The composition and circulation of sentimental discourses became Internet users' vernacular modes of refuting what they considered to be unreasonable verdicts. Even though these discourses were not directly polemical, they effectively laid responsibility for the girls' deaths on the outmoded military arrangement. Young Internet users' impassioned online participation therefore constituted an important political critique that questioned the relevance of agreements conceived in the aftermath of the Korean War and envisioned a politics uninfluenced by that history.

In the development of this collective critique of the U.S.–Korean relationship, online communities offered a space for expressing the younger generation's changed zeitgeist without conforming to the norms of existing political debate. I agree with many critics that individual participants likely did *not* arrive at the vigils with a well-defined understanding of the history behind the Status of Forces Agreement (SOFA) or of the U.S. law behind the trial verdicts; even fewer would have participated in the vigils with the intention of directly challenging the close alliance between South Korea and the United States. Older Koreans, who vividly remembered American benevolence and patronage in times of war and poverty, considered the United States to be beyond criticism. However, for the young Koreans who grew up in a democratized South Korea and who recently experienced national pride during the World Cup, it was unreasonable that the armored vehicle's operators were not held accountable for the accident under Korean law. Online communities offering partial anonymity and easy participation enabled users to share feelings, express their captivation with the deaths, and mobilize like-minded users to attend vigils. The impassioned personal messages and parodies and the photographs of the girls' bodies—as well as the continuous recirculation of those images—allowed young South Koreans to muster their underarticulated yet potent yearnings for a changed status for South Korea, and to channel those yearnings into a critique of the U.S.–South Korean relationship.

The 2002 World Cup: An Unlikely Backdrop

In June 2002 South Korea cohosted the World Cup soccer tournament with Japan, and the South Korean national soccer team advanced all the way to the semifinals. For many Koreans, this achievement attested to South Korea's transition from client state to proud producer of global culture, and they reveled in their newfound national pride. The event eclipsed the girls' deaths, which occurred in the midst of the spectacle, and local residents and anti-American activists tried in vain to draw public attention to the accident. At the time, it seemed that all South Korea cared about was the tournament. The flag-draped revelers and nationalist slogans such as "Great Korea," "Victory Korea," and "We're a strong team" were uneasy objects for me in 2002—they appeared to resurrect the indoctrinated patriotic subject that I once was myself in the early 1980s. In fact, some critics lamented that the "rapture" of nationalism was debilitating critical minds.[1]

However, despite its ambiguous political implications at the time, in the long run the World Cup constituted an important backdrop for the candlelight vigils by reconfiguring public experiences. The event animated the already expanding online space, cementing it as an important element of youth culture. The "Red Devils," supporters of the Korean national soccer team, had originated as an Internet community and drew eighty thousand new members in the weeks after the tournament began—giving the online group a membership of two hundred thousand by the end of June.[2] Additionally, Internet users established and joined fan communities, parody sites, and discussion forums to share information about and responses to games, players, and strategies. The online space emerged as both a community for soccer fans and a prominent coordinator of collective action in city centers.

During the tournament, downtown Seoul—which had previously been a stage for the "national vision"—transformed into a space for popular gatherings and festivity. The street celebration began when the scarlet-clad Red Devils settled into a corner of Kwanghwamun Square to watch matches on the multiscreens atop major press buildings nearby. After the Korean team entered the round of sixteen in mid-June, these street gatherings turned into a de facto festival.[3] The municipal government of Seoul saw an opportunity to showcase South Korea's grassroots dynamism and decided to allow large crowds to congregate in the city center. This newly opened space gave the participants a sense of catharsis emanating from the collective festivities and from the national pride they felt and were able to express. Not only for soccer fans but for young, urban Koreans, the street cheering became a cultural event. When their team played the semifinal on June 25, seven million people (from a total population of only forty-seven million) joined street celebrations nationwide. Throughout the World Cup period, twenty-nine million people participated in the celebrations. In the crowd, teenagers and women were especially visible—a new element for street gatherings in South Korea. As anthropologist Kim Hyŏn-mi suggests, their particular visibility as highlighted in the media might have been an optical illusion against a historical backdrop in which young males dominated public gatherings. However, it is hard to dispute that the safe banner of patriotism and institutional support by the municipal government allayed the gravitas that Koreans had previously associated with occupying the city center.[4]

Early Response: Coming to Terms with Unreasonable Verdicts

As the excitement of the World Cup faded, Internet users belatedly turned their attention to the accident that killed Hyo-sun and Mi-sŏn. It especially kindled interest and attention that South Korea had no jurisdiction in the case under SOFA. Awareness spread rapidly online as users hyperlinked the news alongside photographs of the girls lying dead in the street. Then, in late November, military juries found Sergeants Nino and Walker not guilty of negligent homicide.[5] With the news of the verdicts, the girls' deaths captured the attention of Korea's online community, instantly provoking widespread sorrow and anger. Internet users were transfixed by stories about how South Korean law did not apply in the deaths of two South Korean girls killed in their own country, how the two vehicle operators were acquitted by a jury of American military personnel, and how Korean police guarded a U.S. military base against *Korean* protesters. The stories circulated quickly throughout popular Internet portals, rallying young Koreans. Struck by the perceived injustice of the verdicts, tech-savvy teenagers gathered online to mourn the deaths, calling the girls "sisters and friends." In this emotionally charged environment, one Internet user's proposal for a candlelight vigil continued to circulate well past its intended date, resulting in nightly protests against the terms of the U.S. military presence in South Korea. On December 13, 2002, the six-month anniversary of the accident, more than thirty thousand Koreans mourned the girls' deaths in fifty-seven rallies across the nation, with banners demanding "Retrial of the GIs at a Korean court," "Renegotiation of SOFA," and "Renegotiate the U.S.–South Korean relationship." The peaceful commemorations drew hundreds of thousands of Koreans nightly for more than a year, and influenced the course of the December 19 presidential election.

After the American servicemen were acquitted, U.S. Army officials released a statement declaring that the decisions had been based on "a thorough review of all the evidence." According to the statement, the armored vehicle—a behemoth designed for portable-bridge transport—was the third vehicle in a convoy, and it moved toward the shoulder of the road to avoid a Bradley fighting vehicle approaching from the opposite direction.

Nino, the commander of the vehicle, saw the girls walking on the shoulder and instructed Walker, the driver, to stop. Because of a malfunctioning radio, however, Walker did not hear him. American officials expected that the detailed statement would alleviate the Korean public's mistrust of the U.S. military court, and bring closure to the issue. Instead, many young Koreans were frustrated by the details, particularly that an armored military vehicle killed the girls in a *residential* neighborhood, and that the U.S. military—the responsible party—conducted the investigation. These youths were unwilling to accept "not guilty" verdicts from U.S. juries at trials held behind the closed gates of a U.S. military base.

An outpouring of emotion and disapproval filled the Internet, a vernacular strategy in response to what users considered unreasonable decisions. American jurisdiction struck Koreans as evidence of U.S. highhandedness—in stark contrast to their newfound national pride during the World Cup—and news of the acquittals further fed a growing anti-American sentiment. The verdicts, combined with the dramatic nature of the incident and the closed process of its investigation, were a perfect crucible for speculation and conspiracy theories. Rumors ranged from the two operators knowingly crushing the girls to an extensive cover-up by the U.S. military.[6] Using images, messages, cartoons, and personal reflections, Internet users built a shared interpretation of the girls' deaths as a national tragedy that symbolically represented South Korea's stature as a client state.

South Korea's mainstream media recognized the public's mounting bewilderment and anger. Both the conservative *Chosun Ilbo* and liberal *Hankyoreh* were aware that this outrage stemmed from SOFA, which provided no role for South Korean police in the investigation or for Korean law at trial. Headlines in response to the first acquittal, of Sergeant Nino on November 20, included "Failure of Communication Devices? Cannot Accept a Not-Guilty Verdict" (*Chosun Ilbo*) and "U.S. Court Deceived Koreans, Mounting Demand for SOFA Revision" (*Hankyoreh*).[7] Editorially *Chosun Ilbo* took a hands-off position in reaction to the verdict, stating simply, "We cannot persuade the civic groups to calm down," while *Hankyoreh* defended the mounting antagonism toward the U.S. military as a "natural and justifiable response to the arrogant U.S. forces that disregard Korean public opinion."[8] Both papers acknowledged anti-American sentiment among South Koreans on this specific issue as an understandable response.

However, Internet users increasingly associated the accident not with its immediate legal context but with the broader U.S.–South Korean relationship, in an attempt to identify an accountable entity in the absence of any legally responsible party. Online postings after the verdicts often omitted the military court itself and directly blamed the United States for the acquittals: "The American GIs committed such a brutal crime without guilt. The U.S. is so arrogant"; "They still see us as a desolate country . . . on the verge of a civil war, calling for their intervention"; "Koreans should unify and expel the American troops from Korea. We should boycott McDonald's and Burger King, too."[9] Many Internet users deplored the status of South Korea as a weak underling to the United States: "After all, we're a powerless country"; "I'm sorry that those girls were born in a country that doesn't have the power to protect them"; "We're a colony of America."[10]

Although it is possible to interpret such responses as exaggerated accusations against the United States or as expressions of self-pitying nationalism, I instead see these reactions as Internet users' vernacular efforts to come to terms with the tragic incident by establishing responsibility and accountability. They inserted the girls' deaths into the larger narrative of the historical U.S. presence, which began when the nation was in ruins after the Korean War and continued supposedly because of the division of the two Koreas and ongoing tensions with the North. By situating the accident into this narrative, users collectively made an implicit argument that the girls' deaths were not an isolated incident but a consequence of the obsolete terms of the U.S. military presence.

The broad circulation and recirculation of images during this period— ranging from sentimental to shocking, and from original to heavily Photoshopped—reveals the cultural logic through which Internet users formed a collective and criticized the perceived injustice of the verdicts. In particular, circulation of the girls' funeral photographs marked a belated public attention to their deaths and a shared sense of injustice (see figure 4). The girls' black-and-white school pictures were used in the funeral on June 15, two days after the accident. At that time, local residents and activists were trying to direct public attention to the deaths and to the upcoming trials of Nino and Walker, to little effect. On November 18, the Pan-Korean Community for Two Girls Killed by a U.S. Armored Vehicle (PKC)—a coalition formed by over one hundred civic organizations—demanded that its representatives be allowed to attend the trials.[11] PKC members attempted to enter Camp Casey, where the trials were to be held, resulting in violent

Fig. 4   The main page of *Moim*.

clashes with the Korean police in which several protesters were injured. However, the incident was covered only by progressive newspapers and remained unknown to much of the public.

The turning point came on November 20, when the not-guilty judgments were announced. After the verdicts, Internet users took notice of the original incident. With mounting public interest, the funeral photos circulated rapidly—as the cover image of online communities dedicated to the girls (as in figure 4), as part of user-created online messages (figure 5), or in makeshift shrines in the street. These images were demonstrative "not only of the particular event but also of the conditions of public representation most crucial to understanding the event."[12] As Hariman and Lucaites suggest, iconic images of a period—American examples include the Kent State shooting or the "napalm girl" during the anti–Vietnam War era—should be read more as indicators of public anger and frustration than as mere representations of the events. Similarly, Hyo-sun and Mi-sŏn's funeral photos, combining straight-faced images of the girls in their school uniforms with the black ribbons typical for funerals, accentuate the premature deaths of the teenagers and the public sense of unintelligibility.

In stark contrast with the solemn and formal funeral photos, a graphic photograph showing the girls' bodies crushed by the huge vehicle also went viral. A Yangju photographer and activist had taken the pictures in June and released them on the Web that summer in order to publicize the accident. At the time the images became popular primarily for their gory details, and circulated among forums dedicated to photography, grotesque or shocking images, and humor. However, as criticism within and among online communities increased, pointing out that the pictures violated the dignity of the dead and were so graphic as to be offensive, the images largely disappeared. Only after the verdicts in November did the photos reappear online, this time posted and reposted to rally viewers' emotions against the acquittals. After *Moim* users hyperlinked and reposted the photos, one commented, "I had only heard that the schoolgirls were brutally killed. I just saw the pictures. They are so painful"; another contributor noted, "I saw messages and images from many Web boards, and had a fit of anger."[13] It's impossible to determine exactly how the images reappeared, but responses to them suggest that *Moim* members searched the Web and found the photos after they learned of the verdict. Others then recirculated the images by copying and pasting them to additional Web sites, and still more users came across the images that others had recirculated. No matter how people encountered them, the photos reminded concerned Koreans of their initial shock and helped them to share their anger. This captivation with the pictures suggests that Internet users shared a sense of the importance of the event and an intensity of emotion, even though viewers' interpretations of the accident and assignment of culpability might still have been underarticulated.

Along with circulating the images, members of *Moim* displayed symbols that signaled their collective identity as mourners and protesters. The ▷◁ and ▦ ideograms represented the linen ribbons worn by family members of the deceased at funerals and sometimes for a year afterward. According to a thread on the discussion boards about their origins, these symbols "suddenly appeared on November 29."[14] *Moim* members also adopted user names that expressed their stance toward the tragedy. Some mourned the deaths, taking the forum names "In Commemoration," "Apologies, Sisters," "Pray for You," and "▦In my Memory▦." Others expressed national pride or nationalism, using "▦㉝Girl of Great Korea▦," "2002 Great Korea?," and "Correct the Past." Still others revealed animosity toward the United States, with "Fucking U.S.A," "▦Yankee go home▷◁," "▦Admire Bin Laden," "HateBush," and "Don't Smoke Marlboro." User names, ideograms, and pictures were critical means of affirming their shared sentiment and identity as mourners and advocates of the deceased.

The circulation of messages that sympathized with Osama bin Laden, a symbol of anti-Americanism, similarly reflected an underarticulated yet potent critique of the verdicts. Some contributors to *Moim* adopted user names that included *Laden* or *bin Laden,* and cited his attack on the World Trade Center—for instance, "If the U.S. is not guilty, then Bin Laden is not guilty, either."[15] One post expressed an even more extreme view: "I know it's wrong, but I would understand if Bin Laden attacked the U.S. again. I even anticipate it a little."[16] A parody widely circulated online during this period drew a parallel between the verdicts and the September 11 attack:

> Osama Bin Laden claimed that he was not guilty in the terrorist attack on the World Trade Center. He claimed that he ordered his pilots not to crash into the buildings over the radio, and, finding that the radio did not work, shouted as loud as he could. But the noise around him kept his orders from being transferred to the pilots. The jury found his argument convincing and decided that he was not guilty. The Mujahidin attorney for Al Qaeda presented a re-enactment of the crime scene as evidence and accused the WTC of "blocking the route of the airplanes." In order to ensure fairness in the trial, the jury was composed completely of Al Qaeda members. In the end, the owner of the WTC was convicted for blocking the airplanes' routes.[17]

The author satirizes Sergeant Nino's claim that he tried to point the girls out to Walker, who couldn't hear because the radio had malfunctioned and the vehicle was too noisy for Nino's shouts to carry. The parody also jabs at the composition of the juries—U.S. military personnel—that handed down the acquittals. The seemingly extreme association of the girls' deaths with the 9/11 attacks highlights South Korean Internet users' collective doubt about why the girls died, and the perceived injustice of the verdicts. Parody, as Hariman puts it, will "expose the limits of public speech," while refusing to "discuss, amend, or enact" the object at hand in given terms.[18] Even though parody does not always serve the oppressed (it is a favorite tool for mass entertainment in the modern era), it allows the marginalized to create a space for contesting the dominant view.[19] The viral circulation of the parody above indicates Internet users' refusal to discuss the incident within the given legal discourse. The parody exposes the limits of the legal framework and shifts the ground to the matter of accountability for the deaths. By viewing and recirculating emotional images and extreme parodies, users developed the shared understanding that the South Korean–U.S. relationship made this seemingly unreasonable situation legal, and invited others to attend to the absurdity of the verdicts.

In addition to expressing their grievances with the verdicts, Internet users dedicated messages, cartoons, and Flash videos to the girls. These personal and commemorative messages effectively demanded that Koreans pay attention to history and begin to reform South Korea's political system. Figure 5 shows the first segment of a 120-line message that included images dedicated to the girls. It was created by a then-anonymous Internet user on November 24—two days after the acquittal of Sergeant Walker—and soon copied and pasted into numerous forums, including *Moim*.[20]

Fig. 5   A letter to Hyo-sun and Mi-sŏn, posted on *Moim* © Kang Full.

An English translation of the text reads as follows:

Girls . . .
You were close friends growing up together.
You were best friends.
Holding hands, what did you talk about with each other?
What you wanted to be, your friendship, or boys you'd just passed by?
Looking at the photos of you together, I believe you could have been
    friends for the rest of your lives. . . .
You would have blossomed as you grew up.
You could have devoted attention to your appearance, met boyfriends,
    struggled with the fever of first love, felt anxious about jobs after
    graduation, and fretted about getting older . . . like other girls.
You could have done what others would do.
What could you have become?
Scholars, artists, celebrities, or just honest ordinary people?
. . . And you could have become mothers.
But now these possibilities are all gone.[21]

What captivated readers and made this posting a viral phenomenon was the shared sense of commemoration and guilt. The cartoon offers an imaginary narrative of the lives that the girls could have anticipated. The posting also juxtaposes photographs of the girls when they were younger with the sixty-ton bridge carrier that killed them, and images of their childhood with blurred pictures of the girls' bodies on the street. These contrasts underscore the tragic nature of an accident that took not only their lives but their futures.

By addressing the deceased as "you," the narrative also eliminates the distance between the girls and the reader. The reader is positioned as a friend saddened by the loss of the girls, and as an adult lamenting the loss of a future the girls could have had. Later in the message, the author confesses that South Koreans were at least partially responsible for what happened: "But we forgot what we shouldn't have forgotten. In the middle of the World Cup frenzy, we forgot *you*. In the middle of the presidential election campaign, we forgot *you*." The speaker directly apologizes to the girls for not protecting them, for ignoring their deaths in the midst of a global sports spectacle, and for forgetting them again until the court-martial verdicts recaptured the public's attention. In this narrative the accident becomes a personal event for the author, who invites readers to take part in the girls' lives and deaths.

Despite the potentially controversial message that South Koreans were collectively responsible for the girls' deaths, the posting is not polemic; instead, it maintains a personal and commemorative tone. By highlighting the sentimental over the polemical, the author positioned the images and text to awaken the Korean people's memories of the girls' deaths and make the accident relevant to them.

Another message widely circulated during the same period also shows that commemorative discourses were not merely sentimental but also political, contesting the legitimacy of the verdicts:

> I don't know you.
> I've never seen you.
> But I'm all in tears and filled with remorse.
> My heart's breaking.
> I'm sorry . . . sorry . . . sorry . . .
> "Not guilty."
> I never learned it in school.
> I learned for three years in high school that
> the law is the enforced truth
> that leads people to fairness and propriety
> But "not guilty" . . .
> What is law?
> Moreover, what is this country that demands our toil, taxes, and tears
> and assumes that it protects us?[22]

The message expresses bewilderment at the verdicts, simultaneously addressing the political and legal inconsistencies involved in the decisions. The author points out the irony that even though the victims were South Koreans who died in their own country, their country's law did not apply to them. The author lost confidence in that law, which was supposed to enforce "fairness and propriety." Although it takes the voice of an impassioned personal confession, this posting also deeply questions the law, mainstream politics, and Koreans' historical consciousness—all of which have acquiesced to a system the author regards as unjust.

These emotional images and personal messages captivated users with sorrow over the deaths of the girls. By further circulating the texts beyond the local neighborhood and across online communities, Internet users shared anger and grievances about the verdicts. These shared grievances aren't merely the sum of individual feelings; as Zizi Papacharissi describes, these are nascent political critiques that are "affectively felt and lived prior to, or perhaps in lieu of, being ideologically articulated."[23] Although individuals might have lacked a specific awareness of the convoluted history and current status of the U.S.–South Korean relationship, Internet users captivated with the girls' deaths effectively questioned the existing pact between the two countries and reached an unspoken conclusion: that the current legal framework, which did not allow for the host country's participation in the investigation or trials, was at odds with principles of justice and fairness.

The Candlelight Vigils Begin

On November 26, 2002, *PD Journal,* a television show similar to CBS's *60 Minutes,* aired an investigative report on the U.S. court-martial process titled "Trials Behind Closed Doors: Are They Innocent?"—the first mainstream media investigation into the trials. The show highlighted the South Korean government's reluctance to deal with the aftermath of the girls' deaths, and its acquiescence to U.S. military decisions. Immediately after the show, online communities hosted numerous postings expressing shock and anger toward both governments. "Watching *PD Journal,* I was so outraged." "So angry, I almost broke my TV." "I was so stunned by what I saw in *PD Journal.* A U.S. official said they believed in the Korean government to bring closure to the case, while we don't believe in our government."[24] These responses suggest that many South Koreans learned of the girls' deaths through the show, and went online to find more information about what happened or to share their reactions. Online communities dedicated to the girls quickly expanded, and the volume and pace of online postings increased drastically.

This is the context in which the proposal for a candlelight vigil went viral, capturing Internet users' intense feelings of injustice and their yearnings for an alternative to the unilateral decisions of the U.S. courts-martial. An Internet user named Angma expressed his distress at watching the *PD Journal* report and proposed a candlelight vigil in Kwanghwamun Square on November 30, 2002. He initially posted his idea on the discussion board of *Hankyoreh,* from which it spread to other Web sites and forums. Angma wrote,

Let's show our resolution to the world.
We're the people of Korea who are entitled to enjoy Kwanghwamun.

I cried while watching *PD Journal.*

I finally understood why they [protesters at U.S. military bases] offered such strong opposition.

Some say that when people die, their souls become fireflies.

Let's fill up Kwanghwamun with our souls.

Let's become thousands of lights, with Hyo-sun and Mi-sŏn, and glow in the dark.

6pm this Saturday, let's give up our weekend rest.

Dress in black and bring a candle.

Light it all the way from home.

When someone asks why, tell them you're going to comfort the souls of our sisters who were wrongly killed.

Let's prevail upon Kwanghwamun with candles in our hands.

Let's commemorate Hyo-sun and Mi-sŏn, whom we forgot in the raptures of June [the World Cup soccer tournament].

Will the police restrain us? Still we'll come. Will they beat us? We'd rather be beaten.

We're not like Americans who return violence with greater violence.

I'll be delighted to see only one person.

We'll talk about a Korea where Mi-sŏn and Hyo-sun can rest.

I'll begin with myself.

This week, next week, the week after that.

Let's fill up Kwanghwamun with our candlelight.

Let's extinguish the U.S. violence with our peace.[25]

Angma's call conveys the common feelings of empowerment then guilt that Internet users experienced in celebrating the World Cup in the face of the girls' deaths. Angma calls himself a part of the "we" who watched *PD Journal* and learned the historical origins of the South Korean–U.S. relationship. His post also addresses a feeling that South Koreans shared: the World Cup remained with them as an unforgettable memory of liberation when they took over downtown Seoul to celebrate the national team's victories, and as a newfound sense of national pride. However, the World Cup also evoked guilt because Koreans were too immersed in the spectacle to pay attention to the girls' deaths. The shared sentiments reflected in Angma's call rallied a broad spectrum of South Koreans who would normally not participate in a protest, and formed a collective that would accept responsibility for seeing justice done.

Another appeal of the call stems from envisioning a different reality based on democratic principles as an alternative to the arguably unilateral and unjust U.S.–South Korean relationship. Angma proposes an open discussion of the accident in order to develop a reasonable solution, and presents the vigil as a practice of self-government—an alternative to the unilateral verdicts issued by the U.S. military court. Democratic ideals are juxtaposed with the irony of the South Korean police's decision to protect a U.S. base from Korean protesters. The proposed vigil promised a space in which citizens could "talk about a Korea where Mi-sŏn and Hyo-sun can rest"—a better Korea where the people exert power as members of a sovereign nation. This imagery appeals at once to the sense of powerlessness Koreans felt after the verdicts and to aspirations of becoming agents who would govern themselves by reasonable measures against seemingly unjustifiable "U.S. violence."

The reaction to Angma's post was fervent, and the call to protest attained an iconic status as the catalyst of the vigils. Postings on *Moim* urged others to attend the vigil and called for a wide dissemination of information: "Let's Go to Kwanghwamun!!!!!!!!!!!!!!!!!!!!!"; "Let's meet in front of the U.S. Embassy"; and "One person becomes two . . . two become four . . . Like that, we will fill the entire Kwanghwamun Square with candles."[26] Internet users on *Moim* and beyond continued to circulate Angma's call even after the proposed vigil was held, turning the one event into nightly protests throughout the winter of 2002. The original post became so famous that mass media and even vigil participants mistakenly believed that Angma was the sole instigator of the 2002 vigils. *Oh My News* acknowledged his role by naming him "Person of the Year."[27] However, despite the potency of Angma's post, it was the underarticulated but intense dissatisfaction of young Koreans that circulated the call beyond the proposed date and made the vigils a space for envisioning a democratic alternative to the status quo.

As Angma's call reached increasingly larger audiences, Internet users shifted their demand from the retrial of the American servicemen to the reform of what they perceived to be an outmoded U.S.–Korean relationship. Online postings demanded an official apology from President Bush, a response equivalent to President Clinton's apology in 1996 immediately after the rape of a Japanese girl by three U.S. servicemen in Okinawa.[28] When President Bush issued the long-awaited public apology on November 27, delivered through U.S. ambassador Thomas Hubbard, both the U.S. and South Korean governments expected that mounting anti-American sentiment would end. Instead, Internet users continued to protest the verdicts, laying responsibility for the girls' deaths on the outmoded Cold War arrangement with the United States and on South Korean political leaders who allegedly advanced their own interests ahead of the nation's. In the aftermath of the apology, online posts described the historical influences of the United States in Korea. For example, a post titled "That Is the SOFA" traced the historical development of SOFA and put forth what the author considered its unfair terms; another post, "What the U.S. Has Done to Us for the Past 60 Years," listed the crimes committed by U.S. service members.[29] By the time the vigil was proposed, Internet users had already developed the collective feeling that the girls' deaths were not an isolated incident but something reflecting the deeper historical and political U.S.–South Korea relationship.

In the continuing protests throughout the winter of 2002, the World Cup served as a vernacular trope that inspired younger South Koreans to envision collective action at the vigils. In Angma's call and the commemorative narrative shown in figure 5, the World Cup embodies the rapture and frenzy that blinded Koreans to the girls' deaths. The potent crowd cheering in Kwanghwamun became a reference point from which protesters envisioned both assertive nationalism and the expression of collective action. In reposting Angma's call, Internet users evoked the feeling of powerful collectivity they experienced during the Cup: "Where are the seven million people of the World Cup?"; "Let's show Koreans' power of the World Cup"; "If only we could show a tenth of the energy we had in the World Cup"; "We know individuals got together and created the legend of the five million during the World Cup"; "During the World Cup we had five million people. Let's make it ten million this time!"[30] Contributors even used slogans from the World Cup, such as "Dreams Come True," "Great Korea," and "We're a Strong Team," to urge others to attend the vigils. By remembering the experience of national pride and a potent crowd during the World Cup celebrations in the new context of the vigils, protesters portrayed themselves as cheerful and voluntary actors who would bring justice for the girls' deaths and rectify what they perceived to be an unequal U.S.–South Korea relationship.[31]

The conflation during this period of criticism of the U.S. presence with the trope of the World Cup suggests a telling departure from the dominant protest repertoire of South Korea's social movement tradition during the authoritarian era—a repertoire that did attempt to assert itself in 2002, with minimal results. Immediately after the girls' deaths, the PKC had sought to draw public attention to the incident, holding a number of protests in downtown Seoul well before the candlelight vigil of November 30. However, news of the proposed protests traveled little beyond the social movement circle. PKC activists were close descendants of the original 1980s democratization movement, which risked prosecution on charges of undermining national security or of sympathizing with North Korea by demanding the withdrawal of the U.S. military. The PKC's rallies were therefore more traditional protests involving anti-American slogans and a willingness to engage in violent clashes with police. Even though South Koreans were sympathetic to the group's arguments, most still found participating in such protests unimaginable.

Unlike the PKC-initiated protests, however, the candlelight vigils called for by young Internet users and patterned after the World Cup celebrations showed that these young people envisioned political participation without being confined to the movement tradition of the past. By circulating their objects of captivation—from photographs to parodies to calls for vigils—they laid responsibility for the girls' deaths on the outmoded military arrangement without resorting to the ideologically charged language of anti-Americanism or the aggressive and potentially violent existing social movement repertoire.

Mainstream Media Response: The Vigils as Ideological Anti-Americanism

While young protesters were channeling their anger into a yearning for a strong country and a reformed U.S.–South Korea relationship, mainstream media and politicians were looking for explanations for and solutions to the mounting grievances and what they considered the abrupt eruption of anti-American protests. During this period, mainstream reporting arguably revealed more about the media's ideological stances than about the actual nature of the vigils. *Chosun Ilbo* and *Hankyoreh*—the country's conservative and liberal opinion leaders—shared fundamentally the same view that the vigils were an expression of ideological anti-Americanism and were successors of the 1980s radical activism that criticized the U.S. military presence as a neocolonial occupation of a strategically important region. Both newspapers interpreted online users' grievances as a reflection of anti-American ideology, despite their competing evaluations of this as either dangerous (*Chosun Ilbo*) or necessary (*Hankyoreh*).

Chosun Ilbo, which had initially sympathized with South Koreans' frustration over the verdicts, changed its tone after President Bush's apology on November 27 and demanded that the public accept the apology to provide closure to the tragic case. In an editorial, *Chosun Ilbo* declared the apology "a meaningful step toward the restoration of the Korea–U.S. alliance."[32] The newspaper expressed disapproval of the grassroots grievances as irrational and called for the protesters to stand down, saying that protests "cannot be a solution" but would only worsen the suffering of the victims' families. In another editorial *Chosun Ilbo* urged the public to rationally pursue the national interest: "South Korea and the U.S. need each other, and the U.S. Forces maintain the peace of not only the Korean peninsula but also all of Northeast Asia."[33] As these examples illustrate, *Chosun Ilbo* affirmed the U.S. role as a protector from the military threat posed by North Korea and as a patron of social and economic security. For South Korea, anti-Americanism is "a serious problem" that could jeopardize the country's domestic and international politics, the paper said.[34]

Like its conservative counterpart, *Hankyoreh* considered the grassroots response to be anti-American in the tradition of the 1980s radical social movement.[35] However, the paper maintained its support for the vigils even after Bush's apology, seeing the vigils as a "reasonable reaction" to the fundamentally unequal terms of the U.S. military presence in Korea.[36] On November 24 *Hankyoreh* published an editorial titled "Begin the Renegotiation of Unfair SOFA," rebuking the government for condoning the "absurdly unfair SOFA that excluded the Korean police and court in the investigation of South Korean civilian deaths in our territories."[37] Meanwhile, the newspaper acknowledged that the protests over SOFA "raised a fundamental question of whether a product of the Cold War could be applied to the current situation."[38] The day after Bush's apology, *Hankyoreh* declared that the apology alone without a revision of SOFA was insufficient and that the vigils were still a "legitimate movement to recover the legal and constitutional rights of a sovereign nation."[39]

Interpreting the vigils as a manifestation of ideological anti-Americanism, both mainstream newspapers failed to notice the role of emotional grievances in creating the protesting collective. Although *Chosun Ilbo* and conservative elites were aware of the emotional response to the accident, they thought the trial verdicts and the U.S. presence should be considered strictly political issues, with no role for emotion in making a "rational decision." The paper urged the government to keep "sensationalism and impulsiveness from altering the entire Korean–U.S. relationship."[40] Liberal *Hankyoreh* did not disapprove of the emotional tone of the vigils per se, but interpreted it as coming from the forcefulness of the protesters' ideological demands. *Hankyoreh* often cited online discussion boards, but interpreted the postings simply as public demands for the reform of SOFA and the Korea–U.S. relationship.[41]

These responses from *Chosun Ilbo* and *Hankyoreh* reveal that mainstream media viewed the girls' deaths as a narrowly defined political question that demanded political change: the reformation of SOFA and the U.S.–South Korea relationship. Both newspapers were still wedded to the authoritarian-era model of an ideologically driven social movement and failed to notice the distinct nature of the vigil collective, which was constituted through captivation with the girls' deaths and connected through underarticulated yet potent grievances about the status of South Korea, as reflected in the tragic accident.

In this chapter I have shown that South Korean Internet users were able to mobilize for collective action because they shared a sense that the deaths of Hyo-sun and Mi-sŏn and the subsequent court-martial verdicts were unreasonable. The online discourse after the acquittals of Sergeants Nino and Walker showed that Internet users imagined themselves as advocates for the victims, who had been neglected by their countrymen and by the South Korean government for five months after the accident. Seen through the lens of captivation, the young protesters, who heeded a call from the Internet and poured into the streets, were neither anti-American activists nor impulsive youths, but rather collective actors who tried to come to terms with unreasonable verdicts. It's also understandable that these youths evoked the World Cup street celebrations, because that event was a vernacular symbol of national pride—a pride that protesters sought desperately to recapture in the aftermath of the girls' deaths.

In their attempt to find a responsible party in the absence of any legal culpability, young Internet users concluded that the existing terms of the U.S. military presence rendered South Korea a weakling, which did not correspond to their current national identity. Their captivation with the acquittals and the sustained vigils challenged the narrowly defined political and legal interpretation of responsibility for the girls' deaths, and they demanded a revision of SOFA and the U.S.–South Korea relationship.

The primary political significance of this online discourse lay in the ability of users to share feelings, to circulate their captivation with the deaths, and to mobilize other users to attend the proposed vigils. The commemorative messages, parodies of the verdicts, and photographs of the girls' bodies were Internet users' vernacular strategies for intervening in what they considered to be an unreasonable situation. Through this process, the collective of concerned Koreans challenged legal and political frameworks vis-à-vis the U.S. military presence and envisioned a more equal relationship between the United States and South Korea that would fit the post–Cold War and postauthoritarian environment.

CHAPTER 3

The Internet in Mainstream Politics
Envisioning a New Politics during the 2002 Presidential Election

On December 19, 2002, broad support from voters in their twenties and thirties helped to elect liberal candidate Roh Moo-hyun as president of South Korea. Before the spread of candlelight vigils nationwide in the late fall, many South Koreans had considered Roh too radical, given his background in the democratization movement and his comments that South Korea did not need American troops. However, the acquittal in November of Sergeants Nino and Walker in the deaths of Hyo-sun and Mi-sŏn made candidates' positions on the verdicts and the tragic accident a measure of their patriotism and leadership. Young Koreans, disappointed with the government's perceived acquiescence to the seemingly outdated agreement with the United States, found in Roh's progressivism the hope for a different kind of politics. Online vernacular discourses during the election period portrayed Roh as a metonym for a new democratic politics—responsive to the people and assertive toward outside powers. Meanwhile, Internet users also dissociated themselves from mainstream politicians (who, the online community believed, were absorbed with political games) and assumed a role as conveyors of participatory democracy and voices for silenced victims. Roh's dramatic electoral success gave Internet users a sense that they were stakeholders in the Roh administration and that the candlelight vigils were a form of direct democratic participation distinct from conventional politics.

In this chapter I examine how the politics of captivation that surfaced on the Internet influenced mainstream politics. The contributions of progressive media and online communities to fund-raising and mobilizing for Roh's victory are well documented.[1] However, my focus here is not on the instrumental role of the Internet but on how vernacular discourses induced by the girls' deaths traversed the boundaries of cyberspace and shaped critical elements of mainstream politics (including the standards by which candidates were judged).[2] I argue that Internet and mainstream politics converged when young Internet users—haunted by the girls' deaths and frustrated with existing political and legal solutions—put the tragic accident on the electoral agenda and redefined expectations for the presidential campaign.

Roh's election to the presidency demonstrates how the politics of captivation can introduce a new agenda and enable new approaches for evaluating and envisioning national politics. In 2002 South Koreans—captivated with the seemingly unequal terms of the U.S. military presence—projected onto Roh their yearnings for a political leader. This imaginative and vibrant new politics disrupted conventional politics. I here follow the process through which the girls' deaths became an issue in the presidential election, and, as in chapter 2, I analyze postings on *Moim,* where Internet users actively discussed and reported on the vigils. These postings provide evidence of how an Internet discourse already steeped in the tragic deaths affected the outcome of the national election.

The 2002 Presidential Election

Until March 2002, conservative candidate Lee Hoi-chang, a member of the Grand National Party (GNP), "looked like a shoo-in for the Presidency."[3] He had proven his ability to lead during his tenure in various senior government positions, including Supreme Court justice, prime minister, and 1997 presidential candidate for the then-governing GNP. As chair of the National Auditing and Inspection Office and prime minister from 1993 to 1994, he had won acclaim for his unwavering fight against corruption. This made him the icon of a conservative upper-middle class seeking to imbue South Korean politics with ethics. Lee endorsed conservative policies, including minimal government intervention in the economy, creating jobs rather than supporting the unemployed, and making corporations more transparent.[4]

To offset its low public approval ratings in 2002, the incumbent liberal Millennium Democratic Party (MDP) adopted American-style primaries for the first time in South Korean politics. These party primaries, held between March 9 and April 26, drew national attention by inviting nonmembers to participate.[5] As primary voting began, Roh Moo-hyun was one of several minor candidates, and his background was a stark contrast with Lee's. Roh's father had been a Communist guerrilla during the Korean War, and Roh himself was a self-made man with a low-key style and blunt manner. Although he had no college degree, he passed the bar, and as a labor lawyer represented democratization activists who were persecuted during the 1980s. He was elected to the National Assembly in 1988 as a traditional liberal and served a single four-year term, offering support for policies that included a more active role for government in providing a social safety net, income-tax cuts for lower-income groups, and reformation of family-owned conglomerates. In the 2002 primaries Roh presented himself as a politician with an unusually modest but outspoken manner, and he emerged as an icon of the masses; when Roh won the MDP primary on April 26, his approval rating stood at a record 60 percent. Then, shortly after, a corruption scandal involving MDP members broke and Roh's public approval dropped to a mere 23 percent by June, bottoming out at 18.5 percent in mid-August.[6]

However, Roh's approval rating improved again with growing public attention to the girls' deaths. As Sergeants Nino and Walker went on trial in September, and as mainstream newspapers published accounts of the courts-martial, Roh's approval began to rise, reaching 30.5 percent on October 12. On November 26, days after both sergeants were acquitted, Roh's approval rating reached 42.7 percent. On December 17, four days after the six-month anniversary of the girls' deaths, Roh's approval stood at 43 percent, while Lee's had fallen from 42.4 percent to 34.3 percent in only two months. On December 19 Roh won the presidency by a margin of 2.3 percent, with 48.9 percent of the vote.[7] It's impossible to know exactly to what extent the girls' deaths affected the course of the election, but both conservative and liberal commentators agreed that the fatal accident and attendant anti-American sentiment were determining factors.[8]

Indeed, scholars of South Korean politics viewed the 2002 election as an indication of a new political era in which the traditionally effective red scare (*pukp'ung*) tactic—invoking national security and the potential threat of North Korea—had lost the power to influence younger voters. In previous elections the red scare invariably helped the conservative party, which would vow to reinforce national security; this also undermined the liberal party, which typically stressed the importance of reconciliation with North Korea. However, in 2002 both information about the involvement of Roh's father in the Communist resistance and the occurrence of an armed conflict between North Korean and South Korean warships (the kinds of news that once would have induced a red scare) had a negligible influence on the election.[9]

This new pattern was inseparable from demographic changes and the parallel vibrant Internet discourse regarding national identity and the U.S.–Korea relationship. In 2002, for the first time Koreans in their twenties and thirties accounted for half of the country's thirty-five million voters.[10] As noted in chapter 1, this postauthoritarian generation had no memory of the Korean War or of a credible threat from North Korea. Instead, these voters remembered more contemporary events: the perceived U.S. role in the 1997 Asian financial crisis, President George W. Bush's 2002 "axis of evil" statement, and recent media images of the North Korean famine. These events made the younger electorate skeptical of the United States as South Korea's closest ally and sympathetic toward poverty-stricken North Koreans.[11]

The 2002 election was also marked by grassroots campaigning organized and carried out on the Internet. During the campaign, a Web site called *Rohsamo* ("Love Roh") offered a glimpse of the changing political landscape. *Rohsamo* began in 2000 as an online "fan community" for Roh after his effort to secure a term in the National Assembly failed. Despite the electoral result, Roh's outspoken criticism of the regionalism and conservatism that were splitting the country apart nonetheless won him attention as a man of principle and integrity. As the nation's first large voluntary support group for an individual politician, *Rohsamo* rallied voters during the 2002 primaries and subsequent election by organizing online debates, initiating fund-raising, and mobilizing the electorate.[12] By the end of the campaign *Rohsamo* boasted seventy thousand members and had raised seven billion Korean won (six million U.S. dollars) from two hundred thousand small contributors. Most members were in their twenties and thirties, and many of them had been avid participants in the World Cup street celebrations and the candlelight vigils in memory of Hyo-sun and Mi-sŏn.[13] Such distinctly different generational experiences were apparent in the 2002 election results: 62 percent of voters in their twenties and 59 percent in their thirties voted for Roh, while members of older generations predominantly supported Lee Hoi-chang and his conservative program.[14]

After the Accident: Cynicism toward Mainstream Politics

When the courts-martial of Sergeants Nino and Walker began in September, Internet users—who had just started forming online communities around the girls' deaths—pessimistically predicted that the upcoming presidential election would overshadow the tragic accident, and their cynicism continued throughout the campaign: "For sure, the media won't address the girls' deaths because it's right before the presidential election" and "The corrupt politicians of this country are chasing the presidential election with feverish eyes while ignoring the girls' deaths."[15]

When the two servicemen were acquitted in November, Internet users were outraged that the South Korean government didn't dispute the verdicts. The online community was convinced that South Korea's political leaders were more willing to spurn their own voters than they were the U.S. government. Some young Koreans asserted that they would rather not vote at all in December, claiming that the election would not reflect their views. One lamented, "I wish we didn't have the presidential election. What's the point of electing a leader who can't take care of national issues anyway? It's distressing."[16] Another pleaded, "Do not vote in this presidential election. This is not a sovereign nation so it doesn't need a president. Call it an election for the state governor of the United States."[17] These cynical perspectives pointed to a distrust of the political system and underlined the intensity with which members of online communities expressed their opinions.[18]

The distrust was mutual. As Internet users explicitly targeted the inability of the government to hold the U.S. servicemen criminally responsible for the girls' deaths, mainstream media and politicians openly voiced their suspicion that the vigils were the work of anti-American activists and impulsive youths and so should not be allowed to influence the election. An editorial in the leading conservative newspaper *Chosun Ilbo* on November 29 described the mounting grievances as irrational and advocated disbanding the protests, which "cannot be a solution," and instead called on protesters to "rationally pursue the national interest."[19] Another mainstream newspaper, *JoongAng Ilbo,* made a similar claim: "It is not the time to . . . boost the anti-American craze. . . . We desperately need a rational attitude of distinguishing between the schoolgirls' deaths and the issue of anti-Americanism."[20] Both articles showed sympathy for the Korean public's frustrations but also warned that such emotion should not play a role in politics. Just as Internet users saw the election as a false political event that could not address the real problem of the girls' deaths, mainstream media viewed the vigils as a false political event that should not influence the real politics of the presidential election. For weeks after the verdicts this mutual antipathy widely separated the grassroots campaign on the Internet from the mainstream presidential campaign, until the vigils spread and their influence on the election could no longer be ignored.

Entering the Election: Captivation with Roh and Shifting the Campaign Ground

Although Internet users were frustrated with longtime politicians, they also envisioned a new politics that would address what they considered to be fundamental flaws in the South Korea–U.S. relationship, starting with the agreement on the status of U.S. forces in South Korea. In the minds of many Internet users, Roh was an unconventional politician who would listen to their demands. Roh captivated their imagination with his progressive stance and unconventionally blunt manner, onto which Internet users projected their own desires for a new and responsive politics. Captivation is a "metonymic" process, pointing to the existence of a larger and more complicated entity associated with an object, which can be recognized but perhaps not articulated.[21] Captivation with Roh was similarly not the mere endorsement of a politician but a metonymic expression of underarticulated yet potent hopes and desires for a new politics, which found an anchor in Roh.

Roh's background as a self-made man, a human-rights lawyer, and a dramatic winner in the primaries captivated Internet users—much as young Americans were drawn to the family background and approachable yet eloquent style of Barack Obama in 2008. Since early in the 2002 presidential race, conservatives had heavily criticized Roh for remarks that they regarded as undermining national interests, particularly Roh's statement that South Korea no longer needed U.S. troops and his pledge to be more assertive toward the United States. Politicians and mass media viewed Roh's remarks as political blunders that would alienate voters still sensitive to North Korea. But, as the deaths of Mi-sŏn and Hyo-sun—and a growing anti-Americanism—emerged as a national issue, Internet users began to view Roh's so-called blunders as evidence of forward-looking leadership distinct from that of other politicians. When Roh criticized conservative candidates for presenting photos of themselves with U.S. presidents as evidence of America's endorsement of their candidacy, right-wing critics contended that Roh would undermine the U.S.–South Korea alliance if he were elected. Cyberspace responded differently, however. One user posted on December 1, "As Roh said, Korean politicians brag about taking pictures with American leaders. We have to get rid of these corrupt people first. . . . I honestly didn't plan to vote, but a candidate made moving remarks, and now I will cast my vote no matter what."[22] Another user also took Roh's statement as evidence of an assertive stance toward the United States: "I hope you become the president, reveal the truth of Hyo-sun and Mi-sŏn, receive an official apology from President Bush, reform the U.S.–Korean SOFA, and put the shameless Americans who killed the girls on trial in a Korean court."[23] On the morning of the election another Internet user wrote, "I went to vote. I cast my vote for Number 2 [Roh]. Did you vote? The voting rate is still low. I hope you all go and cast your vote. I hope we elect a person who can talk straightforwardly and be assertive toward the arrogant Americans."[24] To many Internet users Roh was a leader who would stand up to Washington and make independent decisions in South Korea's national interest.

However, it isn't possible to understand how the candlelight vigils affected the national election by looking only at Roh. In the presidential race Roh stood in contrast with Lee Hoi-chang, whose elite education, administrative experience, and conservative views presented him as a metonym for the status quo. Early in the election campaign Lee avoided any explicit statements about the girls' deaths, merely reaffirming the principles of a strong U.S.–South Korea alliance and stating his opposition to any violent protest. However, as the vigils swept the country, Lee began to express sympathy for the dead girls; in December, facing mounting public grievances, he officially lent his support to the vigils. But, by then the move was widely seen as an expedient flip-flop. In a posting dated December 19, an Internet user denounced Lee's plan to attend a vigil: "His father, a government official during Japanese rule, used to oppress Koreans who fought against Japanese rule, and Lee himself prosecuted and killed Korean activists [during the democratization era]. I can't even sleep hearing that he mentioned SOFA reform."[25] The poster was referring to Lee's participation, as a Supreme Court justice, in sentencing anti-American activists to death for setting the American Cultural Center on fire in 1982. To this poster Lee's support for the vigils was hypocritical. Similarly, a post entitled "Angry Speech by Lee Hoi-chang" garnered broad support for its presentation of Lee's family history and past decisions:

> I'll tell you about my family.
> My father worked for the prosecutor's office during Japanese rule.
> My elder brother is a U.S. citizen. My granddaughter is also a U.S. citizen.
> Our family doesn't know the duty of military service.
> Of my eight sons and sons-in-law, no one served in the military, except only one who served for six months.

But I'll become the president and commander-in-chief.

It's funny, isn't it funny? . . .

I love the United States because it's our big brother country.

In 1997 I visited America because I knew I would become the
 president.

I love Japan, too, because it's our father country.

I call their king the Emperor and was invited to his birthday party.

But I dream of becoming the president of Korea.

It's funny, isn't it funny?[26]

This satirical first-person account portrays Lee as someone unashamed of his and his family's behavior, ranging from his sons' exemption from (some say evasion of) compulsory military service to his loyalty to the United States and Japan. In the narrative, he pursues the undeserved roles of representing ordinary Koreans and of being commander-in-chief. In the post, the author repeats "It's funny (*ukkiji*), isn't it funny?" when offering Lee's aspiration to become president despite his background. *Ukkiji* literally means "laughable."[27] By making Lee an object of derision, the parody challenged his image as an elite politician and redefined him as pandering and inexperienced. As with the image surrounding Roh, Lee's personal history and family background became a barometer for his authenticity, an indicator of his ethos, and a measure of his qualifications for the presidency.

Many modern political theorists, from Weber to Habermas to Lippmann, are wary about captivation with politicians. Their concern is that mass media would present a politician to citizens in a way that allows them to identify with the politician, replacing informed and critical discussion of political ideas and issues with an emphasis on personality.[28] In particular, Habermas calls this phenomenon a "refeudalization" of the democratic public: the appearance of the feudal lord validates political decisions without garnering the informed consent of citizens.[29] Indeed, young voters' captivation made Roh and Lee the paragons of progressive and reactionary politics (respectively), simplifying their political stances along the binaries of liberal and conservative, of down-to-earth and elitist, and of anti-American and pro-American.[30]

However, this captivation with Roh demonstrates possibilities beyond those that concerned the political theorists: captivation can serve as the beginning, not the end, of critical political conversation. Roh served as a metonymic figure around which concerned Internet users could share their frustration with conventional politicians and communicate with one another in envisioning a more democratic and assertive nation. The theorists' concerns were primarily with the citizenry's false satisfaction with a leader—when a leader captivates a voter, that voter becomes a consumer of the image, content and unmotivated to critically evaluate politics.[31] In contrast, young Koreans were captivated with Roh outside of mainstream media because of their frustration with existing politicians, and this captivation offered a concrete vocabulary through which they could envision the terms of an alternative politics.

Of course, the Internet can certainly serve as an additional conduit through which false satisfaction spreads faster and more broadly. However, the online space can also be a tool for removing the barriers that isolate citizens into individual consumers who experience grievances and desires as merely private sentiments. The Internet does not necessarily enable political action, but it undoubtedly removes the barriers to finding like-minded others.[32] As in the Korean case, when citizens find—on the Internet or otherwise—that others share frustration with mainstream politics and fascination with a politician, they are likely to exchange these feelings and to develop a vernacular critique of contemporary politics while envisioning something new.

Captivation with Roh and Lee altered the discursive ground of the election. First and foremost, the vigils placed Lee in a unique dilemma. He had two choices: he could endorse the so-called anti-American vigils and damage his relationship with conservative supporters, or he could continue to disapprove of the vigils and risk alienating the voters in their twenties and thirties who constituted more than half the electorate. Lee endorsed the vigils. As a result, conservative critics—including famous conservative opinion leader Cho Gabje—turned on Lee. Cho wrote, "For the right wing, Lee is not a strong leader against the lefties but a flipflopper who betrayed the right and gave in to the left."[33]

In previous elections, conservatives had attacked liberal candidates for being radical and for being naïve about the North Korean threat; liberal candidates had had to prove their belief in liberal democracy and take a firm stance against North Korea. In contrast, by 2002 the burden of proof was firmly on the conservatives, and they risked either losing young voters or contradicting long-established conservative ideology in order to attract them. Lee's situation is evocative of what Shirky called the "conservative dilemma" in the aftermath of the 2010 Arab Spring. For Shirky, when social media increase the shared awareness of a political injustice, conservatives are left with only censorship and propaganda to curb the eruption of mass dissatisfaction. However, in the connected social media environment these options are costly and ineffective compared with the rapidly circulating discourses on the Internet.[34] Shirky is addressing primarily an authoritarian context, which does not apply directly to Lee. However, Lee's dilemma suggests that politicians find it difficult both to control information about themselves (a softer form of censorship) and to pander to voters by changing positions on issues (a softer form of propaganda).

In the 2002 election, the situation in South Korea also provided an opportunity for progressive social movement groups to reach the attention of the general public. During the campaign period, the PKC demanded that presidential candidates sign a pledge to join forces in solving the problems that led to the incident. Many groups in the PKC were descended from organizations that participated in the anti-American movements of the 1980s, which had previously been considered too radical for mainstream politics. However, in 2002 Internet users found that the PKC's efforts resonated with their own demands. A *Moim* user inserted a banner for and hyperlink to the PKC petition page, and wrote the following:

> Now we, the Korean people,
> Should respect the memories of Hyo-sun and Mi-sŏn.
> We have demanded that presidential candidates take action to address
>   the cause of the girls' deaths
> To make public their stance toward the acquittal of the GIs and
> To sign a joint pledge to solve this problem.
> Koreans, visit the home page and ask them to sign the pledge to solve
>   the girls' deaths.[35]

The banner read, "We're looking for a Korean president who will carry out the desire of Hyo-sun and Mi-sŏn." Phrases in the background detailed the major demands of the vigils, including "Punish the killer GIs in a Korean court," "Apology from President Bush," and "Complete revision of SOFA." While mainstream politicians were losing voter support, social movement groups like the PKC were finding new supporters in vibrant online communities.

The convergence of the vigils and the election makes clear in several ways the interaction between vernacular discourse on the Internet and mainstream politics. First, the ethos—the perceived character—of the leader becomes a prominent locus upon which the public projects its hopes and frustrations and envisions political futures. In the case of Roh, his ethos offered a tangible metonym for an underarticulated yet potent vision of a new politics. Alternatively, the public can also be captivated with a villain—as in the case of Lee, on whom Internet users projected their political frustrations. Media theorist Manuel Castells suggests that when a "perception of corruption" is raised in the Internet age, a small incident can easily undermine public trust.[36] The dishonesty that the public perceived in the exemption from military service of Lee's sons and in the U.S. citizenship of his grandchildren ultimately led to questions about his qualifications for leadership.

Second, the politics of captivation can introduce radical political perspectives and marginalized groups into mainstream politics. Bringing marginalized groups into the dominant discursive realm is typically difficult, requiring dedicated strategies to draw public attention and gain recognition.[37] However, widespread grievances that crystallized on the Internet set the agenda for the Korean election, introducing as an issue the status of U.S. forces in Korea (criticism of which was often considered anti-American) and suppressing the red scare strategy. This was not a product of concerted efforts by activists; instead, the vernacular public discourses of the vigils became connected to the election when younger voters were captivated with Roh as a leader who would be assertive toward outside powers. In the introduction to this book I argued that captivation serves as a node for crystallizing underarticulated hopes, fears, and dissatisfaction. The node connects and unifies individuals who might otherwise have divergent identities and political views. At the beginning of the twenty-first century these processes entailed an unusual shift in South Korean politics: criticism of the U.S. military presence had been taboo for decades, but in 2002 this topic nonetheless entered public discourse without being stigmatized as radical or antigovernment.

Resisting Incorporation into Mainstream Politics: Authentic Feelings vs. Political Posturing

Although Internet users projected their hopes for change onto Roh, they also resisted the attempts of mainstream politicians to co-opt the vigils for campaign purposes—Internet and mainstream politics both connected and disconnected through captivation. As the vigils continued, Internet users developed an aggressive criticism of mainstream politics, underscoring their heartfelt feelings and direct experiences at the vigils while distancing themselves from politicians who merely pandered to vigil participants or to critics of the vigils.

The conservative candidate Lee was the primary target of this criticism of mainstream politics, but Internet users also kept their distance from the liberal Roh. At the height of the election campaign in December, the presidential candidates proposed to speak at the vigils, and online forums erupted in heated debate. *Moim* members easily agreed that Lee should not be allowed to participate: "Lee Hoi-chang may come as a Korean, but we can't bear him coming as a presidential candidate"; "I did not propose the candlelight vigil for you. We are not coming to the vigils to support your election campaign."[38] However, no agreement could be reached regarding participation by the more liberal candidates, especially Roh. One user passionately argued, "Neither Lee nor Roh showed even the slightest interest in the girls' deaths before the election!!! They are taking advantage of the two wrongly killed girls for their election campaign."[39] The post's author disapproved of any attempt by the presidential candidates to use the vigils for their campaigns and contended that the vigils should remain separate from the election.

Internet users did acknowledge that some candidates, including Roh, had advocated for a more equal relationship between the United States and South Korea. However, there was still concern that the vigils were rapidly turning into a campaign sideshow. A post on December 8 argued that allowing even one candidate to speak would open the door to the vigils being coopted by the electoral campaign: "What about the other candidates? Everyone else will try to give a speech. . . . Then, what would happen next? Wouldn't it change a voluntary space for the commemoration of the two students into a campaign site? It's not important who initiated the candlelight vigils or who attended more vigils. . . . It's not important who showed support first. It is important that each and every candle is held from the depth of our hearts and that we become unified as one."[40] As this poster alluded, vigil participants had created a "voluntary space" where individuals could contribute equally, free from any political scheme, and express sadness at the girls' deaths and sincere desire for social change. Online postings of this kind show that Internet users conceived of the vigils as an alternative space defined by genuine concern and an unadulterated sense of justice.

The "invisible hand" controversy exemplified Internet users' perceptions of the vigils as sites of spontaneous activism distinct from politics as usual. On December 9 Sŏ Ch'ŏng-wŏn—chair of the conservative GNP and manager of Lee's campaign—asserted, "The current upsurge of anti-Americanism has reached a dangerous level. . . . An invisible hand is systematically spreading anti-Americanism."[41] South Koreans were familiar with this kind of statement from previous national elections—an important tactic in red scare campaigning was the claim that radicals were swaying naïve voters. However, in 2002 Sŏ's gambit did not lead to concern about the candlelight vigils, as he presumably expected; instead, he was disregarded as an anachronistic politician still immersed in the Cold War mind-set. The day he made his statement, more than four hundred messages appeared on Sŏ's home page to dispute it, along with tens of thousands of messages posted in other online communities. Internet users slammed Sŏ's statement, citing it as evidence that the Lee camp was out of touch with public sentiment: "How could a representative of a majority party say this? You will meet the people's judgment for using the two girls' deaths"; "You lost five votes from my family"; "I had thought Lee was the best presidential candidate. . . . Now my family won't vote for you."[42] Yet another *Moim* poster demanded, "Sŏ should reveal the real intention behind the statement and apologize for disparaging innocent Internet users and citizens."[43] The online community considered Sŏ's statement to be a denial of their sincerity. As grievances and demands for apology mounted and became emblematic of politicians' insensitivity to public opinion, mainstream media and even GNP politicians distanced themselves from Sŏ and openly criticized him.

Refutations of Sŏ's assertions often took the form of first-person narratives describing the intense feelings and experiences at the vigils. For example, the day after Sŏ's statement one user wrote, "I have attended the vigils every Saturday as if it was my duty, although I had never been in a protest previously. I ran to Kwanghwamun after transferring on the subway three times, although I am lazy and hate cold weather. Last Saturday, I forgot to bring my own candle and bought a candle for 1,000 won, although I had never bought such an overpriced item. . . . Are you saying that I was manipulated by an invisible hand like a dupe, fool, or puppet?"[44] By describing his attendance at the vigils as an aberration from his usual behavior, the poster presents the vigils as personally meaningful events that only other participants could understand. Similarly, a "mother of two kids" responded to Sŏ's statement with indignation: "All Korean people are mourning and outraged at the deaths of two young lives, who became scars in their parents' hearts. What's your intention in condemning Koreans who are mourning as the girls' brothers and sisters? Why are you calling us hypocrites and dupes manipulated by an invisible hand?"[45] Sŏ was perceived as a heartless politician who was suspicious of people's authentic feelings. These first-person narratives of grief, suffering, and indignation constitute a distinct vernacular discourse that attested to the vigils as a grassroots movement not swayed by political interests.

In a series of vigils held after Sŏ made his statement, protesters both offline and on called themselves "visible hands"; they staged performances that included the waving of hands and adorned posters and placards with the handprints of participants. These efforts were accompanied by graffiti: "Do you finally see the 'invisible hand' of anti-Americanism?"[46] "The invisible hand was me. And my wife, my friend, my colleague, and my family."[47] The visible hand became a recurrent theme in online communities as well. Narratives of personal experiences and emotions maintained the vernacular discourse that confirmed the authenticity of the vigils as a space for concerned citizens unwilling to accept politicians' ideological labels and seeking to remain independent of mainstream politics.

The convergence of online and mainstream politics seen in the captivation with Roh was a temporary connection between the two arenas, rather than an expansion of mainstream politics into the Internet or the Internet becoming a substitute for the existing election campaigns. As the campaigns of mainstream politicians tried to assimilate or delegitimize the vigils, Internet users disconnected the gatherings from "politics as usual" by collectively creating an authentic space marked by intense emotion and firsthand experience.[48]

After the Election: Rapid Disenchantment with the President

On election night younger Koreans—who had been watching Roh take the lead—came to Kwanghwamun Square, the epicenter of World Cup celebrations and the vigils. They watched the election report on the same multiscreens that had shown soccer games that summer.[49] Younger voters came away with a sense of achievement that continued past the election; Internet users claimed ownership of Roh, evoking his victory in the 2002 election in various social and political contexts and encouraging others on the Internet to support and monitor the Roh administration.

Internet users viewed the 2002 election as evidence of grassroots power that can change the course of mainstream politics. A contributor to *Moim* noted in February 2003, "The Republic of Korea has full potential to advance because its people are wise. . . . We achieved democracy thanks to people who shed blood. We defeated rotten politicians by organizing sensible Koreans in the election. We achieved an *Internet election,* the first in the world."[50] For this poster, the 2002 election was the third in a series of historic democratic achievements in South Korea; the first was the democratization of 1987 and the second was the grassroots movement to defeat unqualified politicians in general elections in the late 1990s. In the same vein, when President Roh made progressive moves, Internet users claimed them as their own achievements. When Roh announced his opposition to the war in Iraq in February 2003, a *Moim* post claimed, "We elected the right person! We'll keep building this country."[51] In these posts, *we* (an ambiguous reference to Internet users and to Koreans in general) enabled Roh's victory and were responsible for the future of the administration.

However, the honeymoon between Internet users and Roh was short lived. Even before his inauguration in February 2003, supporters turned on Roh for his statement in January that vigil participants should moderate the tone of their anti-American language. Internet users felt that Roh had become assimilated into the establishment instead of remaining loyal to his supporters, or that he had simply been hypocritical during the campaign. In a message posted on January 16, 2003, one user lamented, "I thought Roh would be different, but he followed the footsteps of past politicians."[52] Roh's supporters continued to monitor every statement or move he made. In January Roh visited a U.S. military base in South Korea, a custom for presidents-elect as a symbol of respect for the U.S.–South Korea alliance. In the guestbook he wrote, "We're good friends." Roh's supporters considered this a sign of his compliance with the status quo and a forsaking of his vow to pursue justice in the deaths of Hyo-sun and Mi-sŏn.[53] This growing disenchantment with Roh culminated in April 2003, when the government decided to send seven hundred noncombat troops to Iraq to support the U.S. military campaign. Roh himself became a target of candlelight protests, along with the U.S. forces in Korea. Online postings during this period claimed, "Please be sensible, President Roh! Return to who you were during the election!!"[54] "I voted for you. Now I feel very sorry for the president's support for sending troops to Iraq. President Roh, you should retract your support for the war."[55] As they criticized Roh's policies, Internet users reminisced about the candidate who had seemed assertive and uncompromising during the campaign.

As members of the online community distanced themselves from Roh after the election, they redefined the vigils as a statement of opposition to mainstream politics, this time *including* Roh. For instance, a self-identified "twenty-six-year-old man" wrote a post titled, "Nothing has changed. Why do we hesitate when nothing has changed?"

> President Roh, the sensational coverage by conservative newspapers,
>   and so on,
> Everyone urges us to stop the candlelight vigils. . . .
> We should fight again.
> We should fight and rise from the bottom. . . .
> As I have done in the past, I will go to the vigil every weekend, set up
>   the stage, distribute candles, and start new fights one by one.[56]

Here the vigils become a symbol of Internet users' steadfastness in the promises they made to the deceased girls, as well as a reflection of posters' concerns about the future of the nation. In this narrative the vigils are a trope of untainted democracy and grassroots power. Similarly, another post describes the candlelight ceremony in Pup'yŏng, a suburb of Seoul, on January 5, 2003:

> Today's candlelight ceremony was a place where we censured President-elect Roh for his statement that we should moderate the vigils, and where we pledged to keep our candles alive until our demands are met.
>   Lee Sul-ah, a ninth-grader and the administrator of an online forum, contended that politicians were disregarding people's demands and frustrating Koreans, and pleaded that we should not extinguish our candles.[57]

Descriptions like this one demonstrate how the vigils took on a more explicitly political tone after the election. Participants now transformed the vigils from a space for vernacular discourse into one where they specifically addressed the actions of the government and President Roh. Although the presidential candidates—including Roh—had withdrawn from the vigils, participants nonetheless retained the habit of intervening in mainstream politics. Events like these also suggest that the vigils served to effect the political socialization of a younger generation of Koreans. At the ceremony described in the post above, a junior high school girl delivered a speech denouncing politicians and encouraging vigil participants to continue their efforts. Even a year before, such political expression from a ninth-grader would have been unheard of. Yet, through the vigils—which coincided with the presidential election and the beginning of the Iraq war—younger South Koreans developed a sensitivity to political issues beyond the girls' deaths and turned themselves into political actors.

Although Roh's supporters accused him of a change of heart, more likely their rapid disappointment was instead the natural conclusion to their abrupt empowerment during the campaign period, and perhaps something to be expected in the popular politics of the Internet era. Younger Koreans had built Roh into a metonymic figure upon whom they projected their nascent yearnings for an assertive leader and a new politics. The captivation with Roh was thus a captivation with images of their own creation. What they remembered from the election, through the metonym of Roh, was in fact Internet users' own grassroots power—which intervened in traditional politics, brought an underdog to the presidency, and maintained genuine political concern without being assimilated into mainstream political activity.

The Roh presidency in the following five years was tumultuous even by South Korean standards, as citizens and alternative media organized on the Internet to become vocal political actors.[58] During his term Roh struggled to meet impossibly high expectations and drew criticism from both sides of the political fence. Conservative media and citizens argued that his drastic expansion of social welfare and higher property tax (often dubbed a "tax bomb" by his opponents) contradicted free-market principles; meanwhile, progressives considered Roh's welfare policies insufficient and criticized him for sending troops to Iraq to support the American military campaign and for oppressing labor activists.[59] Despite their criticism of Roh, however, citizens again supported him in 2004 when the opposition impeached him over a breach of election rules. Internet users interpreted the impeachment as an effort by the conservative party to derail Roh's political agendas, including rapprochement with North Korea, and candlelight protests again filled the streets until the Constitutional Court overturned the move and reinstated

Roh.[60] The candlelight gatherings reappeared when Roh killed himself in 2009, an act that many believed resulted from incumbent Lee Myung-bak's politically motivated investigation of a corruption scandal.

The convergence in South Korea of the candlelight vigils and the presidential election in late 2002 offers a glimpse of the broader convergence between Internet politics and mainstream politics. The vigils were connected to the election through young citizens' captivation with Roh Moo-hyun as an emblem of the new politics they envisioned. This connection, however, was severed during the election campaign when mainstream politicians failed to recognize the authenticity of participants' experiences, and again after the election when Roh supporters grew disenchanted with his performance.

These dynamic connections and disconnections with mainstream politics were not an intentional strategy by activists trying to effect change but rather a natural function of popular online discourses when a controversial or dramatic issue is raised and garners public attention. In the politics of captivation, a figure or issue serves as a tangible metonym through which young people can imagine and communicate political futures beyond those presented by traditional leaders. I've suggested in this chapter that vernacular discourses on the Internet surrounding authentic grievances and desires can lead to the setting of agendas and to changes in political perspectives. Of course, even such an abrupt shift doesn't entirely change the nature of an election. An election is by definition an occasion when competing visions are presented in the hope of drawing voters who identify with one side or the other; the charisma of a candidate has always been a decisive factor on voting day. However, the events detailed in this chapter suggest that online politics has the potential to modify existing standards of judgment and to spread new visions to other voters, offering space for critical discussion regarding a given agenda.[61]

Despite these mixed implications, the convergence of Internet and mainstream politics will almost certainly continue to pose significant challenges for politicians. In the cases of Roh and Lee—and in the parallel case of Barack Obama in the 2008 U.S. presidential election—the individual's personal background and ethos became an important element against which voters evaluated the candidate and projected their hopes for a new leader. Further, because a political figure is a metonymic object of captivation, the Internet discourse surrounding a politician tends to create a larger-than-life image to which the politician is nonetheless held accountable.

As such, the almost-immediate disenchantment among Roh supporters after the election was perhaps a natural consequence of Roh's image during the campaign. Similarly, the American public—and especially younger voters—rallied behind Obama during the 2008 election, setting up Web sites and creating YouTube videos that propagated his slogans of "Hope" and "Change." However, soon after the election, young voters became disillusioned with Obama's performance.[62] Such disillusionment is potentially a mechanism through which the public (including avid supporters of a candidate) can scrutinize a politician while maintaining a critical distance from mainstream politics.

The next South Korean presidential election, in 2007, again demonstrated the temporary nature of connections between the Internet and electoral politics. Conservative candidate Lee Myung-bak garnered broad support by portraying himself as a successful CEO and making promises for economic recovery. As I discuss in chapter 5, Lee won a landslide victory, overwhelming his opponent by a historic 46 percent to only 26; captivation with a leader does not necessarily empower only progressive agendas. However, despite the variable content of captivation, the active and volatile movement—both in support of and against the government—distinguishes contemporary Internet users from masses mesmerized by a charismatic leader. Lee's presidency faced massive disenchantment and resistance from young citizens, much as Roh's did. Mainstream politics cannot completely catch up with the exuberant politics of captivation on the Internet, and the Internet cannot be completely assimilated into mainstream politics.

CHAPTER 4

Remembering the Vigils

The Emergence of a New Repertoire for Youth Activism

In the summer of 2006, I was in Seoul searching for people with whom to discuss the 2002 candlelight vigils. However, by this point South Korea's social atmosphere no longer evoked the vibrancy of 2002. The vigil participants who first agreed to meet with me were those who had already been involved in activism against the American military presence in South Korea. Few who had participated in the vigils as teenagers were locatable. Most online communities dedicated to Mi-sŏn and Hyo-sun were inactive or closed, and opinion polls suggested that South Koreans in their twenties were now as conservative as older generations and concerned more about personal success than social issues.[1] The contrast between 2002 and 2006 made me even more curious about the personal and social meaning of the 2002 nationwide protests. Had participants turned into activists, or were the protests just a blip in the ever-changing scene of Internet politics? In this chapter, I turn to the question of what the 2002 vigils left behind, for both participants and others.

In the end, I recruited thirty young people from college campuses by asking for anyone who remembered the vigils. Even though only a few initially identified themselves as active participants, once at the interview a surprisingly large portion of the students turned out to have frequented online communities and attended the vigils, often to "catch up with top Internet issues," to "experience being with the crowd," to "practice photography," or having "dropped by" while downtown. As I document in this chapter, such casual involvement typified an important feature of the candlelight protests: participation without prior intention or identification with the cause.

I additionally interviewed eight adults, in their forties and older, affili-ated with activist organizations or alternative media.[2] These activists had been devoted to movements against U.S. military bases, national security laws, or oppressive labor policies since the authoritarian era, and were there-fore not the focal point of my research. However, they offer a glimpse into the multiple interpretive frameworks surrounding the candlelight protests. Their recollections suggest that the authoritarian-era protest repertoire continued to influence how young Koreans evaluated the meaning of the then-new candlelight vigils.

The retrospective narratives from the interviewees reminded me of the Rashomon effect (from the Japanese film of the same name), whereby the testimonies of multiple witnesses contradict one another as influenced by each person's past and present.[3] My interviewees' interpretations varied, depending on where they had been in 2002 and where they were in 2006. For some teenage participants, the vigils were festive gatherings, remem-bered as corporeal experiences of occupying city centers and expressing an-ger and sorrow. Others now perceived the vigils as an "anti-American" movement—they had reinterpreted the vigils as a dubious object, and their participation as the naïveté of immature youth.

The vigils are important in South Korea's social movement history *because* of such heterogeneous interpretations. The Rashomon-like narratives suggest that the long-held protest movement repertoire that had been prac-ticed during the authoritarian era was slowly losing its grip, and a new one was in formation. During the authoritarian era, no protester who entered Kwanghwamun could simply ignore the political and social ramifications of being associated with "anti-government" and "anti-American" activism. In contrast, a majority of retrospective narratives in this chapter point to the candlelight vigil as a distinct repertoire, signaling liberation from the legacies of the authoritarian-era movement culture. Prominent themes in the narratives— including online mobilization, casual participation, and the format of a peaceful and festive crowd—constituted a "repertoire" for youth activism, a distinct constellation of social protest tactics and strategies.

In analyzing these retrospective narratives, I attend to how my inter-viewees made sense of the candlelight vigil, which was a novel phenomenon in 2002 but had become a familiar form of protest by 2006. According to social movement scholar Sidney Tarrow, a movement "repertoire" is not merely an instrument for activism but a crucible producing "symbols, frames of meaning, and ideologies" of an era.[4] For instance, the barricades in the

French Revolution of 1848 enacted the refusal to accept state power, and the 1960s lunch counter sit-ins of the American South embodied African Americans' vision of an integrated future. Taken-for-granted practices reveal "deep rules" that prescribe specific ways of living public life, and a shift in these habitual practices signals—and further produces—changes in larger cultural frames.[5]

Retrospective narratives draw attention to the long-term influence of online activism on the participants' subjectivity and movement culture *after* the moment of collective action. In the introduction to this book I argued that the breadth of online activity in general (ranging from the Arab Spring to neofascist enclaves) defies any optimism or pessimism attached to Internet politics. I also proposed that we suspend models assuming an intentional actor and instead attend to the political *effect* generated by the combination of Internet architecture and captivated users within a particular context. The retrospective narratives I examine in this chapter bring the human agent back to Internet politics as a social actor that retains memory from the experience. This approach presupposes neither an activist identity nor intention at that time, nor instant transformation during the period of activism. Rather, this analysis considers that corporeal and affective experiences both online and off could reconfigure the participant's predispositions toward politics and habitual practices in the long term.

Festive Vigils: Fading Political Meanings and Robust Corporeal Memories

When discussing the vigils, many interviewees spoke in terms of what they did and how they felt; their corporeal and affective experiences were at the foreground of their memories, while the political meaning of the vigils remained in the background. In narrating their experiences, they associated the candlelight vigils primarily with two major past events: the 2002 World Cup street celebrations and high school training camps.

In 2002 Ŭn-ha* was a high school student in a small city in eastern South Korea. That summer she learned about Mi-sŏn and Hyo-sun's deaths and the subsequent nationwide vigils through mass media coverage. She and her friends planned the first candlelight gathering in their town and subsequently organized a series of vigils. She recollected the period in detail: her initial shock at the news of the girls' deaths, many nights of making posters and leaflets for the vigils, disapproval from her parents and teachers, the initial indifference from locals, and then eventual approval of her activities as the girls' deaths became a national issue. In 2006 she noted, "The vigils were a very important experience for me. I don't think I could do anything with such passion now. At that time I was a high school student and was shocked that the reality [of the U.S. presence] was so different from what I had known before. I was in my first year in high school and felt a true sense of justice. This propelled me to do the things I did."[6] This period remained important to Ŭn-ha four years later primarily because of the "passion" and "true sense of justice" that shook her worldview but could never be recaptured. Before Ŭn-ha told me her stories, I didn't imagine that she could have been an active leader in 2002. The way she dressed, in a peach-colored skirt, and the way she talked, in high tones, simply didn't resonate with my image of the socially interested students whom I'd personally encountered in college. This expectation, based on my contact with student activists in the 1980s and 1990s, was betrayed again when Ŭn-ha noted that she was no longer involved in activism. In 2006 she had no interest in associating with student activists, and her biggest concern was building a career.

She was the first to remind me that participants and their memories of the vigils might be different from my own expectations. My first memory of the democratization movement was from third grade in 1985, when I was trapped in my school bus surrounded by a cloud of tear gas drifting from a clash at the nearby university. Later, as an undergraduate in the mid-1990s, I heard legendary stories from student activists who had returned to university after years of involvement in the antiauthoritarian movement. The authoritarian-era repertoire was the dominant mode of protest until the early 2000s, with everything it entailed. For those who had participated in high-risk, high-stakes social movements, an activist identity was an integral part of who they were—including how they behaved, spoke, and dressed—and not something from which one could easily dissociate.

Among the vigil participants I interviewed, I met not only dedicated organizers like Ŭn-ha but also many who joined the vigils with little intention of doing so. For example, Chong-su* was waiting for friends in downtown Seoul when he was surrounded by protesters. Si-nae* encountered and joined a vigil at her local train station. Wŏn-hŭi* went to a few vigils not to protest but to practice photography. To borrow Bennett and Segerberg's term, they were "connected" to the vigils without sharing a collective identity.[7] Before 2002 such casual participation in a protest was hardly imaginable. In fact, Chong-su and Wŏn-hŭi insisted that they hadn't actually "participated" in the vigils. Each "joined" or "dropped by" a vigil one night and remained critical toward the anti-American rhetoric. However, that they were able to be part of the protest crowd without identifying with the movement signified a weakening of the ideological commitment associated with dissent.

Instead, this gap in ideological identification was filled with corporeal memories. My interviews typically started with a question: "What were your first impressions of the vigils, either when you saw them on TV or in person?" Every interviewee, participant or not, brought up the World Cup street celebrations to explain impressions of the vigils. Hye-gŭn*, who had been in eleventh grade in 2002, responded, "The vigils were one more time people got together after the World Cup street celebration. Even their scale was similar. Ah, it's really cool that people were united, of one mind, to rebuke the deaths of the two."[8] Three male college students also brought up the World Cup street cheering:

> *Chin-su*: Our people can really come together when they're asked
>   to. . . . We can be of one mind.
> *Ho-wŏn*: I think the World Cup had an impact. [*pause*] What I
>   mean is, previously, we didn't have such a thing. Because a mas-
>   sive number of people gathered at City Hall Plaza for the World
>   Cup, people proposed the candlelight vigils. Because of the
>   World Cup, more people came out, and they had a stronger sense
>   of unity.
> *Si-yŏng*: In the past, throwing Molotov cocktails was part of such
>   mass gatherings, but nowadays we see peaceful gatherings.[9]

These students understood that the draw of the vigils was a function of the intense, cathartic gatherings that soccer fans experienced during the World Cup, paralleling the vigil participants' corporeal and affective memories of "assembly" and "unity." In "How Bodies Remember," anthropologist Arthur Kleinman and literary scholar Joan Kleinman remind us that corporeal experience—which cannot be neatly divided into cognition and affect—is where local social norms and meanings manifest.[10] Similarly, philosopher Edward Casey argues that memory is not contained separately in the mind or brain but instead is ingrained in "bodily movements that accomplish particular action."[11] That is, one does not remember in abstract; instead, childhood is remembered with the childhood home, and war is remembered with the sound and smell of gunfire. For these youths, World Cup crowds made it possible to imagine safe and festive mass gatherings at city centers, supplanting the previous association of protests with violence and fear.

Several interviewees also viewed the vigils as an extension of familiar patriotic campaigns in junior high or high school, such as the disciplinary training camps (*kŭkki hullyŏn*). In the 1970s President Park Chung Hee built youth discipline centers throughout the country that were attended annually by junior high and high school students. Typically, students would go for a two- or three-day camp annually for four or five years, returning with intense experiences of physical exercise, collaborative projects, and etiquette training. These programs taught young Koreans the virtues of patriotism, collaboration, and national unity, and encouraged them to be docile and productive.[12] The training camps transformed national security and development from political ideals into "a state of mind, behavioral style, and a structure of feeling" and instilled these ideals into young Koreans during the authoritarian era and beyond.[13]

In the late 1980s and early 1990s I myself attended such a camp every year between the fifth and tenth grades. Usually, on the final night of camp, students would gather for a candlelight ceremony. Each student held a candle, and a designated speaker (typically one of the instructors at the camp) gave a speech urging us to appreciate the comfort, security, and love we took for granted. Exhausted and complaining about excessive physical activity, we were encouraged and coerced into a sense of indebtedness. The ceremony culminated in an impassioned speech about the love and sacrifice of our parents. By this point girls would burst into tears, and some in the audience sobbed. This process effected a sort of catharsis, and taught students to appreciate authority. I was surprised to learn during interviews for this book that these camps continued into the twenty-first century. Yun-ji*, an eleventh-grader in 2002, recalled her camp experience: "Before going to the vigils, physical confrontation was the first image that came up for me when thinking about a protest. But the candlelight vigils were [*pause*] candles! We used to do the candle ceremonies at camps when we were younger. At the ceremonies, we called, 'Mommy!' [*pretending to be crying*]. During the 2002 vigils I remembered that time, and it changed my attitude."[14] For this young woman, the vigils initially evoked an image of violent protest, the repertoire of South Korea's oppositional movement. However, when she actually went to a vigil, it instead recalled scenes from candle ceremonies during her adolescence. Interestingly, the ideological foundation of the training camp was completely absent from Yun-ji's narrative; instead, the memories of appreciating her mother lingered with her and painted the 2002 vigils as familiar and safe.

Similar experiences connecting the state-run camps and the vigils were also quite pronounced in the following conversation:

> *Nam-hŭi*:* People holding candles at the candlelight vigils looked pious and solemn to me. For me, the images from the candlelight ceremonies at junior high school and the protests in 2002 were similar.
>
> *Hyo-ju*:* Yeah, they looked solemn. I feel that those [images from camp] overlapped with the vigils.
>
> *Myŏng:* And at the ceremonies [at camp], they always asked each person to mention something that we appreciated.
>
> *Nam-hŭi:* The candles seemed to enable that.
>
> *Myŏng:* Candles have been around us for a long time! [*giggles*]
>
> *Nam-hŭi:* Was this [the high school candlelight ceremony] the reason they started the candlelight vigils? [*all laugh*][15]

At a typical vigil in 2002, volunteers from the crowd read letters to the two deceased girls, gave speeches, and staged performances demanding that the U.S. and South Korean governments impose justice for the deaths. Similarly, candlelight ceremonies in training camps featured speeches and performances by student volunteers. The shared pattern of remembrance, appreciation, and indebtedness connects the two disparate ideological spaces. Further, in the passage above, the interviewees talk about the 2002 vigils but often omit specific referents to either the vigils or the training camps, revealing that the vigils and camps were conjoined in their recollections via corporeal memories. The narratives are centered on bodies in place— corporeal memories of holding candles at ceremonies.

In contrast, the progressive media have accused both the training camps and the World Cup of promoting state-driven nationalism. A 2007 op-ed in the progressive online newspaper *Oh My News* questioned the still ongoing camps, asking, "Why should children cry at night holding candles?"[16] The idea behind the camps, the author argues, was that self-discipline, appreciation, and respect could be "trained" through formulaic enforcement, memorization, and submission. For the author, this program attested to the persistence of the "militarized state" despite democratization.[17] Similarly, critical scholars have argued that the World Cup frenzy created a myth in which good nationalism defeats evil nationalism, emotionally rallying Koreans to identify as faithful members of the nation.[18] Progressive scholar Kang Su-dol even warned that the catharsis offered by the World Cup would give uncritical sanction to government pursuit of economic achievement at the expense of justice and equality.[19] These views aptly point out the ideological significance of the school camps and of the World Cup, situating both in a history of state-driven disciplinary spaces that produced patriotic subjects. The youths' corporeal recollections, then, could be seen as evidence of naïveté, or at least ignorance of ideological implications.

However, this naïveté also meant that youths at the vigils could act without considering the ideological ramifications of their actions, in contrast with protesters during the authoritarian era. Forgetting is an integral part of forming a new identity; when an existing vocabulary fades and a new one emerges, we see a glimpse of new identity in formation.[20] In South Korea's previous contestations between state and oppositional ideologies, disregarding the ideological implications of one's actions was impossible—participation in (or withdrawal from) mass events inherently carried political and legal consequences. The forgetting of ideological language therefore suggests that, for the interviewees, the vigils represented a new type of social movement.

The void left by the waning ideological repertoire was filled by corporeal memories of the safe yet potent crowd. Anthropologist Saba Mahmood argues that repeated corporeal performances "train one's memory, desire, and intellect."[21] Similarly, Casey contends that "habitual body memory" orients a person to establish a perspective on what is possible and desirable and changes the nature of aggregate individual experience.[22] The youths at the vigils were South Korea's first generation to experience dissent in a peaceful and festive environment, absent flying rocks, tear gas, and police violence. For many teenagers, their original experience of peaceful mass gathering had likely occurred only during the then-recent World Cup street celebrations. Nevertheless, occupying city centers became "habitual body memories" by the winter of 2002, allowing young Koreans to feel at ease with bringing their excitement and grievances to downtown Seoul and other city centers across the country.

The corporeal vigils as remembered by these interviewees therefore represent a new repertoire and a postauthoritarian subjectivity that departs from the perspective, desires, and attitudes of the authoritarian era. Even though the authoritarian era ended back in 1987, the cultural frames associated with expressing and responding to dissent took time to change. With the vigils, a new set of frames unbound by the previous era finally emerged—a repertoire that included casual participation, freedom from the pressures of ideological sensitivity, and peaceful and festive gatherings.

Ambivalent Political Vigils: The Slow Decomposition of the Authoritarian Repertoire

This postauthoritarian repertoire did not completely replace the previous framework, however. A number of interviewees viewed the vigils from a perspective predicated on the democratization movement that included devoted activism, a physical and social cost for participants, and radical political claims. This framework still exerted significant influence on some postauthoritarian youths, and the "decomposition" of the authoritarian repertoire is (or perhaps now, *was*) therefore clearly a gradual one.[23] That said, two contradictory judgments were made by those who still maintained the perspective of that repertoire: for some interviewees the vigils were too radical because of their anti-American slogans, while for others the vigils were superficial because of the low cost of participation.

One afternoon I interviewed four so-called *pokhaksaeng,* male students returning to college after completing their two-year compulsory military service. With 640,000 soldiers as of 2012, South Korea's military is the sixth largest in the world; all healthy men must serve at least twenty-one months (reduced from twenty-six in 2002).[24] Such returnees are well known for their hard work to obtain good grades, particularly when compared with students who indulge in the freedom of college life prior to military service. These four had been in the military during the vigils of 2002 and doubted the spontaneity of the participants:

> *Hun*:* In the military, we received an enormous amount of educational training about the necessity of U.S. troops in South Korea. Seeing the vigils, I questioned, "Are we better off without the U.S. Army?" Originally, citizens stood up to solve a problem that the government did not properly handle. The beginning was good, but the vigils ended up being too much into anti-Americanism. The vigils served not only Hyo-sun and Mi-sŏn, but also those who were extremely anti-American. Anti-American agitators had to have been at the vigils.
>
> *Chin-su*:* Some people just followed others to the vigils.

Hun: [*simultaneously with Chin-su*] To demand that U.S. troops withdraw from Korea.

Chin-su: I'm sure many just followed their friends, moms, and dads to the vigils.

Si-yŏng: [*simultaneously with Chin-su*] Like, half of them were with a purpose and the other half without a purpose.

Si-yŏng: They [those with a purpose] initiated the vigils and provoked others.

Ho-wŏn: Although we didn't know, they had a purpose to make U.S. troops withdraw.

Hun: North Korean spies (*kanch'ŏp*) could have sent them [*chuckle*].

Si-yŏng: Not exactly spies, but . . .

Hun: They say there are fifty thousand North Korean spies in South Korea [*chuckle*].[25]

For Hun, anti-American demagogues who took advantage of the girls' deaths to incite anti-Americanism were behind the vigils. For Chin-su, vigil participants "just followed" others. As Si-yŏng aptly pointed out, for these returnee students vigil participants were either anti-American demagogues or ignorant masses. Their language is worth considering: "anti-Americanism," "necessity of the U.S. troops in Korea," and "North Korean spies" were terms frequently found in pre-1990s anti-Communist campaigns. These students also told me that during the vigils the military reinforced ideological education (*sasang kyoyuk*) to affirm North Korea as the primary enemy of South Korea as well as the necessity of the U.S. military presence. The military further issued specific instructions to soldiers on vacation not to participate in the vigils. Despite their upbringing in the postauthoritarian era, these returnees inherited the language and narratives of the older protest repertoire, situating the vigils within the traditional anti-American movement.

Meanwhile, an interview with another group of military returnee students implied that the continuation of language from the authoritarian era did not necessarily mean that younger Koreans had also inherited the authoritarian-era cultural perspectives. Some instead negotiated and appropriated those cultural frames to confirm their own maturity and competency. At one of the most prestigious universities in South Korea I met Wŏn-hŭi and Ho-jun.* Wŏn-hŭi volunteered to meet with me, and his friend Ho-jun joined the conversation. My first impression at the interview was that they used English frequently. I was curious whether this reflected the current obsession with English proficiency among Korean college students or their own personal backgrounds, until I learned that both had served in the Korean Augmentation to the United States Army (KATUSA). KATUSA was originally established just after the outbreak of the Korean War in 1950 to augment the fighting forces of the United States. After the armistice in 1953, KATUSA soldiers remained with U.S. units to receive training that was not readily available in the South Korean Army and to improve the U.S. Army's mission capability.[26] In contemporary South Korea KATUSA occupies a unique status in college culture as an object of both desire and derision. South Korean males who have a TOEIC (Test of English for International Communication) score above 780 out of 990 can apply for KATUSA and serve their twenty-one months of military service under the direction of U.S. forces stationed in South Korea.[27] Because in KATUSA physical discipline is less severe and living conditions are better than in the regular South Korean military, many Koreans view serving in KATUSA as a privilege, and some perceive it as an opportunity to hone their English skills. Usually, only students in good colleges and with high English proficiency go to KATUSA. However, because KATUSA lacks male bonding through challenging physical discipline, which many Korean men believe is the core of military life, those who serve in the Korean military often refer to KATUSA with a mixture of envy and disdain as a "fake military." Further, student activists in the past conceived of KATUSA members as traitors who supported the "occupation troops."[28]

As such, KATUSA returnees represent a particular type of college student—high achieving, practical, and favorable toward the United States. In addition, Wŏn-hŭi was interested in pursuing a graduate degree in the United States, which he revealed at the end of the interview. He asked me questions about applying for graduate school and about life in the United States and exclaimed, "I wish I could go where you are now!"[29] He had attended the candlelight vigils and offered an articulate critique of the participants' anti-American sentiment, so I don't think he volunteered to be interviewed only to gain information about graduate school and life in the United States. However, the appearance of "University of Illinois" on the recruiting material (my affiliation at the time) certainly seemed to make him a little more interested in the interview.

Both Wŏn-hŭi and Ho-jun referred to the vigils as an anti-American movement and explained that South Koreans' anti-Americanism originated from ignorance of the United States.

Wŏn-hŭi: Some people seem to know the United States and others don't. Those who know why the United States is in Korea do not have an extreme anti-American sentiment. People who don't know the United States hate the country unconditionally.

Ho-jun: In fact, I used to serve in KATUSA, lived with American GIs, and worked in the human resources department—I was the only Korean in the department. . . . The claims that SOFA is unilateral, needs to be reformed, and the like seem reasonable even though I don't know much. But criticizing the American *people,* for example "Yankee Go Home," isn't. The problem is, Koreans hate American people! . . . In fact, I didn't know the reality before going into the military and learning the "perspective on the enemy," which teaches us that our primary enemy is North Korea and the United States is our blood ally.

Wŏn-hŭi: They [the military] make us memorize the four necessities, why the U.S. troops are stationed in Korea.

Ho-jun: The education wasn't very strict but was recently reinforced, as the younger generation of Koreans felt that they should expel U.S. troops. So, we had to memorize, and take tests from morning to night. But I don't think those kids actually have anti-American sentiment; they're just following what others told them to do.[30]

Wŏn-hŭi and Ho-jun felt that vigil participants had a misguided hatred of Americans, not understanding "why the U.S. is in Korea." This criticism was similar to that of the previous four returnees, but these two established their authority from firsthand experience in KATUSA. Ho-jun highlighted his privileged access to U.S. troops, emphasizing, "I was the only Korean in the department." Wŏn-hŭi had worked for the public relations department in KATUSA. With an inside knowledge of the organization, they stressed their understanding of the U.S. presence—in contrast with younger Koreans, who they felt did not grasp the complexity of the situation and therefore could not properly address the issue. By distinguishing themselves from others in the "younger generation," Wŏn-hŭi and Ho-jun portrayed themselves as mature and cautious members of society. Furthermore, while the previous returnee students upheld views offered by the military, these two interviewees demonstrated their individual competence to criticize both "impulsive anti-Americanism" and a "unilateral SOFA." It might be hasty to conclude that the two represented a turn toward a more pragmatic and competitive individuality after the dominance of ideological confrontation during the authoritarian era; however, their proficiency with English and preparation for future careers, combined with their display of self-confidence at the interview, led me to see them as distinct from the other interviewees.

These interviews suggest that the term "anti-Americanism" (*panmi*) persisted beyond the era of the antiauthoritarian and anti-American movement, through a military culture that reproduced the language and ideologies of official nationalism. Indeed, although my interviewees did not have firsthand experience with the ideological contests of the authoritarian era, they were familiar with the trope of anti-Americanism. I asked, "How did you feel about the girls' deaths?" and "How did the vigils influence your political views?" They answered, "My anti-American sentiment reached its peak,"[31] or "The girls' deaths changed my outlook. But, I wasn't thinking, 'we should be anti-American.' "[32] The term, which had been associated with the oppositional movement during authoritarian rule, nonetheless remained active among some youths even in 2006.

However, although the term "anti-Americanism" itself persisted, the personal meaning associated with it had changed. For the returnee students the vigils were indeed anti-American, but this was not a serious threat to national security—rather, it represented immature youth swayed by ignorant emotion. These young people described the "anti-American" protesters (and North Korean spies as well) as objects of humor. From their position in the increasingly competitive college environment, Ho-jun and Wŏn-hŭi also identified themselves as more mature and responsible than the youths in the street. In this context, college students in 2006 were weaving multiple cultural frames—partly reproducing the authoritarian-era repertoire on the social level and partly confirming their competence and maturity on the individual level.

While some students viewed the vigils as anti-American protests, to others the vigils looked superficial, demanding too little cost compared with the high-stakes social movements of the past. Chu-yŏng* and Ka-in* were friends, both attending a university in Seoul. Chu-yŏng was a senior in high school in 2002 but didn't participate in the vigils because they appeared to be festivals wrongly given the title of protest. She compared the vigils with the World Cup: "The vigils were held not to commemorate the girls' deaths or to protest U.S. troops; they degenerated into an event, a copycat of the World Cup celebration. . . . The participants went to the vigils not to commemorate the deaths but were like, 'Yeah, it will be fun. Let's try the vigils.' They went to the vigils to experience the 'culture of the public square' that they had seen and felt at the World Cup, and to take pictures and post them on their blogs. . . . People seemed to view the vigils as a fun and unusual event they could enjoy."[33] The vigils allowed casual participation, and therefore provided younger Koreans with a space in which to protest without the corresponding fear of punishment. For some Koreans, the vigils became just a festival, not much different from the street celebrations of the World Cup, and high school students participated as a form of liberation from school.

Ka-in had also been a high school senior in 2002 and similarly felt that the vigils were an outing for teenagers even though many claimed it was political action. She went to a vigil with her friends after taking the national university placement test in late November, curious about the gatherings that she'd seen on television but had not been allowed to attend while preparing for the exam. She remembered the event as a "new cultural experience" after a long period of being "locked" in school. Like Chu-yŏng, Ka-in also argued that many, as she did, went to the vigils for reasons other than commemorating the deaths of the unfortunate girls: "Many people believed they should go because everyone else went, and because they wanted to be seen."[34] I suspect that their characterizations accurately describe the motivations of many vigil participants, including those described in the first section of this chapter. The young Koreans who gathered at the vigils indeed came with heterogeneous motives: some to protest the verdict, others to experience the "culture of the public square" as Chu-yŏng put it. Both Chu-yŏng and Ka-in were aware that the vigils were a new form of mass gathering in which youths could participate without any particular devotion to—or even agreement with—the political cause. Acknowledging this new repertoire, they nevertheless evaluated it as a "degenerated" form of protest compared with the movement repertoire of previous generations. In these young women's narratives, meaningful activism was implied to be closer to the traditional oppositional movement in which a protester had to take up an identity as a dissident, which often came with the steep social cost of diminished personal success, alienation from family, or even imprisonment.

These competing interpretations, anti-American or superficial, attest that the authoritarian-era protest repertoire remained as both a lens and a vocabulary through which these interviewees interpreted the 2002 vigils. The then-new candlelight protest was seen either as a variant of the existing protest repertoire or as an insincere movement because it did not properly fit into that repertoire. A movement repertoire changes slowly.[35] The persistence of the older repertoire suggests that the ideological contestation that shaped authoritarian-era activism was still in effect in South Korea.

Anti-American Vigils: The Remnants of the Oppositional Movement Repertoire

In this final section, I turn to the narratives offered by eight activists rooted in the historical radical movement tradition. In 2006 they were among the only people still discussing the girls' deaths, and several volunteered to be interviewed. They had been part of the Pan-Korean Community for Two Girls Killed by a U.S. Armored Vehicle (PKC) in 2002, and after the vigils faded they returned to their respective activist groups, ranging from an organization opposing U.S. bases to a progressive online newspaper to a labor organization. Even though they aren't the focus of this book, they represent important voices in the heterogeneous vigil crowd, and their movement tradition affected young participants' interpretations of the vigils.

Searching for a trace of the vigils, I found that a four-year anniversary candlelight gathering would be held in mid-June of 2006. I went to the train station in a city near where the tragic accident happened in 2002. The square in front of the station was small, but not too small to accommodate the perhaps one hundred participants sitting on the ground, plus passersby who kept a few feet of distance. A group of local unionized taxi drivers on strike at the time were sitting in front of the podium, and the families I sat with turned out to be from a local labor organization. The event started with protest songs originating from the antiauthoritarian movement, after which activists from the local teachers union recited letters to Hyo-sun and Mi-sŏn. Then a dancer performed a traditional *salpuri,* consoling the souls of the deceased. Between the speeches and performances, the host chanted slogans—"U.S. troops withdraw from Korea!"; "Remember Hyo-sun and Mi-sŏn !"; and "Reform SOFA!" I felt as though I were at a 1980s anti-American protest, which I hadn't actually attended but knew well through books, documentary films, and the similar (but smaller) protests of the 1990s with which I had firsthand experience. In this 1980s-like ceremony, only the familiar names of the girls and the candles reminded me of the candlelight vigils that swept the nation in the winter of 2002–2003. The event hardly resembled those in which, just four years previously, hundreds of thousands of young Koreans had filled city centers, waved Koreans flags, and staged fierce yet cheerful performances in protest against perceived injustice.

A few days after the anniversary gathering, I visited Hyŏn-ho*, the host of the ceremony. As I later learned, he was leader of the local branch of an organization rooted in the 1980s radical movement that protested the U.S. military presence, the oppression of human rights, and authoritarianism. He had been closely monitoring the dozens of U.S. army garrisons in the area and criticizing the practices of U.S. forces in Korea well before 2002. In the aftermath of the girls' deaths, he was one of the first activists devoted to the cause. When I visited him, he had been holding sit-ins in front of Ŭijŏgbu's city hall along with a group of striking taxi drivers and his head was shaven—a familiar protest ritual to show determination.

Hyŏn-ho situated the 2002 candlelight vigils within the historic struggle of the democratization movement to liberate the country from U.S. influence and authoritarianism, and he believed that the nationwide vigils were an achievement of South Korea's oppositional movement. "The format of candlelight vigils reflected the efforts of Korea's nationalist-democratization movement (*minjok-minju undong*), which had been striving to join with people instead of resorting to a handful of activists and violent means. . . . Korean social movement currently strives to transform local people into agents (*chuin*) of change and to confront social injustices. Our devotion to this principle enabled us to change the shocking incident [of the girls' deaths] into a movement where everyone could participate."[36] Hyŏn-ho's language pointed to the ideological underpinnings of his perspective even more clearly than his direct interpretations. He described that the vigils were an extension of Korea's "nationalist-democratization movement," which transformed ordinary citizens into "agents of change" in their pursuit of reunification and democratization. These phrases were the terminology of this particular movement sector, which believed that the U.S. neocolonial presence was responsible for Korea's major social ills by dividing North and South Korea and by condoning a dictatorship in the name of regional security against the Communist threat. Activists argued that the nationalist-democratization movement ought to raise people's consciousness in order to build them as agents of political reform. For Hyŏn-ho, the 2002 vigils attested that activists like him had finally achieved their goal after years of "striving to join with people."

Other activists also situated the vigils in the history of the oppositional movement, likening them to the iconic democratization struggles of 1980 and 1987. Po-mun* was a reporter for a progressive online newspaper. He had been critically reporting on the U.S. military presence since the 1990s and reported the girls' deaths immediately after the incident, making his newspaper an opinion leader during the vigils. He viewed the vigils as a descendant of the 1987 democratization movement: "The vigils were an ordinary mode of protest. In the democratization movement in 1987, priests held candlelight vigils."[37] He was referring to the iconic march of Catholic priests in rebuke of the government for the deaths of college student activists. Hong-min*, the director of a nationwide organization opposing U.S. military bases, similarly cited the march, along with the Kwangju uprising in 1980: "During the Kwangju uprising, people held candlelight vigils, and Catholic priests also used candlelight protests in the past. Initially, we didn't expect the 2002 candlelight vigils to become such a massive event. . . . After the vigils went nationwide, I rethought the meaning of the candle. That is, the candle symbolizes resistance, as our ancestors raised a beacon fire when the country was invaded by outside powers."[38] It's worth noting how Hong-min made sense of the massive scale of the 2002 vigils, which he had longed for but "didn't expect." In the vigils he saw the revival of candlelight marches from the period of antiauthoritarian activism. Furthermore, in the "beacon fire" against "outside powers" he traced the vigils' origin back to the nineteenth-century peasant movement against Western colonialism. In the *minjung* discourse, peasant uprisings against Western imperialist expansion in the late nineteenth century are seen as a prototype of the contemporary movement. The 1980 Kwangju uprising and the 1987 democratization protests were landmarks in the *minjung* history, symbolizing the Korean people's voluntarism and resistance to violence from authoritarian and colonial powers.[39] Although Koreans saw few candlelight vigils in the fifteen years after 1987, both Hong-min and Po-mun viewed the vigils as a familiar form of *minjung* protest.

Furthermore, for these activists the 2002 vigils symbolized a promise for future changes and legitimation of their personal commitment in an increasingly depoliticized Korea. Hong-min and his organization were surprised at the scope of the 2002 vigils, and took it as evidence that the Korean people finally supported the organization's effort for the withdrawal of U.S. troops. Hyŏn-ho reported more vividly the personal impact of the vigils: "I was so enthused. I thought, 'Ah, people were really the actors (*chuin*) driving history!' I suddenly, and surely, realized that history does progress, and the agency of that progress resides in the people."[40] For these two activists, the vigils evidenced the long-held faith (and principle of the *minjung* movement) that ordinary people are the driving force behind historical change. Hyŏn-ho, Hong-min, and Po-mun all remembered the vigils as a proud moment in their personal trajectories. In 2006 Hyŏn-ho was involved in protesting against U.S. bases while expanding an alliance with local labor unions and civic organizations. Hong-min's organization was planning to establish branches in America to deliver their grievances against the U.S. presence in South Korea directly to Washington and to protest U.S. military expansion at the global scale. Po-mun was investigating and publishing on the broader subject of the historical U.S. presence in Korea, hoping to revive public interest in a topic that he had seen enter the spotlight four years earlier.

There is a significant discrepancy between these activists' interpretations and those of the young Koreans I discussed in the previous sections. The youths who casually attended the vigils or criticized them for their impulsive anti-Americanism or levity would disagree with the activists' narratives. However, as the Rashomon effect reminds us, such narratives are reasonable in their own right, considering the activists' personal trajectories. In the 2002 vigils they saw a revival of the consciousness of the Korean public. Even though this perspective does not account for the experiences of the youths involved, it significantly affirmed the activists' identities and communities.

Furthermore, it is notable that even in the 2000s this activist interpretive framework was still being passed down to some young students in their early twenties. The following three interviewees adopted elements of this perspective through contact with activist circles in college. In the slowly changing student movement culture, the perception that the legitimate cause of anti-Americanism demanded a steep social price made them agonize over supporting the "right cause" and surviving in the competitive college environment.

In 2006 Su-min*, a senior, was deeply devoted to social justice and to the anti-American movement at her university. She even went to a four-year anniversary vigil in downtown Seoul. The vigil was poorly attended because, as she recalled, it rained hard that day and "most Koreans forgot the girls' deaths." In contrast to "most Koreans," however, she and her fellow activists appeared to remember the girls.[41] She told me that she began to associate with senior students as soon as she entered college in 2002. Usually, student activists were the only people who participated in student councils and cared about the welfare of their juniors in the increasingly individualistic and competitive college culture. Coming from a different region and living near campus, she adopted these seniors as her primary community upon entering university, and she was politically socialized in the student council. During the interview, she didn't mention that she was also deeply involved in a specific student movement at her school, which was known as a stronghold of the nationalist group among *minjung* movement sectors. Mi-rae*, another student from the same school, confirmed after the official interview ended and Su-min left that Su-min was an active member of the group. Even before Mi-rae told me this, however, I'd surmised from Su-Min's perspective and vocabulary that she was involved with that student movement sector, which was rooted in a 1980s oppositional nationalist tradition marked by strong opposition to the U.S. "imperial" power and by the pursuit of reunification.

Along with fellow student activists, Su-min "went to vigils every day during the summer of 2002." She believed that during the vigils the mainstream media denounced activists' legitimate critique of the United States as "mere" anti-Americanism and noted that the South Korean public should distinguish between a total disapproval of the U.S. role in Korea and a reasonable criticism of U.S. policies. She added,

> The U.S. exerts an enormous influence in Korea. [We are] criticizing negative aspects of the U.S. influence—not the entire country but some misguided policies. I dislike America and American products. . . . I heard from my seniors that in the 1990s, they could not drink Coca-Cola in the student council office, and when a person smoked an American cigarette, the seniors broke it. . . . But, it is a misconception that we hate the American people. In fact, what we oppose are misguided U.S. policies, the Hyo-sun and Mi-sŏn incident, and the Iraq war.[42]

Su-min's interpretation of the vigils was contrary to that of her contemporaries, but she shared similar linguistic expressions with vocal critics such as returnee students—"anti-Americanism," a "critique of the United States," and the "withdrawal of U.S. troops." Like the returnee students who recited the language of the military, Su-min appeared to adopt the language of the oppositional movement—both products of the authoritarian period.

Su-min's account of the legendary anti-American practices of past student movements was especially revealing. When I went to college in the 1990s, the anti-American practices she described vis-à-vis Coca-Cola and American cigarettes were long gone. However, I heard the same legends from student activists on campus —except that *I* heard they had occurred in the 1980s. In her narrative, Su-Min frequently noted the role of seniors (*sŏnbae*) and quoted them in explaining the format of the candlelight vigils: "According to my seniors, the recent protests were much different from the past ones. They said that the format and methods of protest became much less intense."[43] This suggests that Su-min became familiar with the narratives of radical and often-violent anti-American protest secondhand as retold by her seniors. The student activist culture, which had served as a reservoir for a progressive worldview and student activism throughout the authoritarian era, declined in the 1990s following the collapse of the Soviet Union and the advent of neoliberal reforms that introduced competitive measures among universities and students. However, elements of the movement tradition nonetheless remained in some student activist communities like Su-min's— but not without tension.

This tension between the movement tradition and new competitive measures hit home for T'ae-ju*, a sophomore in 2006, in deeply personal ways. Like Su-min, he associated with a student movement group as his primary community upon entering university, but, unlike Su-min, he left the group after his freshman year. He heard about my project and e-mailed me, saying that he hadn't been in the vigils but wanted to meet with me. He started the conversation by saying, "I hate protests, but I don't know why. I thought I would find an answer from this interview."[44] I was intrigued by his desire to participate in an interview, and by his personal reasons. Upon entering university he joined the campus broadcast station without know-ing that it had traditionally been associated with a radical sector of the student movement—the same group Su-min was part of. According to him, senior student activists at the station educated him about social problems and brought him to various protests. He was "forced to go to the protests in fear." He vividly described one particular march he attended: "There was no tear gas, but the police used fire hoses. It was a very violent protest. The police shot us with water and the protesters from labor unions threw stones and blocks from the sidewalk [at the police]. What I couldn't bear the most was that such violence kept repeating yet nothing seemed to be changing."[45] He was agitated as he described the scene of the protest at length, attesting to his intense memory of violence. The fear of past protests kept him away from other protests, although he felt that they were for legitimate causes.

For T'ae-ju, another source of fear was the "sacrifice of the future" that he might suffer for participating in an activist movement. At the broadcast station, he was asked to choose between the "right" cause and "selfish" aca-demic pursuit, and felt pressure to sacrifice his future for the sake of social justice. He said, "The broadcast station separated me from other friends and study. I couldn't agree with student activists who ignored study so easily, saying, 'study is not important because injustice is the problem'."[46] As

T'ae-ju encountered in 2006, college students were facing a difficult job market, with a 10 percent youth unemployment rate and diminishing desirable positions.[47] The university was turning into an extension of high school, in that students had to devote their energy to maintain a high GPA and accumulate certificates for the job market. Meanwhile, student movement groups were slow to change. The emphasis on social justice and indifference toward academic success was also part of the 1980s student movement tradition, but had evolved in a period when a degree from a reputable university was sufficient to guarantee a decent job. T'ae-ju knew both worlds—one that demanded full devotion to social justice and another that demanded attention to productivity and competition. His awareness of these two worlds left T'ae-ju split between the "right cause" and his personal future and led him to feel uneasy about protests, including the relatively peaceful 2002 vigils.

In fact, concern about her career similarly led Ŭn-ha (introduced in the first section of this chapter) to dissociate from the student movement upon entering university in 2005. When she saw other student protesters, she drastically reevaluated her "proud" experiences as being merely a reflection of her immaturity at that time: "I entered university and saw people organizing protests. I felt, 'Those are what I used to do naïvely in high school, but I shouldn't do it anymore.' I did those things with such pleasure and excitement in junior high and high school. But I'm partly a member of society (sahoein) already. I felt activism would be a disadvantage for my future career, and even give me a criminal record. I don't think I can ever take action like what I did in high school."[48] Ŭn-ha saw her activist seniors forsaking study and even being arrested for participating in violent street protests, and she realized that they had been typical participants in the 2002 vigils. She repeatedly contrasted her naïveté in high school with the maturity that she later acquired. In the interview, she consistently referred to herself as a "member of society," presenting it as the opposite of having a criminal record and of the "radicals" whom she associated with in high school. The term implied norms that she believed a successful university student should follow in order to become a competent member of society, such as responsibility, observation of the law, and caution—and later, she added English proficiency and other skills with which she could succeed among fierce competition.

In these interviews with Su-min, T'ae-ju, and Ŭn-ha, the vocabulary of the anti-American movement and the fear of sacrifice coexist. They were contemporaries of the other interviewees introduced in the earlier sections, but unlike those who narrated the vigils as personal liberation or freely criticized them, these three young students—like their predecessors in the 1980s—"agonized whether to resist or escape."[49] The coexistence of heterogeneous views within the same cohort suggests that perceptions of the candlelight vigils cannot be accounted for as solely a "youth" or "anti-American" phenomenon.[50] Instead, perspectives on the vigils are better explained by relative distance from the conveyors of the antiauthoritarian repertoire.

The Slow Emergence of a Postauthoritarian Movement Repertoire

Despite varied interpretations, the interviews in this chapter reveal that the vigils were still very much a part of young people's lives four years later. The corporeal and affective memories of fearlessly expressing grievances and occupying city centers remained vivid, even though the captivation with the girls' deaths and with the presidential candidates had been temporary. (One can't be captivated all the time, after all.) Although these youths reinterpreted the political significance of the vigils in various ways depending on their positions in 2006, they all acknowledged the mass candlelight gathering as a habituated mode of expressing underarticulated yet potent feelings. These heterogeneous participants, motives, and practices do not allow a clear characterization along ideological lines. Instead, the vigils are politically significant because they offered a space for what Casey calls "habitual body memory" to form in Kwanghwamun and at other gathering places throughout South Korea.

The interviews I conducted in 2006 contradict the initial picture painted by the media and politicians in 2002—that these teenagers were a new generation of activists equipped with the Internet and an anti-American perspective, or that the youths at the vigils were no different from those at the World Cup. Instead, the interviews in this chapter show that four years later vigil participants had reinterpreted the activism of 2002 in a variety of ways. Even though captivation with the girls' deaths or with the election was short lived, collective and corporeal memories of the safe and potent crowd at the vigils outlived the specific issues. We have seen interviewees who retrospectively associated the vigils with the World Cup street celebrations and with high school training camps. These corporeal associations reflect the erosion of South Korea's hypersensitivity to the ideological ramifications of one's actions and further suggest that the peaceful and festive experience contributed to establishing candlelight vigils as a preferred method of protest for youths. However, we have also seen that the repertoire from the authoritarian era was still at least partially in effect. The coexistence of contradictory interpretations of the vigils among young interviewees—that is, as either too radical or too superficial—signals that the vigils represent a new repertoire that doesn't fit into preexisting ideological frames. The political implications of the vigils reside not in obvious anti-American rhetoric but in rearticulating the corporeal experiences of South Korean youths and in offering space for a new repertoire to form. The significance of the protests cannot be found only in the at-the-moment passion of occupying city centers; instead, the memory remains with individuals long after the moment has passed. In particular, the experiences of voicing underarticulated yet shared passions in a safe space fostered a new repertoire without the necessity of conforming to mainstream political or cultural frames.

By 2006 the establishment of the candlelight protest as a youth protest repertoire had become palpable, and candlelight protests were recurring for various causes. Interviewees spoke of then-recent protests by high school students in 2005. South Korean high school students were—and are—deprived of personal development and free time because of constant pressure to prepare for highly competitive college entrance examinations. In 2005 high school students staged a series of candlelight protests in opposition to a perceived retrogressive revision of the college admissions procedure. At the protests they also contested school hairstyle regulations, a legacy of the military-style discipline that had been implemented for decades. Even though individuals had personally expressed grievances about the regulations, this was the first time high school students collectively protested that particular issue. Ŭn-ha appreciated the new role of the candlelight protests: "Candlelight protests have become a new code for high school students. Their protests were not prompted by adults. Students planned the gatherings on their own and took to the street."[51] Myŏng, who volunteered at an Internet broadcasting station for high school students, said about them, "They grew up seeing candlelight vigils and believe that they are effective. The junior high and high school students constantly bring candles to city squares with all kinds of issues, from the deregulation of hairstyle to the legalization of student council to the demand for voting rights. While the adults have been wondering how to use candlelight protests, the teenagers are already using them."[52] As Casey suggests, the bodies at the vigils remembered the city centers and crowds, and by "feeling at ease" there they made the scene "their own."[53]

PART II

THE MATURATION OF INTERNET POLITICS AND POSTAUTHORITARIAN YOUTH

CHAPTER 5

Internet Activism Transforming Street Politics

The 2008 "Mad Cow" Candlelight Festivals
and New Democratic Sensibilities

On April 6 of 2008, three months after the inauguration of President Lee Myung-bak (2008–2013), a self-identified eleventh-grade student with the handle "Andante" started an online petition demanding that the Korean National Assembly impeach the new president. The petition was posted to *Agora,* an open Internet bulletin board on Daum.net (South Korea's largest online portal). The impeachment petition targeted policies Lee proposed during his election campaign, such as building a pan-Korean Grand Canal, privatizing medical insurance, and increasing competition in education.

> I propose that with ten million signatures we demand the National Assembly impeach President Lee. Lee Myung-bak pledged to serve the people. However, the past three months attest that he does not have the sincerity or will to do so. Instead, he pushed for the construction of the pan-Korean Grand Canal and for immersive English education despite widespread popular resistance. . . . He violently oppressed peaceful marches in the streets and announced American beef import. . . . The president deserted his people and their dignity . . . we cannot stand such a president any more.[1]

On April 18, as the petition neared twenty thousand signatures, the U.S. and South Korean governments finalized negotiations for the resumption of U.S. beef importation, which had been halted five years earlier over concerns about bovine spongiform encephalopathy (BSE)—also known as "mad cow disease." The decision stirred cyberspace because of fear of the fatal disease, whose cause and means of transmission to humans as Variant Creutzfeldt-Jakob disease (vCJD) were not fully known. South Korea's online space was soon inundated with disturbing videos of stumbling and downed cattle, shocking images of vCJD patients' sponge-like brains, and stories about the BSE epidemic in Britain between 1984 and 2009—in which 180,000 cattle were infected, 4.4 million suspect cattle slaughtered, and 166 people killed by vCJD.[2] The Internet also became a font for various scare stories: that Koreans were genetically more vulnerable than other ethnic groups to vCJD or that contaminated beef would likely be served at school cafeterias and in the military where people had no choice but to consume it.[3] Even though Andante's post mentioned the importation of U.S. beef only in passing, the petition has nonetheless obtained an iconic status as the origin of public resistance to the import policy. When Lee signed the beef import agreement on April 18, the heavy traffic on *Agora* surrounding the petition caused the Web site to shut down multiple times, and, overall, *Agora*'s accumulated weekly visitors more than doubled from eighty to one hundred eighty million between early April and early May.[4]

Agora users immediately proposed a "candlelight festival" (*ch'ŏtpul munhwaje*) at Kwanghwamun Square, and *Agora* became the online headquarters for the proposed gathering.[5] The festival was entitled "*You* Eat the Mad Cow," presumably directed at President Lee. The first gathering on May 2 drew fifteen thousand participants to the square, the epicenter of previous candlelight protests.[6] The "beef protest" spread, galvanizing young Koreans with carnivalesque slogans, music and dance performances, and protests in both online and offline spaces nationwide. By May 13 when the National Assembly held a hearing on the U.S.–Korea free trade agreement (FTA), Andante's petition received 1.3 million signatures; from there the candlelight festivals grew nightly, rebuking Lee's policy proposals and demanding his impeachment.

Prominent at the nightly festivals was the overwhelming presence of teenage girls (born in the 1990s and now in junior high or high school). During the early stage of the protests in May, over 80 percent of participants were teenagers, and approximately 70 percent of those were girls.[7] They had already connected with peers through social networking sites such as Cyworld.co.kr (South Korea's equivalent of Facebook, with twenty-two million members in 2008); through highly organized fan clubs for boy bands (including the eight-hundred-thousand-strong club for *Tongbangsinki*, recognized as the largest fan club by Guinness World Records); and through online communities dedicated to humor, celebrities, and gossip. A plausible explanation for the predominantly female presence is therefore the gendered pattern of Internet use—boys went online for games, while girls spent more time on social networking sites and fan clubs for boy bands.[8] The significant presence of teenage girls soon made the "candle girl" (*ch'otpul sonyŏ*) an iconic figure of the beef protest. Although the festivals increasingly drew a broad array of citizens as the gatherings grew and expanded across Korea, the image of girls in school uniforms remained symbolic of the nationwide protests in the spring and summer of 2008—both as actual participants and as icons online and in the streets (see figure 6).

The active role of youths in these protests was not unprecedented, and we've already seen their participation in numerous candlelight protests since 2002. However, the 2008 candlelight festivals significantly departed from previous protests in that teenagers under the voting age (of nineteen) emerged as the original critics of the president and his public policies, well before oppositional parties or activists joined them. Initiated by these teenagers, the beef protest grew to become one of the largest mass demonstrations in South

Fig. 6   Teenage girls at a 2008 protest against U.S. beef importation © Oh My News.

Korea since 1987, eventually inducing multiple apologies from the president and the resignation of eight members of his cabinet.

How did teenagers become the primary instigator of such intense opposition? How did the format of the candlelight vigil, which originally commemorated the deaths of two girls in 2002, evolve into a protest festival? What does this festive yet politically attuned youth activism mean in the broader picture of South Korea's social movement tradition?

I think Ye-jin*, a twentysomething staff member at a youth organization, offered a good answer. When I asked her these questions in 2012, she immediately blurted out, "It's the logic of the Internet manifesting in the street."[9] The "real world" manifestation of these idioms in 2008 was not merely a consequence of successful mobilization online, but rather of Internet activism's power to transform offline politics. Appearing in the streets were new cultural idioms that had been consolidating online: the circulation of captivating objects, the affective networks and temporary alliances surrounding these objects, and the irreverent subversion of authority without fear of persecution.

As such, the 2008 candlelight protests indicate the particular overlap between online and real space, not only in terms of participants but in the modalities of *doing* politics. In the introduction to this book I proposed that captivation thrives on technological innovations enabling users to circulate the texts, images, and sounds that fascinate them, and that this creates a new social space on the Internet. For Korean youth in 2008, who had already witnessed the maturation of Internet-born activism, online domains were a "part of everyday offline contexts."[10] Users increasingly experienced the online space not as "a placeless virtual domain divorced from actual physical places" but as part of organic experiences that weave online activities into other forms of private, interpersonal, and public activities.[11] The candlelight *festival*—a metamorphosis from the solemn 2002 vigils—reflected the "logic of the Internet," transforming the protesters' connectedness, communicative patterns, and sensibilities to the street.

With the overlap of online and offline spaces, the 2008 protests offer a glimpse of new democratic sensibilities. As Ye-jin's carefree response indicates, young Koreans might not have been able to articulate the meaning of their efforts, but they nonetheless intuitively understood that they were undertaking a distinct form of action that was political in nature. Philosopher Stephen Gaukroger reminds us that *sensibility* is not mere responsiveness to the environment, but "a unified phenomenon having physiological, moral, and aesthetic dimensions."[12] Sensibilities make moral behavior a "nondeliberative aspect of one's disposition."[13] The effortless performance of teenagers both online and off already entailed ethical and aesthetic judgments about how to respond to perceived inequity and injustice. This youthful collective and its carnivalesque subversions in the streets reflected nascent political sensibilities as youths moved beyond the demands of institutional democratization (the old democratic agenda). The festive gatherings outmaneuvered the Lee government's attempts to justify beef import and instate neoliberal reform as part of an inevitable global flow and as matters of individual choice.

In this chapter I first discuss the political atmosphere between 2002 and 2008 (which significantly shaped the experiences and expectations of modern Korean youths), then analyze the online discourses and street performances that occurred between April 6 and June 10 of 2008—when beef importation emerged as a national issue and youth-driven candlelight festivals garnered broad support, culminating in the "One Million Candle March" of June 10. In particular, I examine *Agora* and the Daum.net community *Ch'otpul Sonyŏŭi K'oria* (Candle Girls' Korea). These platforms serve not only as sources for online discourses but also as a window into the candlelight festivals themselves, because online slogans, parodies, and performances manifested both in the streets and in various online communities.

Although my focus here is on teenagers, the 2008 protests eventually became an assembly of heterogeneous groups—even more so than the 2002 vigils. Soon this wide array of unlikely protest participants drew attention from the larger public. Beginning in late May, the explicitly political slogans and traditional protest methods of older participants, including college students and members of Generation 386, began to overtake those of the teenage participants.[14] Around the same time, young mothers joined the protests after organizing in online communities dedicated to cooking and parenting. Some came with baby strollers, both to make a statement about the threat of contaminated beef and to deter police violence. They were soon named the "baby stroller brigade." Similarly, women organizing through online fashion communities quickly earned the label "high heel brigade" for their stilettos and stylish outfits.[15] In late May and June, as police began cracking down on the protesters, men who had completed military service came out in uniform to display their patriotism yet opposition to the beef importation, and also to protect student and female protesters. They acquired the label "candle reservists."[16] Meanwhile, online communities of scientists and medical experts began lively debates over the safety of American beef, the human susceptibility to BSE, and the credibility of existing medical and scientific reports.[17]

Two Political Sensibilities: Lee Myung-bak and the Teenagers of 2008

Beef import has traditionally been an important point of leverage for South Korea in trade agreements in order to gain preferential access to the American electronics and automobile markets. Since 2003, when BSE-infected cows were discovered in the United States, the safety of American beef had been debated in South Korea.[18] However, in the public mind the topic was irrevocably associated with President Lee Myung-bak as a consequence of the political atmosphere surrounding the December 2007 presidential election, when Lee's landslide victory on promises of economic growth put an end to two consecutive governments that advocated strong social security and regulation of large corporations. Young voters and teenagers under voting age were critical toward Lee's prosperity rhetoric and were prepared to voice their dissatisfaction.

Lee Myung-bak and Neoliberal Politics

Lee Myung-bak was a self-made entrepreneur and in the 1970s had been an instrumental figure in establishing Hyundai in South Korea and beyond. He debuted on the national political scene as the mayor of Seoul (2002–2006), and his autocratic yet dramatic leadership—the exact qualities that made him a successful CEO—resulted in the city's gentrification and marked improvement in its mass transit system. Lee promised to make South Korea the world's seventh-largest economy and increase GDP per capita to $40,000 by the end of his term in 2013 (while in 2007 it had the fifteenth-largest economy, with $28,000 GDP per capita). Even before the electoral campaign, Lee had been considered a shoo-in with no viable competitor. In the December 2007 presidential election, the historically low voter turnout of only 62.9 percent (compared with 80.7 percent in 1997 and 70.8 percent in 2002, and later 75.8 percent in 2012) and extraordinarily large gap between Lee and the liberal runner-up from the democratic party (46 percent to 26) illustrated the political atmosphere at the time.[19]

Young voters in their twenties were no exception to this conservative turn. College students in the first decade of the millennium keenly felt the consequences of massive deregulation and outsourcing after the 1997 Asian financial crisis, as Min-su expressed in chapter 4. They had to compete for a drastically reduced number of opportunities, and against a globally trained elite who were taking positions in Korean corporations (themselves under pressure to survive globalized market competition). A college degree no longer guaranteed a secure job or middle-class status, and the ideology of competitive individualism became "common sense."[20] Students couldn't afford to set aside career goals and pursue activism, as their 1980s predecessors had, for fear of falling behind. Nor did the postauthoritarian era even require an activist who would fight against authoritarianism. With these changes, the university was transformed "from the stronghold of revolutionary movement to a space of neoliberal domination."[21] Survival in the global economy was a mantra for both the country and the individual.

However, during the electoral campaign, Lee's unwavering lead gave rise to unique online enclaves centered on criticism of his prosperity rhetoric and bitterness toward the public that uncritically accepted it. With names like "Anti Lee Myung-bak," these online communities drew a broad array of citizens who denounced Lee's policies. For them, the pan-Korean Grand Canal, an approximately $20 billion effort to build a 300-mile waterway diagonally across the country, was an anachronistic industrialization-era project designed only to boost the economy, while the privatization of public corporations and deregulation of medical insurance were a neoliberal outsourcing of public service with little consideration for the welfare of the middle and lower classes.[22] In particular, Lee's education policies, such as the deregulation of "special purpose" high schools and the liberalization of university admissions, drew teenagers to these online communities. While Lee presented the changes as increasing opportunity and choice for deserving educational institutions and citizens, concerned students anticipated that the new policies would aggravate competition and disproportionately benefit those who could afford expensive specialized preparations for elite high schools and universities. Immediately after the election, these online communities turned into crucibles for mobilizing the 2008 protests.[23]

American beef importation eventually became the key issue highlighting the class-based nature of Lee's neoliberal projects. For instance, the U.S.–South Korea FTA was expected to meaningfully hurt the typically small and independent South Korean cattle farmers, with the primary beneficiaries being South Korean conglomerates that would gain preferential access to the American automobile, telecommunication, and heavy industry markets. Furthermore, South Korea's upper class would still be able to afford "safe" domestic beef, which was significantly more expensive than its imported counterpart; the choice for the lower classes would be considerably more limited, while students, military service members, and the incarcer-ated would have no choice at all. Despite mounting public concerns about unfair distribution of benefits and risks among wealthy and poorer Koreans, Lee pursued the FTA and continued to emphasize its economic benefits.[24]

Youth in 2008 and Postauthoritarian Experiences

Although it had been only six years since the initial candlelight protests of 2002, that gap was nonetheless long enough to create distinct experiences for the teenagers of 2008. For them, the candlelight protests were already a natural response to perceived injustice. When the first candlelight vigils ap-peared in 2002, participants and observers alike came to terms with the phenomenon by comparing it to the anti-American activism of the 1980s, or to 2002's World Cup street celebrations. These comparisons implicitly characterized the then-new format of vigils as, respectively, radical activism or impulsive youth gatherings with fortuitous political consequences (see chapter 2). In contrast, by 2008 candlelight protests had become a reper-toire in their own right and required no explanation. Ru-mi*, in junior high at the time, captured this change: "They might look radical to the older generation, but for us they are almost a natural response whenever we see something important on the news."[25] By 2008 the candlelight protest had consolidated into a movement repertoire liberated from authoritarian-era ideological assumptions.

Furthermore, while the youths of 2002 faced direct disapproval from their parents, many who participated in the 2008 protests were the children of Generation 386, who fought for (or at least were sympathetic to) the an-tiauthoritarian movement in the 1980s.[26] In my interviews, these teenage participants recalled the protests they attended or viewed in their childhood vis-à-vis the 2008 candlelight festivals. Ch'ang-min*, a ninth-grader in 2008, was a regular participant in the candlelight festivals from their beginning in early May. In explaining his affinity for protests, he described his par-ents, who met in a medical workers' union and remained active in it after their marriage. They brought Ch'ang-min, then in elementary school, to street marches when they couldn't leave him alone in the evening. In 2008 they supported his decision to attend the protests.[27] When I asked Chi-yun*, also a high school student in 2008, about the candlelight festivals, she brought up a 2002 vigil she had attended in sixth grade with her family: "I was there at the New Year's Eve countdown. My family, dad, mom, and older brother, all went. . . . There were lots of people with candles right next to us. They were marching with candles while others were counting down. It was such a bustle."[28] For her, the candlelight protest wasn't an experience of political activism, but of bustling people indistinguishable from the celebratory crowds on New Year's Eve.

As a result of these changes, the formerly strong association between opposition to authority and gravitas had destabilized. Ru-mi recollected the 2004 candlelight protests against the impeachment of Roh Moo-hyun, which occurred when she was in seventh grade: "The impeachment, we had no idea what it was. . . . It's the first time we heard the term. . . . It was all new to us. In my middle school, students used the word everywhere. We told friends on the student government that we would impeach them if they didn't do their work [*laughs*]."[29] The conservative opposition party drove the impeachment, citing violation of presidential impartiality, with the support of a majority in the National Assembly.[30] This unprecedented and highly controversial attempt made "impeachment" a buzzword among students, as Ru-mi recalled. Her parents' generation had risked their safety and future to criticize the authoritarian government, but the idea of taking down the president entered the imagination of young South Koreans as a nonthreatening, viable opportunity, and even an object of jokes. Andante's petition was not nearly as radical to his contemporaries as it appeared to the older generation. Indeed, by early April 2008 junior high and high school students were already holding candlelight festivals against Lee's educational policies, and these evolved to include the beef protest.

"*You* Eat the Mad Cow": Fear of Mad Cow Disease and the Critique of Free Choice

With concern rising about contaminated beef, Internet users soon made the *mich'inso* (mad cow) an icon for their protest—especially the image of a cow with a flower behind its ear, a visual pastiche of the popular comic character of a crazy girl who unashamedly displays erratic behavior (see figure 7). Madness, as in "Mad Cow, Mad Education" or "Mad Cow, Mad Government," quickly became a theme of chants and slogans expressing the immediate threat to young people's lives from both contaminated beef *and* Lee's policies. The trope of madness captured their shared but underarticulated vulnerability to a fatal disease and to extreme educational competition, emerging as a central theme in young Internet users' critique of Lee. The resulting street protests surrounding the slogan "*You* eat the mad cow" highlighted Lee's portrayal of health care, education, and survival in the global

Fig. 7 A visual parody of the U.S.–South Korea summit.

market as matters of personal choice, with little consideration for the unequal access to these resources.

Figure 7 represents the kind of visual parodies that circulated after the U.S.–South Korea summit on April 19, 2008, depicting Lee as interested primarily in his debut on the international diplomatic stage rather than in the feelings of the Korean public. The original photographs from the summit featured Lee and George W. Bush at a podium, shaking hands, strolling together, or riding in a golf cart as in figure 7. As soon as pictures from the summit were released, visual parodies superimposing the mad cow icon over President Bush's face began to circulate. The satirical caption reads,

> Myung-bak is happy now!
> Accompanying and honoring the mad cow,
> Thinking of proudly bringing it back to Korea,
> He is happy!

The narrative conveyed in the original picture was that the American leader acknowledged South Korea's new president as an important partner, and that Lee had successfully employed his diplomatic skills. The visual parody, in contrast, offered the alternative narrative that Lee gladly accepted the importation of contaminated beef—perhaps in order to please Washington or to be recognized as a respectful partner—while turning a blind eye to widespread public disapproval.

The mad cow icon particularly addressed the perceived inequity under Lee's rhetoric of more opportunity and more choice. Lee visited a beef farm on April 26 as a gesture of listening to cattle farmers' concerns about inexpensive American beef; there, he responded that it was the farmers' responsibility to produce quality beef to compete against the American product, saying, "When the GDP per capita reaches forty thousand dollars in ten years, consumers will seek quality beef irrespective of the price."[31] Lee continued that it is "the Korean consumers who decide to choose U.S. beef or not."[32] Lee was alluding to the Japanese model, in which domestic premium beef had become a globally recognized brand. For Internet users, however, these statements were simply evidence of Lee's subscription to a model of market exchange and choice—of both the producer and the consumer—with little consideration either for small farmers whose livelihood was threatened or for the middle and lower classes whose choices were significantly constrained by cost.

The title of the protest, "*You* Eat the Mad Cow," appeared in this context—a refutation of Lee's "free choice" argument. The candlelight festival that began on May 2 depicted the import policy as threatening the lives of Korean citizens. That said, even though visual parodies and the scientific reports circulating online continued to portray American beef as dangerous, the focus of protests both online and off shifted to targeting Lee Myung-bak himself. Protesters held banners directly addressing Lee: "I am too young to die"; "Can we recall the president?"; "President eats Korean beef, and we eat imported beef." Protesters also wore cow outfits and installed sculptures of Lee and the mad cow.

In addition to directly addressing the president, the festivals employed popular slogans and chants criticizing Lee's broader neoliberal policies. Education was the most prominent theme of the early protests; South Korean education had been (and still is) known for the most competition, longest study hours, and highest private education expenditure in the world.[33] Protesters contended against Lee's proposals to introduce additional competitive measures both among students and among schools—policies that led high schools to add another class period before the regular first class, dubbed "period 0." Student protesters brought out banners that read "Our true movers are mad cow and mad education"; "If I died of mad cow disease and could not afford privatized health care, scatter my ashes in the Grand Canal!"; and "Period 0 to students, debt to patients, precarious work to workers, mad cow and GMO for our dinner."[34] The adaptation of a well-known children's song became a popular chant at the beef protests, conveying a similar sentiment:

> When father goes to work, gas price!
> When mother goes to market, mad cow!
> When we go to school, period 0!
> When we go to bed, only four hours![35]

These parodies also addressed the privatization of the universal health care system, the increase of contract workers in lieu of employees with benefits, and the pursuit of the free trade agreement. While Lee presented his policies as inevitable responses to an increasingly globalized and competitive economy, the parodies instead represented these measures as bringing unreasonable hardships to the average citizen. Such Internet-born parodies disrupted the government's framing of competitiveness as a personal and national goal and instead rearticulated beef import, privatization, and extreme academic competition as matters of collective concern.

This protest phenomenon suggests new possibilities for doing politics through the Internet. The overlapping of "mad cow" and "mad education" draws our attention to the convergence of civic, private, and consumptive practices. It's difficult to ascribe to the teenagers at the beef protests any formal intention to critique broader neoliberal politics; instead, what rallied these youths were intense feelings of vulnerability to a fatal disease, anxiety about increasing educational pressure, and the perception of government indifference to their safety. These private, often heterogeneous, motives fostered alliances centering on the object of captivation—here, beef import and the slogan "*You* eat the mad cow."

This protest phenomenon does not allow for easy distinction between citizens and consumers. Participants complained that Lee's rhetoric of "choice" in privatization, deregulation, and free trade in fact failed to afford sufficient choice to consume safe products and quality public services ranging from beef to education to medical insurance. As Papacharissi puts it, "The function of blogging is expressive first, and deliberative only by accident"—the primary motivation of social media users is better characterized as that of a consumer than of a citizen.[36] Accidental, however, does not mean unlikely or arbitrary. A challenge to the status quo is more likely to emerge "as a result of people's dissatisfaction with matters of economics or day-to-day governance than from their embrace of abstract political ideals."[37] Issues that were deeply important and personally relevant to many Koreans— such as health and education—ignited a vernacular critique that unveiled the disregard for inequality underlying Lee's rhetoric of competitiveness.

The convergence of the beef import, educational, and economic issues in the minds of teenagers is an instance of what Anthony Giddens calls "life politics." With the fall of the Soviet bloc and the collapse of ideological contestation, the focus of politics shifted to "life" matters. For instance, a consumer's anxieties and insecurities about food safety are a personal matter to the individual—a matter of health for self and family. Traditional political debate over ideologies is simply not relevant to topics so close to "life," and such personal concerns increasingly influence politics and policy decisions.[38] The youths of 2008 were not activists in the familiar sense of Korea's movement tradition steeped in ideological contestation, but these protesters nonetheless effectively revealed problems with the new market imaginaries by demanding rights as consumers of beef, education, and public services, and their collective concern about limited choice impelled them to speak up against authority.

Evolving Democratic Sensibilities: The Crowd and Carnivalesque Festivals

As the candlelight festivals drew more students and citizens, the government and conservative media described the public fear of BSE as an urban legend (*koedam*) propagated by antigovernment radicals and vowed to aggressively respond to it.[39] On May 14 the South Korean government announced it would obtain the user information of those who posted unsubstantiated information and prosecute them along with initiators of candlelight protests. Andante, the author of the impeachment petition, was one of them. In responding to the spreading beef protest, the government and mainstream media alike drew on the interpretive lens of activist mobilization and conservative-progressive opposition, familiar from the 2002 vigils. The protesters, however, did not respond with the same ideological language; instead, they increased their activities in scope and connectedness both online and in the streets, circumventing government authority with their presence, network, and sense of parody.

Conservative presses quickly attributed the beef protests to "leftists," emphasizing the intentional intervention by radicals.[40] On May 5, three days after the first gathering under the *"You* Eat the Mad Cow" slogan, *Dong-a*

Ilbo published an editorial titled "Leftists Are Taking Advantage of the 'Candle' Yet Again," arguing, "The leftists are gathering under the banner of 'anti-U.S. beef' and 'anti Lee Myung-bak' after failing in the presidential election and again in the general election."[41] Two days later, *Chosun Ilbo* reported on the launch of a coalition against U.S. beef import, concluding that the protesters were "directly and indirectly related to leftist organizations."[42] The paper had already argued in early May that online communities were established with the political objective of "impeaching Lee Myung-bak."[43]

While they ascribed left-wing political intentions to the organized activists, conservative presses depicted the mass participation of youth as merely pathological. The *Dong-a Ilbo* article "Internet Brainwashing" captures this perspective. Here the author laments, "It's deplorable that curious and scientifically minded teenagers are mustered by nonscientific propaganda. More deplorable is the adults who sway them. The Internet is a fitting tool for brainwashing teenagers into anti-Americanism and fear of mad cow disease."[44] A social pathologist invited to comment by *Chosun Ilbo* went on to compare the beef protests to a medieval "witch hunt"; he argued that teenagers' deep frustration with competitive education, combined with propaganda by radicals, goaded them into the irrational decision to stand up against the national interest.[45] In general, the conservative media reflected and further reinforced the long-established lens of intentional political opposition. Their tropes of "leftists" and "pathology" were familiar from 2002, when the vigils were denounced as either mobilization by an "invisible hand" or a copycat of World Cup catharsis.

Unlike the conservative media, progressive publications viewed the young protesters as a new generation of political actors. *Kyunghyang Sinmun* and *Hankyoreh*, two major progressive newspapers, channeled teenagers' voices from the street as counterevidence against the conservative portrayal. The report "Why Do You Insult and Block Our Serious Opinions?" presented interviews with a number of teenagers who claimed that they were "not irrational" and attended protests "not swayed by overblown rumor but because vCJD is incurable."[46] Teenagers were also presented as articulate critics of Lee's "neoliberal policies."[47] A sixteen-year-old girl was reported to say, "We are here not only against mad cow disease. Here we express our stress and discontent related to educational policies such as the immersive English courses, liberalization of regulation, and publication of student rankings."[48] A seventeen-year-old girl attributed her participation to "absurd educational policies."[49] In the reports, the students demonstrated a deliberate criticism of Lee's education policy.[50] With these voices, one article concluded, "the ultimate cause of the so-called urban legends is the government, which pushed for beef import without public consent."[51] For progressive media, students at the protests were expressing their meaningful criticism of beef import, intensive English education, and privatization of public services.

While both the conservative and progressive presses argued about teenage participants' political intentions and the consequent effects, the protesters circumvented such debate and instead *performed* their political critique, blurring the boundaries between online and offline spaces. The day the government announced it would prosecute protest organizers, Internet users brought the real-world format of mass protests online, posting en masse to the bulletin board of the National Police Agency: "I am Andante," "Arrest me."[52] Similar messages appeared on major portal sites, and within days the trend had turned into the "Campaign for Ten Million Arrests," with the goal of protesters being detained in large numbers to outmaneuver the government's efforts to subdue the beef protest.[53]

Parody and subversion had been familiar practices online, appearing in response to controversial political and popular issues under the auspices of anonymity and rapid circulation. However, the beef protesters brought this carnivalesque subversion into the streets, directly speaking back to authority with irreverent humor. As candlelight festivals grew to draw tens of thousands of participants nightly, the Seoul police denied permits for protests in the name of public safety. Citing the illegality of the festivals, riot police shot water cannons to disperse the protesters and arrested them. In response to this police violence, protesters developed creative slogans and performances. For example, protesters chanted "Warm water!" as they were shot by water cannons—a parodic diminishment of violence to simple discomfort from the cold water. Similarly, they rebuked the police for wasting water, chanting "Save water," "Don't waste taxes," and "Send water to those in need."[54] Further, beef protesters established a nationwide network through online communities; as the confrontation between protesters and the police in downtown Seoul became a media spectacle, students from other cities came to Seoul over the weekend to support the protests. These new participants chanted "Give us bus fare" and "I came to Seoul because of you [President Lee]."[55] In a parallel move, as the number of protesters eclipsed the police force, police personnel from other cities were brought in to assist. At a protest in downtown Pusan (South Korea's second-largest city), citizens chanted "Bring back Pusan police!" in support of protesters in Seoul.[56]

Education was a recurrent theme in protester responses to police violence. Police used loudspeakers to ask protesters to send schoolgirls home: "Schoolgirls, it is already too late for you. It is dangerous. Please send the schoolgirls back home." In return, teenage girls responded, "Our evening self-study does not end until midnight"—implying that what exposed them to danger was not the candlelight protests but their own high schools, which enforced an "evening self-study" period until late at night to prepare students for the college entrance exam.[57] Groups of junior high and high school students also chanted, "You are responsible for our final exams!" as they confronted police until late in the evening. Some students brought desks and read books in front of the protest line; "Let us study," they told police.[58] With these responses, young participants deflated the validity of police demands and brought their collective concerns about education to the foreground.

The "hencoop tour," a parody of mass arrests in late May of 2008, exemplifies coordinated online and offline subversion efforts. As the police began detaining protesters by the hundreds nightly, rumors spread online that the police would report the names of students to their schools and to their parents' employers. These rumors initially caused concern among youths about potential disadvantages that they or their parents would suffer. However, during the course of the nightly protests, these mass arrests soon became an ordinary experience. Protesters called it the "hencoop tour," in reference to a riot police bus, which was typically covered in metal lattice similar to a cage. Images of tongue-in-cheek "Free hencoop tour" posters went viral. Figure 8 features such a poster, advertising a "Hencoop tour of Seoul with Podori," in a bricolage of visual components, including a riot police bus against the backdrop of a candlelight festival, the mascot of the Seoul police ("Podori"), and the "Hi Seoul" logo of the annual tourist festival held by city government. The text in the lower left corner presents "tour" information:

Period: Until the renegotiation of mad cow begins
Schedule: departing downtown Seoul at 2 p.m. every day
Route: Various police stations in Seoul
Included: Room and breakfast
Host: Blue House [the presidential residence]
Sponsor: Seoul Police Bureau

The poster resignified the experience of arrest and detention into a "free city tour." In the 1980s the "hencoop bus" had been an object of fear, associated

포돌이와 함께하는 닭장차 타고 서울투어~

기간: 미친소 협상
      다시할때 까지
일정: 매일저녁 2시
      세종로 출발
      우박2일
인원: 제한 없음
행선지: 서울시내
      각 경찰서(랜덤)
혜택: 숙박및 조식 제공
      경우에 따라선 중식도.

참가대상: 미친소 억기싫은 대한민국 국민
행사주관: 청와대   차량및 숙식지원: 경찰청

Fig. 8 Online poster for the "hencoop tour."

with the possibility of incarceration and torture. In 2008, in contrast, the "hencoop tour" presented arrest as a cultural experience, and even as a kind of flash mob occurring at the unusual locations of riot police buses or police stations. The May 28 newspaper article "Do You Know the Exhilarating Hencoop Tour?" begins with a simple but telling conclusion: "Quite a different era." Described in the report are scenes from within the bus and police stations that would appear very eccentric to an older reader—teenagers unafraid of arrest, taking pictures in the bus as if on vacation, and behaving as though the police station were a tourist site.[59] A May 29 article posits the significance of the hencoop tour as either "mockery of state authority or civil disobedience."[60]

However, the crowds did not principally intend to mock state authority or to organize themselves for the purpose of civil disobedience. Rather, they destabilized the work of the state with the scale and scope of their connectedness and communicative patterns. The festive and irreverent crowds in 2008 were not merely a product summoned by Internet communities but a new type of collective that opened a space for outmaneuvering the police with its scale and that rendered state authority an object of satire. In examining the democratic uprising in the Philippines in 2001, Vicente Rafael reminds us that crowds in the street are a "kind of technology itself."[61] For him, excessive attention to the new medium of the cell phone for summoning the crowd underplayed the nature of the crowd itself, which made possible a different kind of experience of becoming one with strangers—envisioning the abolishment of social hierarchy and the overturning of authority. During the 2008 candlelight festivals, belonging to a collective that occupied downtown Seoul and being connected to crowds nationwide enabled protesters to deploy their scale and network to outmaneuver the authorities, demolishing the fear of authority.

This crowd in 2008 was not a Habermasian public or a self-governing collective of citizens, nor was it the emotionally swayed masses that Le Bon or Frankfurt School scholars were wary of.[62] Instead, as a collective, the crowd transformed objects of fear—including water cannons, combat police, and mass arrest—into objects of laughter. Bakhtin reminds us that laughter "demolishes fear before an object."[63] Youth in 2008 revealed new democratic sensibilities, moving beyond the demands of institutional democratization and the solemnity associated with protest. These new sensibilities, as enacted through the carnivalesque, drove intense feelings of belonging to a potent collective and led to speaking back to authority without fear and irreverently subverting politically binding structures, ranging from the police to the neoliberal policies that significantly influenced protesters' perspectives on personal safety and future success.

The Multiple Valences of "Democracy"

In late May of 2008 candlelight protesters circulated online a proposal for a nationwide "One Million Candle March" scheduled for June 10, the anniversary of the famous June 10 democratization protest of 1987. Evoking such an iconic moment in South Korea's democratization movement drew those who had been observing the beef protests with sympathy, particularly Koreans of Generation 386. Some scholars from that generation viewed the recurrence of the theme of "democracy" as an indication that the 1980s democratization movement had been resurrected, or was at least fuelling the 2008 protests.[64] However, "democracy" as a trope for young protesters had a different valence. Politicians and progressive intellectuals were excited about the beef protest as an effective means of influencing institutional politics, repealing the FTA, and even impeaching the president. In contrast, democracy as evoked by the younger participants marked demands for more open and direct communication with government, as well as their grievances toward Lee's use of procedurally lawful measures to contain the protests.

As the candlelight festivals drew broader public support in May, many self-identified participants of Generation 386 supported the continuing activism of students and were apologetic about previously condoning Lee's "undemocratic" or "autocratic" decisions; young protesters in turn responded with gratitude for the older generation's achievements in democratization. For example, a posting on June 1 by "Alice"—a self-identified eleventh-grade schoolgirl—received more than three thousand responses on *Agora*. Titled "This democratization is what my dad achieved in the basement interrogation room," the post portrays Lee Myung-bak as an opponent to democracy who is reversing her father's achievements.[65] On a similar theme, Article One of South Korea's constitution was adapted as a song and chanted widely starting in mid-May: "The Republic of Korea is a democratic republic. Its sovereignty resides in the people, and all state authority emanates from the people." As police were increasingly deployed to contain the protests, protesters invoked democracy as an ideal lost amidst the government's suppression of what they considered to be legitimate demands.

As the beef protests became increasingly framed as a movement for democracy, mainstream politicians, religious groups, and progressive intellectuals came to support the cause. In particular, the oppositional Democratic Party and activists against the FTA joined the crowd, citing a need for leadership at the powerful yet unorganized protests.[66] On June 2 a group of one hundred university professors offered a joint statement rebuking beef importation and the Grand Canal project.[67] The Catholic Priests for Justice, a group that played an instrumental role in the 1980s democratization movement, released a public statement on June 8 criticizing beef import and the Grand Canal for "putting the socially and ecologically weak at risk."[68] Growing support from these respected organizations pointed to the success of the youth-driven protests. Nevertheless, these older activists' visions of identifying leadership, securing legitimacy, and achieving institutional change coexisted awkwardly with the goals of younger participants.

The clash between old and new democratic understandings became especially visible around "Myung-bak Fortress" on June 10. The Seoul police had not given permission for the proposed One Million Candle March, citing the need to protect government buildings and the presidential residence. To prevent crowds from gathering there, police blocked the entrance to Kwanghwamun Square with shipping containers stacked fifteen feet high. However, on June 10 protesters nonetheless gathered before the container wall—three hundred thousand people according to the police report, five hundred thousand according to civic groups.

The protesters promptly named the container wall "Myung-bak Fortress," alluding to Lee building the wall to fend off protesters, much as a premodern fortress would resist enemies. The container wall could not be crossed, but was soon repurposed into a canvas for graffiti, posters, and banners. In particular, the banners "A Government of Communication? Is this MB's Communication?" (visible in figure 9) and "Congratulations! Myung-bak Fortress, the new landmark of Seoul" were installed atop the wall. Later that day, after an impromptu free debate in front of the container wall, the protesters decided to build a "citizens' fortress" out of packing-foam cubes to use as a platform for free speech. (The white stairs visible in figure 9 are the result.) The barrier afforded protesters a veritable online forum—except offline, and created by the government itself—on which verbal, visual, and performative parodies took place. The standoff and subsequent ascent of "Myung-bak Fortress" was called "Myung-bak Battle" (*taech'ŏp*).

Ironically, the growing popular appeal of the candlelight festival marked the beginning of the end, and the participation of activists and politicians in particular jeopardized the position of young participants in a

Fig. 9 "Myung-bak Fortress" © Oh My News.

number of ways. More familiar faces took a prominent role, and the police declared that "professional" protesters were influencing the festivals and inciting violence.[69] As clashes between police and activists escalated, some protesters thought that teenagers should be protected. The military-trained "candle reservists" assigned themselves the role of protecting young protesters, saying, "Students should not get hurt. Your parents wouldn't want it. . . . Trust adults once"; and "Students, please do not come within five meters of the reservists' scrum. Instead, you use your weapons—keyboard, camera, and the Internet—to fight against them. No country sends students to war."[70]

Furthermore, debates about securing the political legitimacy of the candlelight protests altered their dynamics. While Myung-bak Fortress was blocking Kwanghwamun Square, argument erupted among protesters regarding whether to break through the wall of containers and enter Kwanghwamun or remain peacefully outside. Some maintained that the protest should remain peaceful to protect its legitimacy, while others contended that they could (and must) take down the obstacle that breached the constitutional right to freedom of assembly. In the end, the protesters decided to remain peaceful. However, the debate itself demonstrated that the protests had become constrained by the binary of peace and violence—options foisted by mainstream political ideology.[71]

The June 10 protest was an apparent success. Lee's approval rating plummeted to 7.4 percent nationwide (and only 3 percent in Seoul, the epicenter of the beef protest), and he publicly apologized for the second time, accompanied by the resignation of his chief of staff and seven other cabinet ministers.[72] Lee also promised additional negotiation with the United States. Opposition politicians, activists, and civic groups joined together in Lee's moment of weakness to channel the power of the crowd into tangible political changes. However, it was now clear that there was little more to be gained by protest, and the candlelight festivals began dying down in late June.[73]

In the trajectory of the beef protest, teenage participants began withdrawing right at the height of the protest's institutional influence. This attests that what was conveyed in the young protesters' slogan of "democracy" differed significantly from the meaning of the word for older activists. For teenagers in 2008, the trope of democracy was not a foundation for entering into institutionalized politics but a means to speak back to authority and critique its activities—independently and outside of the institution. When the protests shifted to more institutional goals, teenagers lost interest. As Raymond Williams reminds us, no generation speaks the same language as its predecessor—a new generation adds, deletes, and modifies language.[74] The new ideal of democracy in South Korea perhaps represents this evolution at work.

It was Ye-jin who remarked blithely that the 2008 festivals were bringing the idioms of the Internet out into the streets. Such festivals might seem to youth participants to be natural extensions of familiar practices on the Internet; however, as communication scholar Mimi Sheller describes, new technologies bring about significant social changes not so much because increasing numbers of social actors join a "network" but because new "persons" and "places" are constantly "emerging" out of new modes of connectedness.[75] In the broader scope of South Korea's social movement tradition the carnivalesque protests and the young protesters' comfort with them indicate the emergence of new democratic sensibilities. These sensibilities represent a significant departure from those of protesters of the previous generation, for whom political changes were associated with direct influence on institutional politics.

In this chapter I showed how the teenagers of 2008 spoke back to authority with parody and subversion, both on the Internet and in the streets. That these practices were not confined to the Internet—which offered anonymity, ease of circulation, and participation without necessarily agreeing with the cause—suggests that the Internet didn't merely mobilize youths, but also contributed directly to reshaping their way of *doing* politics. The crowds in Kwanghwamun might not have formally intended to criticize Lee's larger neoliberal trajectory, but they nonetheless formed an alliance centering on the perceived threat to their health and education, effectively criticizing the underlying disregard for class inequity. They also destabilized the authority of the state by transforming objects of fear—including riot police, water cannons, and mass arrest—into objects of laughter.

These candlelight protests inform recent debates regarding the role of the Internet in activism, suggesting a shift in attention from the Internet's instrumental role to how its long-term use by local actors *reshapes* their political experiences and expectations. The 2008 candlelight festivals, and in particular their significant transformation from the solemn 2002 vigils, suggest that low-risk protest or feel-good activism (so-called slacktivism) is *not* an antithesis of meaningful protest. Rather, young users growing up familiar with the logic of the Internet—the circulation of captivating objects, the affective networks and temporary alliances surrounding those objects, and the irreverent subversion of authority without fear of persecution—have begun to embody that logic in the real world.

CHAPTER 6

Youth at the End of the Candlelight Decade

The young Koreans I interviewed in 2011–2012 were born between 1989 and 1993, and experienced the 2008 protests as teenagers. That intense summer left these young people with unprecedented experiences of being liberated from school, of criticizing the government, and of occupying city centers. Even though my interviews were conducted only ten years after the initial candlelight vigils of 2002, and only five or six years after my 2006 interviews, the youths introduced in this chapter nonetheless experienced the protests very differently. My interviewees in 2006 were actively coming to terms with the then-novel format of the candlelight vigils, interpreting them as anti-American protests, as a copycat of high school candle ceremonies, or as festivals that fortuitously had political influence. In contrast, the younger students' memories of the 2008 candlelight festivals were instead primarily *personal* narratives about their past selves, present identities, and future aspirations, rather than stories about the social or political meaning of the protests.

In this chapter I pay particular attention to seven youths for whom the 2008 protests were a significant part of their lives—for reasons related to both participation and nonparticipation. By 2012 these youths had witnessed the maturation of youth-initiated, Internet-born protests over the course of a decade. They felt at ease complaining about politics and judging policy against the ideals of community and democracy they experienced during the protests. It is especially interesting that almost no reflection on the Internet as a tool or on the candlelight protest as a format appears in these youths' narratives—by this point, the Internet-born candlelight gathering had been established as a repertoire that required no explanation. Individuals were able to act in public without being hypersensitive to the ideological ramifications of their participation, which in chapter 5 I called a "new democratic sensibility." However, this shift nevertheless did *not* mean that these students were entirely free to express their dissenting views; they commonly experienced significant pressure from school, the job market, and financial burdens. Surrounded by apolitical and career-driven peers, many felt that they were deprived of an outlet for expressing their political views.

The narratives of the seven young Koreans introduced in this chapter suggest that a new way of *doing* politics had manifested in the street to shape individual sensibilities. These individuals developed their own critical perspectives, attentively monitored issues of life politics, and distanced themselves from existing ideological lines. Perhaps most significant in the interviews was that these young participants retained affective and corporeal memories of belonging to an alternative community or of voicing their independent thoughts as defining moments of their *personal* maturation. The content of these memories varies, of course—ranging from sudden awareness of the brutality of official education to experiencing an alternative community, to the burden of progressive views imposed by a teacher, to the realization that candlelight protest had become a cliché. However, with all of these memories, the students developed what they considered to be unique political views and came to see themselves as independent thinkers.

Moving On, but with a Sense of Community

The four individuals I introduce in this section were the archetypical "candle girls," actively organizing their peers online and participating in the street protests of 2008. Captivation with the imminent threat of contaminated beef originally induced them to join the candlelight protests; however, by 2012 their most prominent memories were the significant and unique experiences of belonging to an alternative community, and their fears associated with the cause had faded. Even though the exigencies of school, family, and work had dictated their lives before the 2008 protests and resumed shortly afterward, the experiences of ideal community and direct democracy remained with these young people and continued to serve as standards against which to evaluate politics even in 2011 and 2012—despite their various trajectories having brought them to very different places, from a peace organization to university to a secretarial position.

The Candlelight Protests as the Beginning
of an Alternative Path: Ta-jŏng

In 2012 Ta-jŏng* was a full-time staff member at a nonprofit organization known for advocating alternative values against war, environmental degradation, and overcompetitive education.[1] As soon as she sat at the table she exclaimed, "The candlelight protests changed my life!" Over the following two hours Ta-jŏng—in 2008 a typical tenth-grader in suburban Seoul—passionately described how the candlelight festivals had opened an unexpected path for her that included boycotting the college entrance exam and joining an activist organization as an employee. She began with the day in April 2008 when she first encountered news about mad cow disease.

> The mad cow investigation was airing on *PD Journal*. Cows jam-packed in a tiny cell, eating fodder made of cow product, staggering and falling. Words can't express how I felt at the time. Intuitively I felt that it was my story in school, how we were educated. Locked up in a small classroom, we consider other students only as competitors. I immediately related to the cows. A sense of crisis came upon me. I couldn't stay and tolerate the school. The image of us [reflected by the cattle] was so sad. That's probably why I . . . *we,* took to the street.[2]

Ta-jŏng's reflection was poetic. She identified with the faltering and downed cattle and was struck by the similarity of their conditions with those of her classroom, seeing both as crammed cells in which captives were devastated by cannibalism. The images of the cattle captivated her, resulting in a changed perspective of the school environment, which until that moment she had endured without question. It certainly isn't news that South Korean children spend the longest hours in school and are the unhappiest in the world, as repeated surveys have found.[3] Yet, this hadn't come to Ta-jŏng's awareness prior to 2008. That said, she might not have fully developed the poetic parallel between cattle and students at that exact moment in 2008; I suspect her organization and the peers she met after joining offered an environment in which to fully appreciate the connection. However, her captivation with the faltering cattle was a form of underarticulated knowledge and judgment regarding the dehumanizing environment and destructive competition that Ta-jŏng associated with "cannibalism."

In recollecting the beef protests, Ta-jŏng continued to talk about how she could no longer fit in at school and instead felt a sense that she belonged in the protest crowds.

> For the first time, I had the experience of people helping each other and unifying with no reservation. There were a number of moments when I felt that life was supposed to be like this. . . . Being shot by a water cannon or even marching with candles in hand, we all shared the experiences. Some friends at school asked whether I was pushed around or hurt in the crowd. In fact, it's the quite opposite when you're at the scene. It's seeing and walking with one another, not dashing to a celebrity or pushing others aside. . . . Every day was revolutionary for me. Listening to those kinds of things [criticism of the South Korean and U.S. governments] for the first time, talking to strangers for the first time. Memories of such experiences, I am sure, would also be with others who were at the protests.[4]

For Ta-jŏng, the beef protests weren't only about the fear of contaminated beef in her school lunch or even the free trade agreement itself. What stood out in her narrative was a series of "first experiences"—taking the subway by herself, talking to strangers, and being part of a crowd—that were "like a revolution every day." After these experiences, Ta-jŏng felt increasingly distant from her peers at school. Her sense of belonging to the protesting crowd evokes literary theorist Lauren Berlant's idea of the "intimate public." Ta-jŏng was "magnetized" by the idea of coexisting with and caring about others, and she developed an affective sense of belonging to a collective.[5] Even though Ta-jŏng did not have formal membership in the protest crowd, this sense of belonging nonetheless helped her to perceive her nascent "disappointment" with school and to imagine an alternative life unrestrained by the existing educational system.[6] An intimate public might not have a direct effect on institutional political changes, but it nonetheless enables individuals to imagine forming a collective. In contemporary commodity culture, individuals exist as isolated consumers whose needs and desires are satisfied by products designed for comfortable consumption. Even resistance is rendered a lifestyle choice, satisfied by a countercultural style.[7] Belonging to such an alternative "intimate public" is perhaps all that one can do when rebellion is futile or co-opted. Furthermore, this sense of connection offers individuals "fantasies of transcending, dissolving, or refunctioning the obstacles that shape their historical conditions" and therefore helps them to adapt to the world without completely accepting the dominant perspective.[8]

Ta-jŏng's sense of belonging to the protest gave her dreams of transcending the typical paths prescribed for her cohorts in the competitive educational system. As her attachment to the protests grew, her connection to school decreased: "I hated the way school taught and forced us. Teachers said every day, like, 'You must become one who eats not with a spoon and chopsticks but with a fork and knife.' They forced this type of thought and lifestyle, and I had no motivation to defeat others to survive in that environment."[9] In this example, the teacher is motivating students to endure the incomparably long study hours and severe competition as a means to achieve an upper-class and cosmopolitan lifestyle—represented by a "fork and knife." The other path is to a lower-class lifestyle—"spoon and chopsticks"—through mediocre school performance. Although politically problematic, such promises for freedom and affluence were nonetheless common in the rhetoric of delayed gratification at high schools. After the protests, Ta-jŏng began to question these promises, and to imagine a truly alternative life. She decided to forgo the national university placement test in her senior year (eventually persuading her parents to allow it) and instead joined a nonprofit organization focused on antiwar and environmental initiatives. While I don't think the 2008 protests instantly transformed a studious and docile schoolgirl into a full-time activist, Ta-jŏng's experiences in the city center undoubtedly showed her that an alternative path was possible.

As Ta-jŏng talked about that intense summer, during which she commuted daily from a suburb to Kwanghwamun, I wondered about her relationship with her parents. In South Korea's competitive education market, most believe that one's college determines the opportunities for the rest of one's life—including career, marriage, and comfortable middle-class status. When I asked about her parents' reaction to all of this, Ta-jŏng responded with a mixture of humor and seriousness:

> Phew! You'd need to stay up all night to listen to my story about my parents [*laughs*]. My parents were adamant and didn't listen to me, dismissing me as a kid. . . . It was truly difficult to change anyone, including myself. Words were useless. Seeing me as a changed person would speak louder than words. . . . I decided to show that I was a mature person. . . . Before the candlelight protests, I was a very good daughter

[*laughs*]. For the first time, I expressed my opinions to them. We had so many arguments, and they grounded me, with some hitting involved. I wrote many letters to them. Being face-to-face didn't solve anything, and they didn't listen to me. So, I wrote letters and went to the protest.

As she was speaking, Ye-jin, a colleague at Ta-jŏng's organization, interjected: "On the Internet, people said that the parent fortress was higher than Myung-bak Fortress." Both young women laughed and nodded. Myung-bak Fortress, the fifteen-foot-high wall of shipping containers that blocked access to Kwanghwamun, was considered the epitome of President Lee Myung-bak's refusal to listen to mounting public grievances.

Despite this political reference, Ta-jŏng's narrative of criticizing the educational system and choosing to live as an activist is perhaps most significant for the *absence* of politics and ideological legitimation. In South Korea's social movement tradition, identity as an activist had previously been inseparable from personal dedication to the cause of democracy, justice, and national liberation. In contrast, Ta-jŏng's narrative is most noteworthy for moments of captivation with the competitive educational environment and the potent crowd. Even though the alternative community with which she identified dissolved at the end of the protests, Ta-jŏng's memories remained with her and allowed her to continue on a new path.

Losing Touch with Politics: Chi-yun

Chi-yun is the same age as Ta-jŏng and, like her, traveled to Kwanghwamun from a suburb of Seoul in 2008. She had been a member of a youth organization that demanded the abolition of "period 0," the mandatory daily study hour before the first class in the morning, and she organized candlelight festivals against President Lee's proposed educational policies (see chapter 5). She learned about the danger of BSE-contaminated meat and the beef protests through *Agora* and other online communities dedicated to celebrity news and humor. Chi-yun attended her first protest out of curiosity, but fascination with the collective festivity brought her back to Kwanghwamun throughout the summer, despite more serious moments.

When I first went to the protest, it was really fun. It was a festival, and people were ready to enjoy the atmosphere. They performed, sang, danced, brought musical instruments, and we all had a blast. We just had fun, rather than protesting. . . . On June 10, the air was scary. Somehow I was trapped in the crowd when the citizens were confronting the police. We were caught between protesters and the police, and I was at a loss how to get out of there. Police were right in front of me, right there, and behind me were citizens. People around us shouted to open a way for us, and let us go safely.[10]

Chi-yun's memories revolved around vivid descriptions of a few memorable scenes from the protests. She spoke with surprising calmness about the water cannons she faced, about Myung-bak Fortress, and about how her teachers pressured students not to go to Kwanghwamun. It was difficult for me to understand how she spoke casually about being trapped between the police and protesters. Yet, it was clear that Chi-yun hadn't seriously envisioned the possibility of being hurt or persecuted—consequences that I personally associated with dissent from protests in the 1980s and 1990s. Instead, her story about the initially "scary" night of June 10 ended when the protesters—with the permission of police—opened a path for her.

Even after such intense experiences, Chi-yun remained active in the protests and unafraid of voicing her criticism—in the way that progressive media celebrated as characteristic of a new generation of activists. She paid attention to Lee Myung-bak's policies with a critical eye and engaged in political debates at school: "Since the beginning of the Lee government, we [teenagers] were interested in politics. Lee's plan for the Grand Canal and the insider trading scandal were topics of debate among my friends. . . . I thought that such a scandal should disqualify him from the presidency, but some of my friends still thought that he was the best person to revive the economy." She was also an opinion leader among her classmates and persuaded indifferent peers to attend the protest with her. For Chi-yun, the protest was a personally meaningful event that made her attentive to politics and developed her critical political views: "I hadn't been to any protest before then. Until junior high school, I hadn't thought I'd be interested in politics. After the protests, I became more interested in politics, because I participated in it. It was an important moment—I felt I was part of politics and history."

By 2011, however, Chi-yun had lost touch with politics and was surrounded by politically indifferent peers. She was majoring in Japanese language at a rural university two hours from Seoul, and we arranged to meet near a bus terminal in Seoul on her way to visit her parents for the weekend. When she said that she didn't visit home every weekend and my interview was a big reason for her to come back to Seoul, I wondered if I'd pressured her to interview with me. However, after listening to Chi-yun speaking passionately for more than ninety minutes, I had the strong impression that she was simply keen to open up about the 2008 protests and about politics—topics she otherwise had little opportunity to discuss.

Her university—which had opened only two years before—was all residential in a small rural town and emphasized practical training that would give its students a competitive edge in the job market. Except for a few prestigious institutions, the reputation of a university in South Korea is determined by the number of graduates who land full-time jobs after completing their programs, and students are keenly aware of ever-increasing competition in the job market. The classes and atmosphere at Chi-yun's university reflected this. Her fellow students rarely discussed current affairs, let alone politics. No one read the newspaper, and televisions in communal areas of her residence hall were always tuned to entertainment channels. As she put it, "They aren't at all interested in history. They have no knowledge, no common sense. It's outrageous." Yet, she understood and even sympathized with their indifference. "Their major concern? They have no concern other than their obsession with job prospects. . . . They just don't care, because the economy hit bottom a few years ago. Even though it's a bit better nowadays, they're very busy providing for themselves. The tuition is high and their parents are financially struggling, so they don't care about anything else. All they think is 'Ah, I want to live comfortably.' "

So, while she complained that few at her university were interested in politics, Chi-yun also understood that students (including herself) couldn't *afford* to pay attention to politics. Indeed, Chi-yun's tuition fees were a significant financial burden on her. Because her department awarded tuition waivers to only the top three students in a given class of twenty, she had to compete directly against her peers. She also worked part-time at a retail store near the university, taking time and energy from her studies. With her new academic focus, Chi-yun would perhaps appear to be politically indifferent to those around her at school; however, she remained attentive enough to politics to offer criticism. In fact, these complaints about her competitive school and politically indifferent peers strike a delicate balance of criticizing but not dissociating from the environment in which she must survive. Acquiescing at school but complaining in private enabled Chi-yun to adapt to the university environment while keeping emotional distance from her politically indifferent peers.

That Chi-yun nonetheless maintained a critical attention to politics became clear when she comprehensively listed the protests that she did *not* attend. The 2008 beef protest was the last protest she attended. When a candlelight festival to criticize Lee's neoliberal policies broke out in 2009 on the anniversary of the 2008 festival, Chi-yun was going to school seven days a week to prepare for the college entrance exam. In the same year, after the death of former president Roh Moo-hyun, citizens set up altars and held candlelight vigils, protesting what they saw as the politically motivated investigation behind Roh's corruption charges. Chi-yun did briefly visit an altar, but couldn't stay until the vigil held later that evening. She became agitated when speaking about the 2010 protests during the G20 summit in Seoul, when an artist was arrested and prosecuted for depicting Lee in street graffiti as a mouse. She exclaimed, "The prosecution showed that we didn't have free speech. They [the government] controlled the press. That's why people called Lee autocratic. Whoever spoke up was arrested." Chi-yun had clearly kept paying attention to politics, even though she couldn't afford to participate in any of the protests.

Chi-yun is an example of the inversion between high school and university that I discussed in chapter 5. Until the late 1990s, the first year or two of college had typically been dedicated to exploring new experiences, with unprecedented liberty to party, engage with political causes, or pursue individual interests. However, after the market restructuring to address the Asian financial crisis, the South Korean university became focused on extreme preparation for the competitive job market and was even more anxiety inducing than high school because the array of necessary qualifications was constantly shifting.[11] Chi-yun's narrative shows just how little space for activism and experimentation remains at the university level. Yet, she also retained powerful memories of active involvement during her teenage years. Her comprehensive list of protests she had not attended and her obvious yearning for political conversation suggested strongly that Chi-yun remained politically attuned and had maintained her critical perspective.

The Candlelight Protests as an Ideal of Participatory Politics: Su-rin and Min-ji

Su-rin* and Min-ji* became close friends in high school over a shared interest in Japanese anime. They were regular participants during the 2008 protests, when both were in eleventh grade. Afterward, Su-rin followed her hobby by majoring in animation at university, while Min-ji attended a two-year junior college and later worked as a secretary. When I met them in 2011, they were still close friends. Min-ji was preparing to retake the college entrance exam after becoming disenchanted with her first secretarial job, while Su-rin was still a student and working part-time in the neighborhood where they grew up. According to them, neither had been interested in politics prior to the beef protest. As Su-rin described,

> It was no joke, both the beef import and overall politics. Politics was a subject of everyday conversation in my class, and that's how I learned about it. Frankly, for me the protests were half outings with friends and half novel activity. But, after going to a few protests, I realized that they were no joke. I wanted to express my view as a citizen. . . . And I hated how politicians misrepresented us—as just young students. They said we didn't know, and we had better study. Frankly, those who went to the protests weren't ignorant. Particularly those who joined later, after the protests became popular, knew what they were going for. Calling them ignorant or rebuking them was . . . a kind of oppression of free speech.[12]

Su-rin originally participated in the protests only out of curiosity. Then, in the street, she deeply felt the fear of contaminated beef and identified with the protest crowd. At the same time, she developed a critical view of mainstream media and politicians, who she felt misrepresented the protesters as impulsive youths mobilized by false rumors.

Min-ji vividly recalled the night that completely altered her outlook on the candlelight festivals: "I went to a small protest in my town. . . . What was really impressive was, people did it voluntarily. A student in his school uniform came to join the festival. He threw his bag at a street corner, and served water to people. He brought a large water jar. It was a really hot day in May and everyone was thirsty. He was not the only one; there were others like him as well."[13] Su-rin interjected, "That's a touching story!" What made the moment so touching was the sense of community expressed by the student's voluntary service to his fellow protesters. Spontaneous participation and care for fellow participants provided Min-ji with a sense of community in the middle of the protest. For both girls, the protests were their first encounter with an "ideal" form of participatory politics, and attending expanded their previous understanding of politics as purely institutional. The protests remained with the two as a moment of archetypical community, which existed only briefly but left lasting memories.

After a few intense weeks in 2008, the girls returned to the routine of minding their personal futures; however, they remained politically attuned. When I asked Min-ji and Su-rin about the meaning of the 2008 protests, they didn't talk about abstract political ideas. Instead, they described a concrete transformation in themselves and their peers.

> *Min-ji:* They made us rage, made us rage against politics. Beforehand, students had been excluded from politics. Adults used to say "None of your business" to us when it came to politics. Although we hadn't expressed our opinions, we in fact had been interested in politics all the time. They [the protests] were the turning point that kindled that interest.
>
> *Su-rin:* Political fence-sitters enable autocracy. Autocracy is facilitated by fence-sitters. . . . The protest was a hopeful sign that junior high and high school students weren't indifferent to politics.[14]

The two girls discovered that they were "interested in politics all the time" after encountering mass media's misrepresentations of them in covering the protests. It was telling that Su-rin held fence-sitters in particular, who are politically indecisive, responsible for autocracy. The complaint again evokes Berlant, who sees complaint as a method of surviving and adapting to the world without being completely subsumed by it. For these two girls, the memories of the candlelight protests remained as ideals of participatory politics, allowing them to "blame" flawed attitudes while "maintaining some fidelity to the world" in which citizens turn a blind eye to politics.[15] The 2008 protests were a crucible for political socialization in which these young Koreans developed a sense of what politics should look like.

Much like the two previous young women, Min-ji and Su-rin were animated and engaged—they talked almost nonstop for two-and-a-half hours, far exceeding my expectations. Min-ji was especially excited to discuss political topics. "I was a secretary working for a high-up in politics. A secretary often works for someone with an opposite political view. It's inevitable. We cannot really choose who we want to work for. It was a big source of stress for me. . . . I was distraught, because I would never be able to express my political views at all. . . . Now I feel so recharged, expressing what I had to keep inside for many years."[16] For both Su-rin and Min-ji, attending the protests marked an evolution of political awareness that stayed with them well after their participation in activism had ended.

The participants of the 2008 vigils were often in very different places by the time I met with them. Like Chi-yun, Su-rin and Min-ji had no one in their college or workplace with whom to discuss politics. Furthermore, Min-ji even had to hide that she once attended protests, and that it had been a personally meaningful experience. By 2012, three of the four young women interviewed in this section had moved on to college and the job market and been forced to step back from politics. Even Ta-jŏng, who opted out of the competitive track and embraced her political side, experienced continuing struggles with her parents.

Nevertheless, the 2008 beef protests remained an important part of their life trajectories and continued to offer a sense of connection with those who shared their passion for justice and concern for others. A survey of teenage participants offers a glimpse of the new sense of belonging that the beef protest perhaps offered. Sociologist Lee Hae-jin found that over 70 percent of those who experienced a candlelight protest before mid-June (when it was absorbed into mainstream politics) attended more than one protest, and that the biggest motivation for repeated participation was meeting with other participants (22 percent) or friends (22 percent), followed by online community members (17 percent).[17] These results suggest that the experience of spontaneous crowds and the sense of attachment to fellow participants significantly contributed to transforming a casual visitor into a regular participant.

This feeling of connection does not mean that a visitor necessarily becomes an activist. However, the sense of belonging was a different kind of *doing* politics. The vocabulary of abstract ideology and disputed legitimacy missing from these narratives does not entail that the protests were merely transient events that just happened to have personal significance. Rather, for these young women, the beef protests were their first contact with and participation in politics, and as a result they became attuned to politics. As the interviews suggest, for them politics was more than simply voting: it included active monitoring of lawmakers, public debates, voluntary participation, and care for fellow citizens. For Ta-jŏng, activism became a way of life. Even Su-rin, Min-ji, and Chi-yun—whose biggest concerns were future job prospects—nonetheless energetically complained about politicians and expressed deep concern about current political issues, while imagining and embodying a politics predicated on active monitoring.

Entrepreneurial and Comfortable with a Minority Opinion

Kŏn-ho, Bin-na, and Ch'an-ki* came from more comfortable backgrounds than the young women interviewed in the previous section, and when I interviewed them they were attending reputable universities in or near Seoul. Like the four young women, they remembered the candlelight protests as important moments in their personal trajectories. Unlike those four, however, they also expressed specific political perspectives during the interviews and identified themselves as holding minority opinions within their generation. I was intrigued that *all* of the youths I discuss in this section, despite their diverse political views, considered themselves ideological outsiders. Their strong emphasis on taking a unique path suggests that some young Koreans are carving out their own spaces for bringing together justice and personal aspirations in the competitive university environment.

Self-Correcting Conservative: Kŏn-ho

Kŏn-ho was a sociable young man who had started university just three months before I interviewed him in 2012. He hadn't attended the 2008 protests because he lived in a suburb, too far for a ninth-grader to travel alone to downtown Seoul. However, he was happy to meet with me on a Saturday afternoon, and even felt a sense of duty to do so: "I decided to come out for this interview because I thought that predominantly progressive people would come and sway your view. The conservative view needs to be heard [*laughs*]."[18]

Contrary to his present conservative identity, Kŏn-ho was in fact one of those youths rallied by the news on the Internet in 2008. He recalled, "Reflecting on myself at that time, I was a victim. No, not a victim, but a fool. I believed what I saw on the Internet, and even wrote online myself." Even though he didn't join the street protests, Kŏn-ho actively participated in online discussions regarding the joint threats of contaminated beef and Lee's neoliberal policies. Four years later, however, he actively distanced himself from his previous perspective. In retrospect, he felt that he and his peers were prompted to attend the 2008 protests by an exaggerated threat of BSE and unsubstantiated rumors. Nor did he see the street protests as meaningful political participation. He remarked, "Young people uploaded pictures from the protests on their social network sites and took them as the emblems of a conscientious citizen. They wanted to build this image of a good citizen. Also, the protests were nothing more than musical concerts that featured celebrity singers. Young people went for those concerts."

Kŏn-ho's narrative then shifted to how he became conservative. An important turning point came in high school, when he felt pressure from a progressive teacher and sought to become an independent thinker: "In my senior year, I was the only one applying for a journalism major. A social studies teacher liked me very much and advised me to listen to *Nakk'omsu* [a progressive comedic radio program, roughly equivalent to Jon Stewart's *Daily Show*] or to plan to work for [progressive newspapers] *Hankyoreh* or *Kyunghyang*. He was almost putting pressure on me, and I didn't like it." Kŏn-ho was exposed to a progressive viewpoint on Korean history from the new high school social studies and history curricula implemented in 2002. This was a sea change compared with the authoritarian era, when only one official history textbook was available and a progressive perspective had typically been associated only with politically active college students. Six years after this curriculum change, Kŏn-ho felt pressured by his teacher to adopt the new progressive view.

In 2012 Kŏn-ho criticized youths who identified as progressives, noting that they were swayed by the same imposed progressive views and made the same mistakes as Kŏn-ho himself did in 2008. He distanced himself from those who indiscriminately criticized the government: "This government has done things to be both commended and criticized. But progressives are blindly attacking it. . . . A good citizen who cares about the country must give credit to what the government does well and criticize what it doesn't." Kŏn-ho was proud to have taken a sense of objectivity from his teacher, if not a progressive perspective, and to have become an independent thinker. His critique of the 2008 protests was a way of asserting his maturation as a critical citizen in his own right.

Kŏn-ho was also passionate about his future plans, which were very different from those his teacher recommended. His entrepreneurial talent and array of achievements were impressive even at his young age. In elementary school he had worked as a volunteer reporter for *Children's Dong-a Ilbo*, a publication for children from one of South Korea's major newspapers. In high school he was fascinated by Magnum Photos, a photography group founded by Robert Capa and Henri Cartier-Bresson known for their documentary photos from war zones. Kŏn-ho decided that his lifetime goal was to establish a nonprofit fund to support young creative artists in photography, film, and fashion. During our conversation, it became clear that Kŏn-ho had already mapped out his immediate future. He was planning to attend a summer program at a film institute and then to work full-time as a photographer's assistant for the following year: "No matter whether it's directly useful for my future career, I want to try as much as possible. I'm trying to broaden my social network—making friends with photographers, socializing with artists through online communities." Even at nineteen, Kŏn-ho had impressive plans for obtaining skills and qualifications toward his goal and was already aware of the importance of building a social network. Furthermore, he seemed to have the ability to enjoy every situation: "I tried to enjoy school, even high school"; "I enjoy learning new things"; "Unlike other people, I enjoy working. I don't find it difficult. I find working fun." He contrasted himself with other youths: "You know, people of my age want both freedom and money. When you take on a part-time job, then you lose freedom in order to earn money. But in my case, I think everything entails responsibility, and I'm fine with being compliant and trying my best."

Kŏn-ho was more complex than simply the rare conservative voice he presented himself as at the beginning of the interview. In his narrative of turning from an active online participant to a critic of the 2008 protests, he was an independent thinker who resisted the authority of his teacher and found his way to a worldview that is unusual among his generation. Similarly, his aspiration to establish a nonprofit organization and his current preparations for reaching that goal defy any simple classification of Kŏn-ho as either a practical or progressive youth.

Entrepreneurial Activist: Bin-na

In 2012 Bin-na was a college junior attending a branch campus of an elite university. Her experience with the candlelight protests came in 2010, during the Seoul mayoral election, when she worked as a paid intern for a progressive candidate who held candlelight gatherings in downtown Seoul in lieu of typical campaign rallies. Even though Bin-na fondly remembered the peaceful and beautiful candlelit scenes in the city center, she felt that the format of candlelight protest had become a cliché, meaningless as activism. In contrast, she discussed a campaign she herself had initiated, and the array of global justice movements about which she was passionate. The ingenuity and pride she expressed as she spoke about her own project, as well as the surprising confession of loneliness about not belonging to any group, offered a glimpse of the privilege and burden of being an independent thinker and activist in postauthoritarian Korea.

In 2011 the South Korean government decided to build a naval base in Kangjŏng, a fishing village on Cheju Island near rare marine fauna. The issue grabbed national attention after fierce contestation by locals and activists against damage to wildlife, and against military armament of a strategic site near North Korea and China. Bin-na felt strongly about the issue. She gathered fellow students and started "the Kangjŏng Project"—an effort to raise money at her university by making and selling chicken wings (which have the same pronunciation in Korean as the village, *kangjŏng*). She was enthusiastic as she described the project:

> We did fund-raising for Kangjŏng village by selling chicken wings. "Save Kangjŏng through kangjŏng." I did it with my friends. I wanted to do something for the village. I didn't want to just send money or write on the Internet. These things weren't appealing to me. . . . I wanted to do something more meaningful, and came up with the Kangjŏng Project. . . . The project was what we were able to do as college students. We didn't have much money to send. . . . I was so happy to do the Kangjŏng Project. I was happy. Kangjŏng villagers had to pay a lot of fines for protesting the naval base—I was able to help them.[19]

Bin-na's original plan had been to pursue the project only during her university's spring festival, but she continued afterward. Through this effort, she gained a sense of participating meaningfully in the movement against the naval base. In contrast, she was skeptical of the candlelight protests: "I doubt I would have participated in a candlelight protest for Kangjŏng, had there been one. . . . Candlelight protests have become places where people visit. Of course the protests express something important, but many people go just to see, without taking concrete, meaningful action." In Bin-na's mind, the candlelight protest had become a tired form of activism, a cultural experience that anyone could visit without significant impact for either the participant or the social issue at hand.

It was already clear from her reasoned criticism of the candlelight protest that Bin-na had become an independent thinker and developed her own unique trajectory. In 2012 she continued to pursue activism: she was interested in international humanitarian aid and already participating in a number of direct efforts, including a staff position with a nonprofit organization. However, despite aspiring to work in the field of human rights, she did not identify as a progressive—or even really as an activist. Bin-na instead felt that she belonged to neither the activists nor the career-oriented students on campus.

> I'm almost amazed at how others categorize me, and how the categories differ. . . . To some people I'm an activist because I care about society. But to my activist friends I'm a skeptic because I constantly question whether I can really help those on the other side of the globe. . . . I do what I believe is right, but at the same time I care about my GPA. For me it's a matter of personal values, but others see me as an oddball. I haven't been able to really belong anywhere.

Career-driven students around Bin-na were envious of her volunteer work with an internationally recognized NGO and her six months of full-time staff experience in Africa. For them, Bin-na had accumulated unique and valuable qualifications in a job market hungry for globally sophisticated employees. Among her activist friends, she was similarly the unconventional one. She wouldn't join them in criticizing the government or attending street protests, but instead planned her own campaigns—such as the Kangjŏng Project. Bin-na saw herself as an outsider, and felt a burden of not fitting into existing categories.

Like her peers, I also found it difficult to place Bin-na into the "usual" categories. Bin-na's criticism of South Korea's neoliberal education restructuring was sharp. She pointed to the ever-increasing pressure to learn foreign languages, obtain certificates, and build social networks—referring to university as "the fourteenth, sixteenth grades" and arguing that it had become an extension of high school instead of being a space for independence or intellectual pursuit. Critical as she was, Bin-na nonetheless found herself at the forefront of this competition, having foreign language skills and exceptional credentials along with a degree from a prestigious university.

Elite Lifetime Activist: Ch'an-ki

Ch'an-ki was attending a university in Seoul when I met him in 2012. He held a leadership role in a nationwide student movement group, but nonetheless felt that his personal trajectory was atypical for an activist. He was self-motivated and entrepreneurial, in a sense combining Kŏn-ho's entrepreneurial mind with Ta-jŏng's devotion. Ch'an-ki described that he originally became an activist in his first year of high school in 2005. He struggled to adjust to a competitive environment in which the only focus was the college entrance exam and joined an online youth community for friendship. There, he encountered the then-emerging issue of hairstyle deregulation and watched as the issue eventually led to high school students' candlelight protests. Through the online community he was further connected with a youth activist organization and later with a group of political activists. During high school he played a prominent role in advocating for the voice of students in educational decisions, and he served as a leader in a watchdog group during the election of superintendents at the city's Office of Education. He recalled how his parents, both high school teachers, were embarrassed that their son openly denounced the candidates and criticized the role of teachers.

When the beef protests began in his first year of college, Ch'an-ki attended frequently. His narrative combined explanations of political meanings with his corporeal memories. Before the protest, he'd been paying attention to negotiations for the free trade agreement, along with other social justice issues. He explained that "anti-American activists had already been planning protests against the free trade agreement," and that the beef protest became a prominent issue as the activists "took it up as a popular agenda."[20] Ch'an-ki attended the protests with the perspective that they were part of a political movement against the FTA, and that mass participation in the protests was a consequence of activists' successful appeals to the larger public. His narrative attributed the protest to successful mobilization by activists, which struck me as a reflection of his current affiliation with activist groups.

However, even though Ch'an-ki was politically motivated, many of his most prominent memories from the protests were of festivity. "At the protests, my friends were arrested, and elementary school students were arrested [*laughs*]. It's funny. Isn't it [*laughs*]? Minors were released soon after their arrest. What a disappointment. Among us, we looked for pictures floating on the Internet the day after the protests and found us captured in them. It was fun. We said, 'Here you are,' 'You look ugly' [*laughs*]." Even though Ch'an-ki used ideological language to *explain* the protests, he *narrativized* memorable moments from the protests in corporeal terms. The protests and arrests were described as more a rare cultural experience than political persecution, and the students' immediate release from police detention made for a disappointingly short-lived adventure. Despite Ch'an-ki's sharp ideological criticisms, the playfulness that he experienced during the protests remained with him.

Like Bin-na's, Ch'an-ki's academic credentials could be considered those of a practically minded student. He was majoring in international studies at one of the most prestigious and expensive private universities, where classes in his field were taught in English. His program was known for its cosmopolitan, upper-class association, with students who typically had lived abroad, had studied abroad for years, or had received intensive preparation for English proficiency. Although encountering student activists at prestigious universities in South Korea is not unusual, English proficiency is associated with the more entrepreneurial, career-focused student.[21] Students in Ch'an-ki's program in particular were considered politically conservative or apolitical, given their class background or extensive stay in a foreign country. This tendency was confirmed by Ch'an-ki himself, who noted, "I don't really fit into the culture. They go to nothing but fancy bars, and even reserve an entire bar for a birthday party. It bothers me."[22] It was impressive that Ch'an-ki had entered the program without experience studying abroad, and that he continued to be involved in student activism even against the dominant student culture of his peers.

Furthermore, Ch'an-ki returned to the student activist group even after completing his military service in 2011. In chapter 4 we were introduced to returnee students, who obtained a vocabulary of anti-Communism and an appreciation for national security during their military service, after which they focused on practical matters to prepare for their careers. In particular, KATUSA (Korean Augmentation to the United States Army) is typically a path for entrepreneurial and practical students who aim to hone English skills while serving, and who similarly do not hold a critical view of the U.S. military presence in South Korea. Contrary to these popular associations, Ch'an-ki completed his military service with KATUSA but returned to activism afterward. When I asked Ch'an-ki about his future plans, he responded, "I'm not sure what exactly I'll do. I'll probably be somewhere involved in a kind of activism." He envisioned himself as a lifetime activist. However, his trajectory thus far suggests that Ch'an-ki might be a different breed of activist, who pursues activism as a career based on personal preferences and passions—with less concern about a political cause or moral imperative.

I initially attempted to understand Kŏn-ho, Bin-na, and Ch'an-ki through the familiar distinction between the activist and the practically minded student. As recently as 2006, young people's views of the candlelight protests and politics in general were rather predictable—those who completed military service (like Hun and his three friends), and especially those who served with KATUSA (like Wŏn-hŭi and Ho-jun), criticized activism as naïve and ignorant. However, Kŏn-ho, Bin-na, and Ch'an-ki's narratives defy such a facile distinction. Kŏn-ho retrospectively criticized his impassioned online participation as foolish and now identifies as conservative, but he envisioned—through his entrepreneurial preparation—starting a nonprofit for independent artists. Bin-na appeared to others to be an extremely competitive person because of her unique set of qualifications, yet she identified as a near-ideal activist who pursued her passions genuinely without being swayed by the views of others. Ch'an-ki was determined to pursue what he considered the unusual path of becoming a professional activist. These three entrepreneurial youths have all developed what they feel are unique political perspectives, and they view themselves as independent thinkers. Indeed, they even envisioned other modes of meaningful participation that transcended the candlelight protest.

The retrospective narratives of these seven young people show that experiences surrounding the 2008 protests have more complex and nuanced meanings to the participants than some critics argued. In 2008 critics touted the Internet and teenagers as "Generation Web 2.0," "keyboard warriors," "digital journalists," and builders of an "alternative public sphere."[23] Social media, online communities, and personal mobile devices were expected to strengthen participatory democracy, and tech-savvy youths were expected to transform themselves into critical citizens and producers of information. Some expected that these teenagers would become the true successors of Generation 386, offsetting the political indifference of twentysomethings shuffling through the tight job market.[24]

   This enthusiastic projection has not come to pass. However, memories from action-packed moments in the street nonetheless remain, informing political dispositions, and the routinization of the Internet-born protest presents a notable backdrop for these new sensibilities. References to the Internet and to the format of the candlelight protest largely disappeared in the retrospective narratives. Once, the Internet had been an exciting new tool, and young participants debated the nature of the 2002 vigils in retrospect, drawing on the familiar forms of radical street demonstrations and celebrations. By 2012, however, the format demanded no interpretation or justification. Even though many individuals outgrew their own candlelight protest phase—as most interviewees discussed in chapter 4 did—teenagers at any given moment are drawn to the Internet and then to the streets when an issue arises and captivates them. By the end of a candlelit decade, young Koreans routinely interacted with authority and other citizens. Criticism of the government was possible, parodies of official discourses became popular (both online and off), participation in protest demanded no personal sacrifice, and finding like-minded people was easy.

Against this backdrop, belonging to a peaceful yet potent crowd remained with my interviewees as experiences of an alternative community. The connection they felt with the spontaneous and caring collective in city squares continues to influence them as personally transformative memories, even though it was not directly related to institutional change. Although Chi-yun, Min-ji, and Su-rin might have appeared to be politically indifferent in their school or workplace, they were nonetheless critically appraising politics against their own standards of passionate engagement in the streets.

Furthermore, these young people each wove the experiences of the protests into their coming-of-age narratives and established themselves as independent thinkers—while defying the traditional binary of conservative and progressive. We are now seeing entrepreneurial activists like Bin-na and Ch'an-ki, as well as critical conservatives like Kŏn-ho. Such heterogeneous identities among participants suggest that young Koreans who experienced Internet-born, youth-driven candlelight protests underwent a kind of political socialization through which they developed their own ethical and aesthetic judgments about how to respond to perceived injustice.

The ideological void left by the collapse of authoritarianism hasn't (yet) been filled by another political paradigm, but instead points to a more open-ended future. The once-new repertoire of the candlelight protest is already being met with skepticism about its effectiveness and democratic value, as Bin-na and Kŏn-ho's observations demonstrate. However, the protests nonetheless had an impact on how both participants and observers have come to approach politics and democracy: all of the youths presented in this chapter envisioned more personally meaningful political activity without being confined to an established political discourse of any stripe. I expect their engagement will continue.

Conclusion

The Ignition of the Internet and Its Aftermath

The emergence and maturation of the candlelight protests in South Korea between 2002 and 2012 established the Internet-born, youth-driven protest as a new repertoire for activism, with few of the ideological preconceptions and limits once associated with dissent. This repertoire signals (and facilitates) changes in larger cultural frames in political practices, characterized by casual participation without a preexisting activist identity, temporary alliance among citizens, demand for government openness and transparency beyond formal democratization, and direct response to—and irreverent parody of—mainstream politics.

These practices made visible the "decomposition" of gravitas associated with authoritarian-era politics, fifteen years after the fall of the regimes.[1] The postauthoritarian transition documented in this book is therefore not a clean break but a gradual, local, participatory process mediated through shared experiences. Nor does the transition mean simply that the ideological paradigms of the previous era yielded to another set of ideologies. Instead, with the maturation of the candlelight protests, taken-for-granted ways of doing politics were changed in at least three areas: the *discourse* young Koreans generated about domestic and international politics, the *practices* they embodied online and off, and the *social context* in which actions took place, most prominently in Kwanghwamun Square.

As such, postauthoritarian youth is not a new self-proclaimed identity or a demographic group. Instead, it is defined by changes in experience (and not necessarily worldview or ideology), or what Raymond Williams calls "what is actually being lived, and not only what is thought is being lived."[2] In fact, the narrative generated by South Korean youth often didn't align with the practices they embodied. For instance, teenagers who propagated "anti-American" slogans in 2002 imagined their protest through the model of recent street festivals, and the familiar trope of "democracy" during the 2008 beef protests actually conveyed a yearning for a transparency and accountability that goes beyond institutional politics. Furthermore, the previously incommensurable experiences of antigovernment demonstration and school camp merged in these new experiences. The old framework dictating vocabulary, practice, and identity was failing, and new frameworks free from existing boundaries formed in response.

However, while the candlelight protests succeeded in effecting both political change and a new social awareness in South Korea, many of the youth uprisings that swept the Middle East, North America, and Europe in 2009–2011 subsided with less concrete results. As a *Time* article remarks, the enthusiasts have now realized that young protesters need to move beyond their moment of excitement to the "dull but essential business of governing the squares and grownups."[3] The first wave of these Internet-born protests ebbed, leading to mixed results for each country's domestic and international politics.

Then, what are the consequences of this intense but short-lived activism? What counts as success? The specific South Korean case doesn't answer these questions, which apply only in discrete social and cultural contexts. However, the ten-year evolution of candlelight protest in South Korea does raise fundamental questions that can help us to understand the different local and particular manifestations of youth-driven dissent. The following three questions look into the discourse, practice, and context of the new protest repertoire, specifically addressing the communicative dynamics of the Internet and its influences on both participants and the connection between online and offline spaces. The fourth and final question looks to the future, reflecting on the long-term influences of short-term "viral" activism. Taken together, these questions illuminate the larger cultural ignition process which takes place via captivation and its aftermath and through which we can speculate about the future of this new form of activism.

What are the underlying grievances, fears, and hopes that fuel the formation of this collective action?

I offer this question in lieu of the one most commonly raised about Internet-born protests and their participants: *What is the role of the Internet in the protests?* Or, perhaps, *What do the protesters want?* These questions valorize new technologies and intentional, committed actors while leaving little room for citizens who participate from time to time, or who electronically forward material about the issue at hand *without* participating in street protests. However, the protests in South Korea suggest that these aren't really the right questions. Focusing instead on the grievances, fears, and hopes of participants asks critics to acknowledge the distinct dynamics of Internet politics— the *politics of captivation*—that enables scattered users to express similar opinions, forge temporary alliances, and make judgments without any social pressure to conform to established political discourse. Thinking about this highlights preexisting local conditions and dissatisfactions even though participants might not be able to fully articulate them either online or in the streets.

This direction also draws attention to the local and historical context in which the politics of captivation takes place. It wasn't solely the Internet or anti-American activism that gave rise to the unprecedented scale of mass protest against the U.S. military presence in South Korea. Instead, what ignited the Internet was nascent criticism of the state of national politics. In 2002 young Koreans were captivated by the deaths of two teenage girls and regarded both the accident itself and the subsequent courts-martial of the vehicle's crew as reflecting the subordinate status of South Korea—in stark contrast with the national pride young Koreans had experienced during the recent World Cup soccer tournament. Korean teenagers rallied in 2008 because they feared that BSE-contaminated beef would be served in their school cafeterias. However, underlying the perhaps-exaggerated fear of contracting mad cow disease was anxiety about what people saw as the government's disregard for their safety and about increasing loss of control over their daily lives as the result of international free trade.

When Internet users transform an issue into an object of mass attention by propagating and recirculating ideas (both reasonable and exaggerated), that issue becomes a metonym for underarticulated yet widely shared fears, anxieties, or hopes. An issue that captivates public attention is "far from being a simple, straightforward representation of the 'facts'" and is instead an "index that is necessarily rich with imagination and feeling."[4] Seeing a "viral" phenomenon as a metonym for underlying sentiments better explains why certain issues—like the girls' deaths or beef importation— induce protest, while other significant and shocking events only faintly ripple on the ever-changing surface of the attention economy. Attention to captivation illuminates "emergent" practices and relationships that are shared but not yet registered in mainstream politics and media.[5]

In the recent case of the Arab Spring, addressing underarticulated sentiments highlights the process through which the story of Mohamed Bouazizi drew the attention of both other Tunisians and people in neighboring nations, eventually leading to mass protests in a number of countries in the region. Bouazizi's story captivated youths who identified with a young man struggling to feed his family while forced to pay bribes in order to continue earning money.[6] Although few Internet users who disseminated the story— or even protesters who took to the streets—expected to overthrow the government, they nevertheless harbored potent grievances about their economic situation (Tunisia had 30 percent unemployment at the time) and authoritarian rule. The Bouazizi story lit up the Internet, reaching those who shared similar experiences and inspiring them to organize for protest.

In 2011 *Adbusters*—a Canadian magazine for those "who want to advance the new social activist movement of the information age"—drew the attention of young Americans who had been quietly sharing their grievances about an economic system they believed favored the elite. The magazine was best known for its antibranding campaigns and parodies of advertising to reveal how corporations foster consumer desire for branded goods (the famous "Joe Chemo" ad parodying Camel cigarette advertising was from *Adbusters*).[7] Despite the magazine's success, its acclaimed strategies were nevertheless criticized as becoming "just a different brand" for upper-middle-class liberal consumers.[8] However, the magazine's call to Occupy Wall Street on September 17 captivated young Americans well beyond its typical readership, and the one-day protest turned into a long-term campout in city centers across the United States. As CNN noted during the 2012 presidential campaign, although the Occupy movement had fizzled by then, it nonetheless significantly influenced mainstream politics by putting on the agenda "rising income inequality, tax policies that favor the rich, growing influence by large corporate interests in elections and the reckless deregulation of financial institutions that resulted in the 2008 crisis."[9] Even though the Occupy movement wasn't successful in a traditional sense—for instance, it lacked a clear leadership structure, did not articulate its demands, and had little immediate impact on politics—it *was* effective in highlighting economic inequality, which had long been hidden under the American ideal of meritocracy.[10]

The politics of captivation also demands that critics recognize and interpret Internet users' criticisms, which are often expressed in "vernacular discourses" and seldom conform to the conventions of mainstream political debate.[11] South Korean youths in 2002 and 2008 didn't systematically articulate their criticism of how the U.S.–South Korea relationship evolved, or of the neoliberal policies they opposed. However, the visible targets of young Koreans' activism—particularly the U.S. military presence in 2002 and President Lee Myung-bak's pursuit of free trade in 2008—were metonyms for larger political forces. In the case of the Arab Spring, implicit in the circulation of Bouazizi's story was criticism of a government that presided over a failed economy while maintaining dominance through police power. Meanwhile, the Occupy movement targeted politicians and corporations that protesters believed operated in a predatory manner to promote business interests rather than the interests of the people, facilitating the concentration of wealth among those who were already wealthy.[12]

Although the examples here have been tied to the pursuit of progressive change, the politics of captivation can also undermine important societal values. The Internet makes it easier to form a group "without social approval" under the protection of anonymity.[13] Similarly, extremist politics thrives on the Internet, offering simple (or simplistic) explanations and solutions for complex social problems. In countries from Scandinavia to Italy to Australia, far-right nationalism and hostility toward immigrants circulate online and captivate citizens as comfortingly simple solutions for ongoing economic difficulties and increasing unemployment.[14] This phenomenon can significantly undermine the rights of minority groups and is not merely a matter of individual pathology but a cultural product in the connected world.

These cases in South Korea and beyond suggest that widely shared dissatisfaction is capable of erupting on the Internet at an unexpected moment, even when it goes unrecognized by mainstream media or politics. The politics of captivation implies a more volatile popular political process that exposes to public scrutiny the larger problems revealed by a specific issue, eventually challenging conventional politics without being confined to existing political fault lines.

How do participants remember their temporary involvement in protest?

Although I've argued that collective action brought about through the Internet is likely to be made up of temporary alliances rather than communities with stable membership, it is certainly possible that the Internet could transform citizens politically and sustain political changes. In response to this possibility, critics often ask, *Are the participants a new generation of activists?* However, this line of discussion privileges the identity of "activist"— which, as we've seen, is itself potentially an outdated notion. Instead, it is more relevant to consider the potential long-term effects of temporary alliances on individual participants, without assuming that a particular type of enlightened citizen would—or should—result.

The retrospective narratives documented in this book show that many Korean teenagers participated in protests (both online and in the streets) without a formal objective in mind and afterward returned to their competitive schools and workplaces. Even though they didn't become permanent activists protesting broader U.S. patronage or neoliberal reforms, they nevertheless had in common an experience of political socialization through which they came to view themselves as independent thinkers with a critical perspective toward politics. The 2002 vigils awakened Ŭn-ha, well before her peers, to the reality of the U.S.–South Korea relationship (see chapter 4). For Ta-jŏng, the experience of belonging to an alternative community in 2008 allowed her to decide not to attend college, which was the path prescribed by her family and by society. In contrast, Kŏn-ho was proud to have distanced himself from his progressive teacher and to have become an independent thinker, resisting pressure from both peers and adults (see chapter 6).

Furthermore, in many cases the vivid memories of occupying city centers and being part of a peaceful and festive crowd remained with participants and observers, destabilizing the association between dissent and fear—a powerful mechanism that had deterred Koreans from joining protests during the authoritarian era. Ch'ang-min and Chi-yun, who actively participated in the beef protests in 2008, recollected their comfort with activism in corporeal terms. Ch'ang-min was familiar with street marches from those he experienced in elementary school with his labor-union parents; Chi-yun had participated in a 2002 vigil with her family when she was only eleven years old. Their familiarity with street marches led them to join the 2008 protests without consideration for (or fear of) any legal or political consequences of participation. This was a dramatic shift from the authoritarian era, when downtown Seoul was closed to protesters and entering the space involved physical and social sacrifice.

For critics, the retrospective narratives offer a vantage point from which to gauge the impact of Internet activism and its transformative influence without assuming a particular subjectivity for the participants—for example as activists, as a multitude, or as consumers of "slacktivism." The long-term impact of these protests transcends any immediate institutional change and is instead mediated through individuals, whose memories from the street affected their later trajectories. For example, Ta-jŏng's memories of being part of a potent crowd empowered her to resist the "cannibalistic" competition at school and find an alternative path. At the same time, the experience of activism also has the potential to induce cynicism—as in Kŏn-ho's case, where he critically reappraised his impulsive online activism during junior high school and refashioned himself as a cautious conservative (see chapter 6). For South Koreans, these memories completely changed the character of dissent, from a commitment that demanded devotion and sacrifice to an object of play and casual participation.

How do online and offline spaces overlap and reconfigure each other?

By the end of the candlelight decade, the Internet was no longer a "virtual" space separated from the "real" world, nor merely a tool to empower youth to *enter* the real world. Therefore, I offer this question in lieu of *How does the virtual public sphere operate?* or *What is the impact of the Internet on real-world politics?* These inaccurately assume a concrete dichotomy. Furthermore, familiar monikers implicitly (or explicitly) entail a discursive realm separated from the real world. For instance, "virtual public sphere" and "cyber salon" evoke the ideal of people leaving behind bodies and associated privilege or stigma and interacting as minds.[15] In contrast, labels such as "cesspool" brand the Internet as a haven for slander and misinformation that fail to find a home in the real world.[16]

Instead, the question above brings attention to how the two spaces are *interconnected* and evokes a backdrop for activism that cannot be reduced to either online or real-world efforts. Furthermore, this perspective brings renewed attention to space as not just a context for political action but also an element in politics integrated through corporeal memory. In the progression of the South Korean candlelight protests, the online and offline spaces evoked and transformed one another in a number of ways. In 2002 the experience of reveling in national pride during the World Cup let Internet users imagine a street protest to reclaim national self-determination (see chapter 2). In 2008 Kwanghwamun mirrored online forums and became a canvas for parody as citizens mocked the water cannons ("Warm water!") and mass arrests (the "hencoop tour") (chapter 5). In the progression of the candlelight protests, cyberspace and physical space converged in modes of expression and techniques of protest. The experience undoubtedly empowered youth in the new millennium to enter the protest space, but it also transformed the *nature* of the space. In recurring protests throughout the candlelight decade, young Koreans developed new ways of inhabiting both the Internet and the "real" world.

This overlapping of online and offline spaces is not a unique phenomenon for the South Korean case. Contemporary users experience the Internet as part of their daily routine, fluidly traversing and blurring boundaries between the virtual and real words, especially with the increasing use of mobile technology. A user can be in a publicly accessible online space but still communicate through a personal device with personally connected partners. For Hjorth and Arnold this serves as a context for new kinds of practices, which they call "mobile intimacy"—the intimate but public character of interactions at the intersection of physical and virtual space builds "a sense of reciprocal commitment and obligations to the collective."[17] Similarly, Sheller proposes that the overlapping of contexts gives rise to "mobile publics," which are characterized not by static identity as a member of the public but by the "capacity to take on an identity that is able to speak and to participate in specific contexts."[18] These concepts suggest that the weaving together of spaces transforms the relationship between user and space, and deserves further attention.

As I write this in 2015, both South Korea and the world at large have seen the establishment of a particular format of Internet-born protests: mass occupation of city centers with increasing degrees of carnivalesque subversion. From the Tahrir protests, literary scholar Brian Edwards concludes that "the 'temptation of reading for meaning' should be resisted," and suggests instead that "critics ought to pay greater attention to 'the proliferating copresence of varied textual/cultural forms in all their mobility and mutability.'"[19] Indeed, Tahrir Square, Wall Street, and La Puerta del Sol have taken on a new significance. Even though the expression of citizens' grievances has now largely ceased, the occupation of these sites by people chanting "We are all Khaled Said!"; "We are the 99 percent!"; or "*¡No nos representan!*" remains in the memories of both participants and larger audiences. I expect that these locations will be the locus of future carnivalesque gatherings.

Of course, Internet-born youth protests do not always generate a repertoire that allows easy participation: protests in Bahrain and Syria were quickly and violently restrained, and the protesters' efforts subsumed under armed conflicts between opposing political or ethnic groups. Corporeal memories from *these* experiences are likely to evoke fear—much as Kwang-hwamun was associated with fear and dissent during South Korea's authoritarian era.

How does Internet-born activism shape expectations for politics?

Significant political change takes place only gradually, as the result of concerted and accumulated actions. In South Korea, the two major waves of protest in 2002 and 2008 met with limited success in bringing about changes to institutional politics; however, these protests nonetheless reshaped expectations with regard to the "physiological, moral, and aesthetic dimensions" of political experiences—"sensibilities," as Gaukroger calls them.[20] The 2002 candlelight vigils did not immediately lead to reform of the U.S.–South Korea relationship, nor did the 2008 protests force the South Korean government to ban the import of American beef. However, both efforts established new expectations for popular politics among youth, and had an impact in larger precincts as well. The 2002 vigils nurtured the nascent yearning for an assertive national identity unfettered by outside powers, set agendas for the upcoming presidential election, and made "red scare" campaign tactics a thing of the past. In 2008 the fear of mad cow disease created what philosopher Sung-gi Hong calls "a changed structure of public debate"—namely, a distrust of the government's ability to appropriately consider matters of social importance and the consequent coalition of the Internet and private experts in investigating critical public issues.[21]

In 2015 the Internet-born candlelight protest is now a predictable response to any controversial issue, and through it citizens question the operation of government authorities and demand transparency. Recent examples of controversies include the suicide of former president Roh Moo-hyun in 2009, which many believed resulted from President Lee Myung-bak's "vengeful corruption investigation"; the alleged involvement of South Korea's National Intelligence Service in the December 2012 presidential election; and the failure of maritime police and the government to appropriately investigate the deaths of more than three hundred students after a ferry sank in early 2014.[22] Bin-na is not the only one to conclude that the candlelight protest is now so frequent and familiar as to have become a cliché (see chapter 6). However, it does also appear that the habituation of examining government decisions and expressing criticism in the vernacular language serves to keep institutional politics more responsive to the public interest.

Furthermore, Internet-born youth protest in South Korea is already evolving beyond the repertoire of candlelight protests, suggesting that post-authoritarian youth politics is not confined to one particular format. In December 2013 a student posted a handwritten letter to a bulletin board on his university campus that began, "I just wanted to ask everybody. How are you all doing? Is it okay for you to ignore social issues since it's none of your business?" The letter then listed a raft of national issues, ranging from mass layoffs of striking railway workers to the government's attempts to unseat opposition lawmakers, to the construction of electricity transmission towers in rural villages that have caused health problems. He asked again, "Are you doing all right?" and signed his name.[23]

The letter soon became an Internet phenomenon as its image circulated broadly on social media and a community page of the same title was established on Facebook. The Facebook page has received more than 261,000 "likes," and its broad circulation and the enthusiastic responses to it soon led to a mass gathering in downtown Seoul called "Are you doing all right?" (*Annyŏngdŭl hasipnikka?*).[24] Other Internet users posted—online, in the streets, at high school and college campuses—their own open letters, responding, "I am not doing well."[25] The handwritten letters list the authors' own reasons for not doing well, ranging from the overly competitive educational environment to increasingly dire career prospects for young Koreans, to the loss of the social safety net, to corrupt politicians. Such letters became a "nationwide phenomenon spanning generational, regional, and class divides."[26]

These youths were likely not activists in the traditional sense; postauthoritarian South Korea doesn't need devoted activists to fight authoritarian regimes. Nor did the extremely competitive environment allow youths to become activists while temporarily setting aside their personal goals. However, the young Koreans who made "Are you doing all right?" a national phenomenon were political actors addressing such injustices as illegal labor practices, corruption, and environmental degradation. The now-familiar dynamics of the candlelight protests—casual participation and temporary alliance, advocacy for democratic principles, and direct response to (and irreverent parody of) the government—continue in new forms of expression. These efforts paint the figure of a popular politics that might be volatile at times but that nonetheless subjects the exercise of power to scrutiny: it is an expression of collective voices in response to matters that captivate them.

Notes

Introduction: Igniting the Internet

1   Anthony Capaccio and Nicole Gaouette, "U.S. Adding 800 Troops for South Korea Citing Rebalance," *Bloomberg Business,* January 7, 2014.

2   Howard W. French and Don Kirk, "American Policies and Presence Are Under Fire in South Korea, Straining an Alliance," *New York Times,* December 8, 2002, 20.

3   "Korean Anger as U.S. Soldiers Cleared," *BBC,* November 22, 2002, sec. Asia-Pacific.

4   See, for example, Seung-Hwan Kim, "Yankee Go Home? A Historical View of South Korean Sentiment toward the United States, 2001–2004," in *Strategy and Sentiment: South Korean Views of the United States and the U.S.–ROK Alliance,* ed. Derek J. Mitchell (Washington, DC: Center of Strategic and International Studies, 2004), 24–35; Sook-jong Lee, "Anti-Americanism in Korean Society: A Survey-based Analysis," *Joint U.S.-Korea Academic Studies* 14 (2004): 183–204.

5   For instance, Hae-joang Cho Han concludes, "Without the World Cup, the movement to revise the SOFA (Status of Forces Agreement), the anti-American/peace movement following the death of two young schoolgirls by an American military truck, would not have been possible." Hae-joang Cho Han, "Beyond the FIFA's World Cup: An Ethnography of the 'Local' in South Korea Around the 2002 World Cup," *Inter-Asia Cultural Studies* 5, no. 1 (2004): 21. See also Gyuchan Jeon and Tae-jin Yoon, "Cultural Politics of the Red Devils: The Desiring Multitude Versus the State, Capital and Media," *Inter-Asia Cultural Studies* 5, no. 1 (2004): 77–88; Seoung-Tae Hong, "The World Cup, the Red Devils, and Related Arguments in Korea," *Inter-Asia Cultural Studies* 5, no. 1 (2004): 89–105.

6   As noted in the following section, Alfred Gell's anthropological account of the function of artwork uses the concept of *captivation* and inspired my discussion. In media studies, James Ash uses the term to explain the relationship between computer game and body. Alfred Gell, *Art and Agency: An Anthropological Theory* (Oxford: Oxford University Press, 1998); James Ash, "Technologies of Captivation: Videogames and the Attunement of Affect," *Body & Society* 19, no. 1 (2013): 27–51.

7   Michael Barkun, *A Culture of Conspiracy: Apocalyptic Visions in Contemporary America* (Berkeley: University of California Press, 2003).

8 Marlies Glasius and Geoffrey Pleyers, "The Global Moment of 2011: Democracy, Social Justice and Dignity," *Development and Change* 44, no. 3 (2013): 547–567.

9 Blake Hounshell, "The Revolution Will Be Tweeted," *Foreign Policy,* June 20, 2011; Liz Else, "The Revolution Will Be Tweeted," *New Scientist,* February 6, 2012; Brian Lenzo, "Will the Revolution Be Tweeted?," *International Socialist Review,* July 2013.

10 Malcolm Gladwell, "Why the Revolution Will Not Be Tweeted," *New Yorker,* October 4, 2010. See also Jon B. Alterman, "The Revolution Will Not Be Tweeted," *Washington Quarterly* 34, no. 4 (2011): 103–116.

11 Gerard Delanty and Patrick O'Mahony, *Nationalism and Social Theory: Modernity and the Recalcitrance of the Nation* (Thousand Oaks, CA: Sage Publications, 2002).

12 Yuka Hayashi, "Japan's Nationalist Movement Strengthens," *Wall Street Journal,* August 14, 2012. I thank Sungyun Lim for drawing my attention to this phenomenon.

13 Evgeny Morozov, "The Brave New World of Slacktivism," *Foreign Policy,* May 19, 2009.

14 Many scholars have explored how activism, subculture, and independent media on the Internet form counterpublics—groups with marginalized or oppositional identities—that contest mainstream norms and develop alternative styles of political behaviors or norms of speech. See, for example, Catherine Helen Palczewski, "Cyber-Movements, New Social Movements, and Counterpublics," in *Counterpublics and the State,* ed. Robert Asen and Daniel Brouwer (Albany: State University of New York Press, 2001), 161–186; Juan Francisco Salazar, "Articulating an Activist Imaginary: Internet as Counter Public Sphere in the Mapuche Movement, 1997/2002," *Media International Australia, Incorporating Culture & Policy* 107 (2003): 19–30.

15 Daniel C. Brouwer and Robert Asen, introduction to *Public Modalities,* ed. Brouwer and Asen (Tuscaloosa: University of Alabama Press, 2010), 16.

16 See, for example, Manuel Castells, *The Information Age: Economy, Society and Culture, The Power of Identity,* vol. 2 (Oxford: Blackwell, 1997); Mark Poster, "Cyber Democracy: Internet and the Public Sphere," in *Information Subject* (London: Routledge, 2013), 95–116; Mark A. Smith and Peter Kollock, *Communities in Cyberspace* (New York: Routledge, 1999).

17 Herbert A. Simon, "Designing Organizations for an Information-Rich World," in *Computers, Communication, and the Public Interest,* ed. Martin Greenberger (Baltimore: Johns Hopkins University Press, 1971), 40–41.

18 Richard A. Lanham, *The Economics of Attention: Style and Substance in the Age of Information* (Chicago: University of Chicago Press, 2006), 165.

The term *attention economy* was originally coined by Thomas Davenport and John Beck in 2002. Thomas H. Davenport and John C. Beck, *The Attention Economy: Understanding the New Currency of Business* (Boston: Harvard Business Review Press, 2002).

19   New media scholar Jay Bolter argues that in the hypertextual environment every trajectory defines "an equally convincing and appropriate reading," and the multiplicity of trajectories creates the Internet as a discursive space with "no univocal sense." Jay David Bolter, *Writing Space* (Hillsdale, NJ: Lawrence Erlbaum, 1991), 25.

20   In a similar vein, new media scholar George Landow argues that the center of a community "exists only as a matter of evanescence" in the hypertextual environment. George P. Landow, *Hypertext 2.0: The Convergence of Contemporary Critical Theory and Technology*, 2nd ed. (Baltimore: Johns Hopkins University Press, 1997), 70.

21   Jiyeon Kang, "A Volatile Public: The 2009 Whole Foods Boycott on Facebook," *Journal of Broadcasting & Electronic Media* 56, no. 4 (2012): 562–577.

22   Immanuel Kant, *The Critique of Judgment*, trans. J. H. Bernard, 2nd ed. (London: Macmillan, 1914); Plato, *Gorgias* (Baltimore: Agora, 1994); Max Weber, "The Nature of Charismatic Authority and Its Routinization," in *Max Weber: On Charisma and Institution Building*, ed. S. N. Eisenstadt (1922; Chicago: University of Chicago Press, 1968), 48–65.

23   Marx's notion of "commodity fetishism" is central to the Frankfurt School's critique of popular culture. Margaret Cohen, "Walter Benjamin's Phantasmagoria," *New German Critique* no. 48 (1989): 87–107; Jürgen Habermas, *The Structural Transformation of the Public Sphere: An Inquiry into a Category of Bourgeois Society*, trans. Thomas Burger and F. Lawrence (1962; Cambridge, MA: MIT Press, 1989); Max Horkheimer and Theodor W. Adorno, *Dialectic of Enlightenment: Philosophical Fragments* (1947; Stanford, CA: Stanford University Press, 2002).

24   Guy Debord, *The Society of the Spectacle*, trans. Donald Nicholson-Smith (New York: Zone Books, 1995). In "'Sighting' the Public," Cara Finnegan and I argue that the fear of mesmerizing images and the equating of images with passive spectatorship are deeply embedded in modern public sphere theory. Cara A. Finnegan and Jiyeon Kang, "'Sighting' the Public: Iconoclasm and Public Sphere Theory," *Quarterly Journal of Speech* 90, no. 4 (2004): 377–402.

25   Evolutionary biologist Richard Dawkins explains the propagation of ideas using analogies to biological and computer viruses, arguing that religious ideas spread by tricking people to accept them and pass them on. Richard Dawkins, *The Selfish Gene*, 2nd ed. (Oxford: Oxford University Press, 1990); Richard

Dawkins, "Viruses of the Mind," in *Dennett and His Critics: Demystifying Mind*, ed. Bo Dahlbom (Oxford: Wiley-Blackwell, 1993), 13–27.

New media scholars Henry Jenkins, Sam Ford, and Joshua Green as well as Limor Shifman criticize the importing of biological assumptions into the cultural transmission of ideas, and instead propose explanations with a focus on users' motivations and satisfaction in spreading a message. See Henry Jenkins, Sam Ford, and Joshua Green, *Spreadable Media* (New York: New York University Press, 2013); Limor Shifman, "An Anatomy of a YouTube Meme," *New Media & Society* 14, no. 2 (2011): 187–203.

26 I appreciate Robert Asen and Sam Collins for their valuable input regarding the distinction between captivation with an image and with an idea. This difference is critical for regarding captivation as a psychological and cultural process.

27 Gell, *Art and Agency*.

28 Anne D'Alleva, "Captivation, Representation, and the Limits of Cognition: Interpreting Metaphor and Metonymy in Tahitian Tamau," in *Beyond Aesthetics: Art and the Technologies of Enchantment*, ed. Christopher Pinney and Nicholas Thomas (Oxford: Berg, 2001), 90.

29 Robert Hariman and John Louis Lucaites, *No Caption Needed: Iconic Photographs, Public Culture, and Liberal Democracy* (Chicago: University of Chicago Press, 2007), 10.

30 Ibid., 11.

31 Gell, *Art and Agency*; Raymond Williams, *Marxism and Literature* (Oxford: Oxford University Press, 1977), 121; Kent A. Ono and John M. Sloop, *Shifting Borders: Rhetoric, Immigration, and California's Proposition 187* (Philadelphia: Temple University Press, 2002), 12–13. See also Cara A. Finnegan, "Recognizing Lincoln: Image Vernaculars in Nineteenth-Century Visual Culture," *Rhetoric & Public Affairs* 8 (2005): 31–58; Gerard A. Hauser, *Vernacular Voices: The Rhetoric of Publics and Public Spheres* (Columbia: University of South Carolina Press, 1999).

32 Michael Warner, *Publics and Counterpublics* (New York: Zone Books), 61.

33 Ibid., 89.

34 Dilip Parameshwar Gaonkar and Elizabeth A. Povinelli, "Technologies of Public Forms: Circulation, Transfiguration, Recognition," *Public Culture* 15, no. 3 (2003): 388.

35 Benedict Anderson, *Imagined Communities: Reflections on the Origin and Spread of Nationalism* (London: Verso, 1991); Habermas, *Structural Transformation of the Public Sphere*.

36 Katy Steinmetz, "And Oxford's Word of the Year Is . . . ," *Time*, November 18, 2013.

37 Shifman, "An Anatomy of a YouTube Meme," 190.

38 Hariman and Lucaites, *No Caption Needed*, 10.

39   Alice E. Marwick and danah boyd, "I Tweet Honestly, I Tweet Passionately: Twitter Users, Context Collapse, and the Imagined Audience," *New Media & Society* 13 (2011): 122.

40   Larissa Hjorth and Michael Arnold, *Online@Asia Pacific: Mobile, Social and Locative Media in the Asia-Pacific* (Oxon, UK: Routledge, 2013), 7, 12.

41   Linda Herrera, *Revolution in the Age of Social Media: The Egyptian Popular Insurrection and the Internet* (London: Verso, 2014), 7.

42   Hjorth and Arnold, *Online@Asia Pacific,* 13.

43   Clay Shirky, *Here Comes Everybody: The Power of Organizing without Organizations* (New York: Penguin, 2008), 262.

44   Bronisław K. Malinowski, "The Primitive Economics of the Trobriand Islanders," *The Economic Journal* 31, no. 121 (1921): 1–16; Marcel Mauss and W. D. Halls, *The Gift: Forms and Functions of Exchange in Archaic Societies* (New York: W. W. Norton & Company, 1954).

45   Jenkins, Ford, and Green, *Spreadable Media.*

46   Yi Kil-ho, *Urinŭn DC* (We are DC) (Seoul: Imagine, 2012).

47   Zizi A. Papacharissi, *Affective Publics: Sentiment, Technology, and Politics,* Kindle ed. (New York: Oxford University Press, 2014), 564.

48   W. Lance Bennett and Alexandra Segerberg, *The Logic of Connective Action: Digital Media and the Personalization of Contentious Politics* (Cambridge: Cambridge University Press, 2014), 16.

49   Sidney Tarrow, "Review of the Logic of Connective Action: Digital Media and the Personalization of Contentious Politics," *Perspectives on Politics* 12, no. 2 (2014): 469.

50   Victoria Carty and Jake Onyett, "Protest, Cyberactivism and New Social Movements: The Reemergence of the Peace Movement Post 9/11," *Social Movement Studies* 5 (2006): 229–249; Cass Sunstein, *Republic.com* (Princeton, NJ: Princeton University Press, 2001); Magdalena Wojcieszak, "'Don't Talk to Me': Effects of Ideologically Homogeneous Online Groups and Politically Dissimilar Offline Ties on Extremism," *New Media & Society* 12 (2010): 637–655.

51   Guy Redden, "Changing Times Again: Recent Writing on Globalization, Communications and the New Activism," *Social Movement Studies* 4, no. 1 (2005): 99–103.

52   Barry Wellman, "Changing Connectivity: A Future History of Y2.03K," *Sociological Research Online* 4 (2000).

53   Colin Sparks, "The Internet and the Global Public Sphere," in *Mediated Politics: Communication in the Future of Democracy,* ed. W. Lance Bennett and Robert M. Entman (New York: Cambridge University Press, 2001), 75–95; Nicholas Vinocur, "Charlie Hebdo, Satirical Weekly, Publishes Cartoons of the Prophet Mohammad," *Huffington Post,* September 19, 2012.

54   Howard Rheingold calls these "smart mobs," underscoring their intelligence and efficiency based on shared information, connections, and the ability to coordinate—in contrast to what *mob* usually evokes. Howard Rheingold, *Smart Mobs: The Next Social Revolution* (Cambridge, MA: Perseus, 2002).

55   This idea is inspired by actor-network theory (ANT), developed by John Law, Michel Callon, and Bruno Latour in the 1980s. ANT proposes that society be studied without privileging certain actors (typically human or technological), and paying attention to how relationships are formed and effects are generated. ANT asks the researcher to observe the interaction of actors (sometimes referred to as "actants") with a suspension of presumptions, explicitly distancing the actor from intention or motivation. This approach is particularly productive for Internet research because it defies both the humanistic and structuralist approaches, which respectively valorize the user or the technology as a determinant. Bruno Latour, *Reassembling the Social: An Introduction to Actor-Network-Theory* (Oxford: Oxford University Press, 2005); John Law, "Notes on the Theory of Actor-Network: Ordering, Strategy and Heterogeneity," *Systems Practice* 5 (1992): 379–393. See also Nick Couldry, "Actor Network Theory and Media: Do They Connect and on What Terms?" in *Cultures of Connectivity*, ed. Andreas Hepp et al. (Creskill, NJ: Hampton Press, 2008), 93–110.

56   Kurt Andersen, "Person of the Year 2011: The Protester," *Time,* December 14, 2011.

57   John Keane, "Monitory Democracy and Media-saturated Societies," *Griffith Review* 24 (2009): 16.

58   Manuel Castells, *Communication Power* (Oxford: Oxford University Press, 2009), 240.

59   Sook-Jong Lee, "The Rise of Korean Youth as a Political Force," *Brookings Northeast Asia Survey 2003–2004*, 2004. See also Ki-suk Cho, "The Ideological Orientation of 2008 Candlelight Vigil Participants: Anti-American, Pro-North Korean Left or Anti-Neoliberalism?," *Korean Journal of Politics* 43, no. 3 (2009): 125–148; Seung-Hwan Kim, "Anti-Americanism in Korea," *The Washington Quarterly* 26, no. 1 (2002–2003): 109–122; Pyung-won Kong, "Change in the Political System of Republic of Korea (ROK) and the United States (U.S.)-ROK Relationship" (PhD diss., West Virginia University, 2005); Sook-jong Lee, "Anti-Americanism in Korean Society"; Eui Hang Shin, "Correlates of the 2002 Presidential Election in South Korea: Regionalism, the Generation Gap, Anti-Americanism, and the North Korea Factor," *East Asia* 21, no. 2 (2004): 18–38.

60   Progressive political critic Yong-min Kim published an op-ed, "You're Hopeless," in a university newspaper and stirred up controversy about the

political indifference of college students. Available at Kim Yong-min, "Nŏhŭinŭn hŭimang'i ŏptt'a" (You're hopeless), *Kim Yong-Min's Blog*, June 14, 2009. Chŏn Sang-jin, "2008nyŏn ch'otpul hyŏnsange taehan sedaesahoehakchŏk koch'al" (A generation sociological consideration on 'candlelight protest'), *Hyŏndae chŏngch'i yŏn'gu* (Journal of contemporary politics) 2, no. 1 (2009): 5–31.

61   See Song Ho-geun, *Hankuk, musŭn iri ilŏnago itna?: Sedae kaldŭnggwa chohwaŭi mihak* (Korea, what is happening: The aesthetics of generational conflict and concord) (Seoul: Samsung Economic Research Institute, 2003).

62   An Sŏn-hŭi, "Sahŏe chuyŏk tt'ŏorŭn p'i sedae" (Generation P: A new leader of society), *Hankyoreh*, June 9, 2003.

63   For instance, Do-Hyun Han, "Contemporary Korean Society Viewed through the Lens of the Candlelight Vigils," *Korea Journal* 50, no. 3 (2010): 14–37; Kim Se-gyun, "Han'gukŭi chŏngch'i chihyŏnggwa ch'otpul sedae" (Korea's political terrain and the candle generation), *Munhwa/Kwahak* (Culture/Science) 63 (2010): 47–65; Sim Kwang-hyŏn, "Sedaeŭi chŏngch'ihakkwa hankuk hyŏndaesaŭi chaehaesŏk" (Generation politics and the reinterpretation of contemporary Korean history), *Munhwa/Kwahak* (Culture/Science) 62 (2010): 17–71.

64   Gill Jones, *Youth* (London: Polity, 2009), 31.

65   Kim Sa-kwa et al., "20 tae yaegi, tŭrŏnŭn poassŏ?" (Have you ever listened to twentysomethings?), *Ch'angjak kwa pip'yŏng* (Creation and criticism) 38, no. 1 (2010): 269–299.

66   Agora P'yeindŭl, *Taehanmin'guk sangsik sajŏn Agora* (Common sense of the republic of Korea: Agora) (Seoul: Yŏu wa Turumi, 2008); Andrew Eungi Kim, "Civic Activism and Korean Democracy: The Impact of Blacklisting Campaigns in the 2000 and 2004 General Elections," *The Pacific Review* 19, no. 4 (December 1, 2006): 519–542; Yong Cheol Kim and June Woo Kim, "South Korean Democracy in the Digital Age: The Candlelight Protests and the Internet," *Korea Observer* 40, no. 1 (2009): 53–83; O Yŏn-ho, *Taehanmin'guk t'ŭksanp'um Omainyusŭ* (Oh My News, a Korean specialty) (Seoul: Humanist, 2004).

67   Yi Mun-jae and Ch'a Hyŏng-sŏk, "02nyŏn olhaeŭi inmul haengdonghanŭn netijŭn" ('02 'person of the year' is the activist-netizen), *Sisa Journal*, December 23, 2002.

68   Yoonkyung Lee, "Democracy without Parties? Political Parties and Social Movements for Democratic Representation in Korea," *Korea Observer* 40, no. 1 (2009): 27–52. See also Choi Jang-jip, "Ch'otpul chiphoewa han'guk minjujuŭi ott'ŏkk'e polgŏsin'ga" (How to view the candlelight protest and Korean democracy), in *Proceedings of Ch'otpul chiphoewa Han'guk minjujuŭi* (The candlelight protest and Korean democracy) (Seoul 2008); Sung-gi

Hong, "A Look at the Changes in Debate Structure in Korea through the Candlelight Vigils," *Korea Journal* 50, no. 3 (2010): 100–127.

On a different note, a number of critical scholars viewed the 2008 beef protests as a turning point that drew public attention to "risk politics," in which the human-caused environmental risk of mad cow disease compelled political action. Chŏng Jin-sŏng, ed., *Wihŏm sahoe, wihŏm chŏngch'i* (Risk society, risk politics) (Seoul: Seoul National University Press, 2010).

69 Tangdae Pip'yŏng, ed., *Kŭdaenŭn wae ch'otpurŭl kkŭsyŏnnayo* (Why did you put out the candle?) (Seoul: Tangdae, 2009).

70 Edward Casey suggests that habitual memories are individually and socially transformative. According to Casey, habitual body memories orient a person to develop a perspective on what is possible and desirable, and repeated contact with a scene allows for "feeling at ease" and thus domesticating the space. Edward Casey, *Remembering: A Phenomenological Study,* 2nd ed. (Bloomington: Indiana University Press, 2000), 192.

71 Political philosopher Danielle Allen theorizes "habits" as the substance of citizenship, in that habits—not written rules—dictate how citizens behave in the public sphere, exerting rights and practicing duties. Danielle S. Allen, *Talking to Strangers: Anxieties of Citizenship since* Brown v. Board of Education (Chicago: University of Chicago Press, 2006). See also Paul Connerton, "Cultural Memory," in *Handbook of Material Culture,* ed. Christopher Tilley et al. (London: Sage, 2006), 315–324.

72 The method is also influenced by actor-network theory. See Kang, "A Volatile Public."

73 For more details about the collaboration and tension between participants organized on the Internet and traditional activists during the 2002 candlelight vigils, see Jinsun Lee, "Net Power in Action: Internet Activism in the Contentious Politics of South Korea" (PhD diss., Rutgers University, 2009).

74 For an analysis of women participants in the 2008 protests, see Yeran Kim, "Kamsŏng kongronjang: Yŏsŏng k'ŏmyunit'i, nŭkkigo malhago haengdonghada (Affective public sphere: woman communities feel, speak and act)," *Ŏllon kwa sahoe* (Media and society) 18, no. 3 (2010): 146–191; Kim Yŏng-ok , "Yŏsŏngjuŭiŭi kwanjŏmesŏ pon ch'otpul chiphoewa yŏsŏngŭi chŏngch'ijŏk juch'esŏng" (The candlelight protest and political subjectivity of women from the feminist perspective), *Asia yŏsŏng yŏn'gu* (Journal of Asian women) 48, no. 2 (2009): 7–34; Young Ok Kim, "Understanding the Candlelight Demonstration and Women's Political Subjectivity through the Perspective of Changing Publicity," *Korea Journal* 50, no. 3 (2010): 38–70.

75 William Labov, *Language in the Inner City: Studies in the Black English Vernacular* (Philadelphia: University of Pennsylvania Press, 1972), 366.

76 Stanton Wortham, *Narratives in Action* (New York: Teachers College Press, 2001).

77 Richard Bauman and Charles Briggs, "Poetics and Performance as Critical Perspectives on Language and Social Life," *Annual Review of Anthropology* 19 (1990): 59–88.

78 W. Lance Bennett, "Review of *The Language of Contention: Revolutions in Words, 1688–2012*," *Perspectives on Politics* 12, no. 2 (June 2014): 472.

Chapter 1: South Korean Youth in the New Millennium

1 Chi-yun, interview by author, Seoul, South Korea, July 8, 2011.

2 *Millennials* refers to those who entered adulthood at the turn of the twenty-first century, according to the Pew Research Center. Pew Research Center, *Millennials: Confident. Connected. Open to Change*, 2010. The term *digital natives* comes from Marc Prensky, "Digital Natives, Digital Immigrants Part 1," *On the Horizon* 9, no. 5 (2001): 1–6.

3 Ch'oe Hyŏng-ik, "Hankukŭi sahoe kujowa ch'ŏngnyŏn chuch'eŭi wigi" (The Korean social structure and the crisis of youth subjectivity), *Munhwa/Kwahak* (Culture/Science) 37 (2004): 69–85.

4 So Yŏng-hyŏn, "Pullyang chŏngnyŏn taemangron" (Hope for mischievous youth), *Naeilŭl yŏnŭn yŏksa* (History for tomorrow) 40 (2010): 26. See also Hong Sŏng-t'ae, "Kŭndaehwa kwajŏngesŏ ŏrininŭn ŏttŏk'e charawannŭn'ga: Han'guk sahoeesŏŭi ŏrini tamnonŭi pyŏnhwa" (How children grew up in the modernization process: Changes in the discourse on children in Korean society), *Tangdae pip'yŏng* (Contemporary criticism) 25 (2004): 245–255.

5 Dafna Zur, "The Construction of the Child in Korean Children's Magazines, 1908–1950" (PhD diss., University of British Columbia, 2011), 5.

6 So, "Pullyang chŏngnyŏn taemangron."

7 Kang Chŏng-ku, *Hyŏndae Hankuk sahoeŭi ihaewa chŏnmang* (Understanding contemporary Korean society) (Seoul: Hanul, 2000), 90. See also Ko Yŏng-bok, "4wŏl hyŏkmyŏngŭi ŭisik kujo" (The structure of consciousness in the April Revolution), in *4wol hyŏkmyŏngron* (On the April Revolution), ed. Man-gil Kang (Seoul: Han'gilsa, 1983).

8 Gi-wook Shin, "Nation, History, and Politics: South Korea," in *Nationalism and the Construction of Korean Identity*, ed. Hyung Il Pai and Timothy R. Tangherlini (Berkeley: University of California Press, 1999), 155.

9 Ch'oe, "Hankukŭi sahoe kujowa."

10 The appropriation of ancient history was also a matter of contention between North and South Korea, as each claimed to be the sole legitimate nation-state on the Korean peninsula. When Rhee declared the establishment of the Republic of

Korea (South Korea) in August 1948, he made the mythical founding day of the original Korean nation in 2333 BCE a national holiday celebrating "five thousand years of Korean history and culture." Hyung Il Pai and Timothy R. Tangherlini, "Introduction," in *Nationalism and the Construction of Korean Identity* (Berkeley: University of California Press, 1998), 2–3.

11 Yi Hyŏn-hŭi, *Saeroun Han'guksa* (New history of Korea) (Paju: Jimmundang, 2005).

12 Man-gil Kang, "Contemporary Nationalist Movement and the *Minjung*," in *South Korea's Minjung Movement: The Culture and Politics of Dissidence,* ed. Kenneth M. Wells (Honolulu: University of Hawai'i Press, 1995), 38.

13 Namhee Lee, *The Making of Minjung: Democracy and the Politics of Representation in South Korea* (Ithaca, NY: Cornell University Press, 2007), 6.
    See also Nancy Abelmann, "Minjung Movement and the Minjung," in Wells, *South Korea's Minjung Movement,* 119–153; Chungmoo Choi, "The Minjung Culture Movement and the Construction of Popular Culture in Korea," in Wells, *South Korea's Minjung Movement,* 105–118; Chŏn Sang-bong, *Han'guk kŭnhyŏndae ch'ŏngnyŏn undongsa* (A history of the contemporary Korean youth movement) (Seoul: Duri media, 2004).

14 Namhee Lee, *The Making of Minjung,* 10. See also Mi Park, "South Korea: Passion, Patriotism, and Student Radicalism," in *Student Activism in Asia,* ed. Meredith Leigh Weiss and Edward Aspinall (Minneapolis: University of Minnesota Press, 2012), 125–151.

15 The death toll was 230 according to the government's report, but a 2005 report by the families of those who died placed the count at 606. Bae Myŏng-jae, "Ch'ŏngsonyŏn 41 myŏng dŭng hangjaeng chung 165 myŏng samang" (165 died during the uprising including 41 teenagers), *Kyŏnghyang Sinmun,* May 15, 2005.

16 Bruce Cumings, "Anti-Americanism in the Republic of Korea," *Joint U.S.-Korea Academic Studies* 14 (2004): 213.

17 Yi Ŏ-yŏng, "Chiralt'an, sagwat'anŭl kiŏk hasimnikka?" (Do you remember tear gas bombs?) *JoongAng Ilbo,* June 9, 2007.

18 Han Hong-ku, "Han Hong-Ku ŭi yŏksa iyagi: 10 man nyŏn ŏchi kamok sarirŭl pŏrŏtta" (History by Han Hong-gu: we saved jail time worth 100,000 years), *Hankyoreh* 21, December 20, 2002.

19 Jesook Song, *South Koreans in the Debt Crisis: The Creation of a Neoliberal Welfare Society* (Durham, NC: Duke University Press, 2009), 9.

20 Hyuk-Rae Kim, "The State and Civil Society in Transition: The Role of Non-Governmental Organizations in South Korea," *Pacific Review* 13, no. 4 (2000): 595–613; Hagen Koo, "Civil Society and Democracy in South Korea," *Good Society* 11, no. 2 (2002): 40–45; Seungsook Moon, "Carving

Out Space: Civil Society and the Women's Movement in South Korea," *Journal of Asian Studies* 61, no. 2 (2002): 473–500.

21 Young-a Park, *Unexpected Alliances: Independent Filmmakers, the State, and the Film Industry in Postauthoritarian South Korea* (Stanford, CA: Stanford University Press, 2014), 13–14.

22 Kim Min-sik, "1980 nyŏn 5 wol Kwangju, p'oktong kwa minjuhwa undongŭi ch'ai" (Kwangju in May 1980, the difference between a riot and a democratization movement), *Oh My News,* May 18, 2007.

23 Chalmers A. Johnson, *The Sorrows of Empire: Militarism, Secrecy, and the End of the Republic* (New York: Metropolitan Books, 2004), 89.

24 Bruce Cumings, "The Asian Crisis, Democracy, and the End of 'Late' Development," in *The Politics of the Asian Economic Crisis,* ed. T. J. Pempel (Ithaca, NY: Cornell University Press, 1999), 17–44; Chaibong Hahm, "Anti-Americanism, Korean Style," *Issues and Insights* 3, no. 5 (2003): 9–22; Byung-Kook Kim, "The Politics of Crisis and a Crisis of Politics: The Presidency of Kim Dae Jung," in *Korea Briefing, 1997–1999: Challenges and Change at the Turn of the Century,* ed. Kongdan Oh (Armonk, NY: M. E. Sharpe, 2000), 34–74.

25 Young-a Park, *Unexpected Alliances,* 13. See also Meredith Woo-Cumings, "South Korean Anti-Americanism," *Japan Policy Research Institute Working Paper* 93 (2003).

26 James V. Feinerman, "The U.S.-Korea Status of Forces Agreement as a Source of Continuing Korean Anti-American Attitudes," in *Korean Attitudes toward the United States: Changing Dynamics,* ed. David I. Steinberg (Armonk, NY: M. E. Sharpe, 2005), 196–219; C. S. Eliot Kang, "Restructuring the U.S.–South Korea Alliance to Deal with the Second Korean Nuclear Crisis," *Australian Journal of International Affairs* 57, no. 2 (2003): 309–324.

27 Hong Yŏng-rim, "Yŏron chosa: Miguk hogamdo" (Opinion poll: Koreans' image of the United States), *Chosun Ilbo,* March 4, 2002.

28 Katharine Moon, *Protesting America: Democracy and the U.S.–Korea Alliance* (Berkeley: University of California Press, 2013), 223.

29 Sim Kwang-hyŏn, "Chabonjuŭi apch'uk sŏngjang kwa sedaeŭi chŏngch'i pip'an" (A critique of the capitalist compressed development and of the politics of generation), *Munhwa/Kwahak* (Culture/Science) 63 (2010): 15–46.

30 Jiyeon Kang and Nancy Abelmann, "The Domestication of South Korean Pre-College Study Abroad in the First Decade of the Millennium," *Journal of Korean Studies* 16, no. 1 (2011): 89–118; Jeong Duk Yi, "Globalization and Recent Changes to Daily Life in the Republic of Korea," in *Korea and Globalization: Politics, Economics and Culture,* ed. James B. Lewis and Amadu Sesay (London: Routledge, 2002), 10–35.

31   For instance, Chu Ŭn-wu, Kim Chong-yŏp, and Kim Yŏng-kyŏng take the
      former critical perspective, while Ko Kil-sŏp takes the latter. Chu Ŭn-wu,
      "Chayuwa sobiŭi shidae, kŭrigo naengsojuŭiŭi shijak" (A decade of freedom
      and consumption, and the onset of cynicism: The Republic of Korea, its
      conditions of everyday life in the 1990s), *Sahoewa Yŏksa* (Society and
      history) 88 (2010): 307–344 ; Kim Chong-yŏp, *Sahŏejŏk chouljŭng kwa
      naengsojuŭi* (Social manic depression and cynicism) (Seoul: Munhak
      Tongne, 2001); "Han'gugŭi chŏngch'isedaee kwanhan kyŏnghŏmjŏk
      yŏn'gu: 'Minjuhwa sedae' wa 'sinsedae' ŭi pigyorŭl chungshimŭro" (An
      empirical study of Korean political generations: The "democratization
      generation" and the "new generation"), *Tonghyang kwa chŏnmang* (Journal
      of Korean social trends and perspectives) 41 (1999): 119–133; Ko Kil-sŏp,
      "Ch'ŏngnyŏn munwha, hokŭn sosu munhwaronjŏk yŏn'gu e taehayŏ" (On
      the study of youth culture or subculture), *Munhwa/Kwahak* (Culture/
      Science) 20 (1999): 145–172.
32   Jesook Song's monograph and edited volume offer excellent analyses of both
      the macro-level social changes and the ethnographic accounts of various
      groups, including workers, families, and women. Jesook Song, ed., *New
      Millennium South Korea: Neoliberal Capitalism and Transnational Movements*
      (New York: Routledge, 2010); Song, *South Koreans in the Debt Crisis*.
33   "South Korea Youth Unemployment," TheGlobalEconomy.com, accessed
      June 20, 2014.
34   Hagen Koo, "The Changing Faces of Inequality in South Korea in the Age of
      Globalization," *Korean Studies* 31, no. 1 (2007): 1–18. See also Cumings, "The
      Asian Crisis"; Martin Hart-Landsberg and Paul Burkett, "Economic Crisis and
      Restructuring in South Korea: Beyond the Free Market-Statist Debate," *Critical
      Asian Studies* 33, no. 3 (2001): 403–430; Iain Pirie, *The Korean Developmental
      State: From Dirigisme to Neo-Liberalism* (New York: Routledge, 2007).
35   Kang and Abelmann, "Domestication of South Korean." See also Nancy
      Abelmann, Jung-Ah Choi, and So Jin Park, eds., *No Alternative?:
      Experiments in South Korean Education* (Berkeley: University of California
      Press, 2012); Kang-shik Choi, "The Rising Supply of College Graduates and
      Declining Returns for Young Cohort: The Case of Korea," *Global Economic
      Review* 34 (2005): 167–180.
36   Chang Sun-wŏn, "Ch'ŏngnyŏn sirŏptyul ŏttŏke kyesan halkka?" (How is
      the youth unemployment rate calculated?), *E Daily*, March 21, 2012.
37   Statistics Korea, *2009 Han'guk ŭi sahoe jip'yo chuyo kyŏlkwa* (2009 major
      social indices in Korea).
38   Nancy Abelmann, So Jin Park, and Hyunhee Kim, "College Rank and Neo-
      liberal Subjectivity in South Korea: The Burden of Self-development," *Inter-
      Asia Cultural Studies* 10, no. 2 (2009): 229–247.

39 Michael Hadzantonis, *English Language Pedagogies for the Northeast Asian Learner: Developing and Contextually Framing the Transition Theory* (New York: Routledge, 2013), 115.

40 Kim Se-gyun, "Han'gukŭi chŏngch'i chihyŏnggwa ch'otpul sedae" (Korea's political terrain and the candle generation), *Munhwa/Kwahak* (Culture/Science) 63 (2010): 47–65.

41 Wu Sŏk-hun and Pak Kwŏn-il, *88 manwon sedae* (Generation 880-thousand won) (Seoul: Redian, 2007).

42 So, "Pullyang chŏngnyŏn taemangron."

43 Antonio Incorvaia and Alessandro Rimassa, *Generazione mille euro* (Milan: BUR, 2006); "Greece's Lost Generation," *Now Public News,* May 22, 2008; Ediciones El País, "1,000 Euros a Month? Dream On . . . ," *El País,* March 12, 2012; "More Signs That American Youth Are a Lost Generation," *The Atlantic Wire,* September 22, 2011; Michael Zielenziger, *Shutting Out the Sun: How Japan Created Its Own Lost Generation* (New York: Random House, 2006).

44 O Myŏng-ho, *Han'guk chongch'isaŭi ihae* (Understanding Korea's political history) (Seoul: Orum, 2006).

45 Mirae Hankuk, "Chŏnkyojo, sahoe isyu tt'aemada kyeki suŏp charyo ollyŏ" (KTU publishes curriculum for every social issue), *Mirae Hankuk* (Future Korea), November 11, 2005. See also John P. Synott, *Teacher Unions, Social Movements and the Politics of Education in Asia: South Korea, Taiwan and the Philippines* (Burlington, VT: Ashgate, 2002).

46 Myŏng, Interview by author, Seoul, June 17, 2006.

47 Kŏn-ho, interview by author, Seoul, June 2, 2012.

48 Bin-na, interview by author, Seoul, June 5, 2012.

49 Yi Mun-jae and Ch'a Hyung-seok, "02nyŏn olhaeŭi inmul haengdonghanŭn netijŭn" (02 'person of the year' is the activist-netizen), *Sisa Journal,* December 23, 2002; see also T. Y. Lau, Si Wook Kim, and David Atkin, "An Examination of Factors Contributing to South Korea's Global Leadership in Broadband Adoption," *Telematics and Informatics,* WSIS Special Issue: The World Summit on the Information Society (WSIS) from an Asian-Pacific Region Perspective 22, no. 4 (2005): 349–359.

50 The cost further decreased to less than twenty dollars in 2006, although it bounced back to thirty-eight dollars in 2007. However, in 2007 the fee was fifty-three dollars in the United States, sixty in Canada, and forty in Japan. Dal Yong Jin, *Korea's Online Gaming Empire* (Cambridge, MA: MIT Press, 2010), 22.

51 Andrew Moran, "OECD: South Korea High-Speed Internet Penetration Rate Tops 100%," *Digital Journal,* July 23, 2012; Organization for

Economic Cooperation and Development (OECD), "OECD Broadband
Statistics Update," *OECD,* July 18, 2013.

52 Tim Kelly, Vanessa Gray, and Michael Minge, *Broadband Korea: Internet
Case Study* (International Telecommunication Union, March 2003).

53 Guido Ghedin, "Social Media in South Korea: How Facebook Won
Cyworld," *Digital in the Round,* April 4, 2013.

54 Dal Young Jin argues that in the late 1990s the growth of PC bangs
(Internet cafés) equipped with high-speed Internet connections and online
games contributed to the vibrant Internet culture among young Koreans.
Jin, *Korea's Online Gaming Empire.*

55 Yi Chong-wŏn and Yu Sŏng-ho, *Ch'ŏngsonyŏn dul'ŭi onlain keim iyong silt'ae
yŏn'gu* (Study on youth online game use) (Seoul: Korean Youth Development
Institute, 2003).

56 "Kirok ŭro ponŭn o mai nyus 10 nyŏn" (10 years of Oh My News), *Oh My
News,* last modified 2010, accessed May 3, 2014.

57 Pak Chi-hwan, "Simin kija 7man yŏ myŏng, kijon ŏllonkwa ch'abyŏlhwa"
(70,000 citizen reporters, a big distinction from the existing press), *Sinmun
kwa pangsong* (Press and broadcasting), December 2011, 68–73.

58 Charles Ess and Fay Sudweeks, *Culture, Technology, Communication:
Towards an Intercultural Global Village* (Albany: State University of New
York Press, 2001).

59 Hyeongseok Wi and Wonjae Lee, "The Norm of Normlessness: Structural
Correlates of a Trolling Community," in *Proceedings of the 2014 ACM
Conference on Web Science* (New York: ACM, 2014), 275–276; Yi Kil-ho,
Urinŭn DC (We are DC) (Seoul: Imagine, 2012).

60 Agora P'yeindŭl, *Taehanmin'guk sangsik sajŏn Agora.* For the role of political
polemics on Agora, see Jeong-ho Kim, "The Internet and the Public in South
Korea: Online Political Talk and Culture" (PhD diss., University of Illinois,
Urbana–Champaign, 2012).

61 Pak Chi-in, " 'Kwang'upyŏng' Agora t'oronbang chohoe 5200 man kŏn"
("Mad cow disease" Agora page view reached 52 million), *Consumer News,*
May 9, 2008.

62 Chŏng In-hwan, "Pusi panghan pandae kisŭp siwi" (Flash protest against
Bush's visit), *Hankyoreh,* February 15, 2002.

63 Don Kirk, "America on Thin Ice in South Korea," *New York Times,*
March 1, 2002.

64 Hwang Ho-t'aek, "Kamsangjŏk panmi juŭi" (Sentimental anti-Americanism),
Dong-a Ilbo, March 25, 2002.

65 Hahm, "Anti-Americanism, Korean Style"; Jeffrey Robertson, "The Anti-
American Blowback from Bush's Korea Policy," *Foreign Policy in Focus,*
January 2003.

66 "Police Go on Nationwide Alert to Prepare for Massive Crowds," *Korea Times,* June 9, 2002.

67 Ho-young Lee, "The Configuration of the Korean Cyberspace: A Tentative Study on Cultural Traits of Korean Internet Users," *Sahoe kwahak nonch'ong* (The journal of social sciences) 12 (2010): 123–153; Paik Wuk-in, "Saengsanjŏk p'aerŏdi rŭl wihayŏ: Ttanji ilbo rŭl pogo" (Toward productive parody: The case of Ttanji Ilbo), *Tangdae pip'yŏng* (Contemporary criticism) 6, no. 3 (1999): 486–489.

Chapter 2: The Birth of the Internet Youth Protest

1 Kwon Hyŏk-pŏm, "Wŏltŭk'ŏp 'kungmin ch'ukche' pŭllaekhol ppallyŏ tŭrŏgan taehanmin'guk—tongnipchŏk chisŏngŭn ŏdie innŭn'ga?" (The Republic of Korea subsumed under the "national festival" of the World Cup—where are independent intellectuals?), *Tangdae pip'yŏng* (Contemporary criticism) 20 (2002): 62–89.

2 "Pulgŭn angmawa wŏldŭk'ŏp sedae" (The red devils and the World Cup generation), *National Archive,* accessed July 17, 2013.

3 Ch'oe Wŏn-sik, Kim Hong-jun, and Kim Chong-yŏp, "Chŏngdam: Wŏldŭk'ŏp ihu han'gukŭi punhwawa munhwa undong" (Interview: Korean culture and cultural movement after the World Cup), *Ch'angjakkwa pip'yŏng* (Creation and criticism) 117 (2002): 14–54.

4 Kim Hyŏn-mi, "2002nyŏn wŏldŭk'ŏpŭi yŏsŏnghwawa yŏsŏng p'aentŏm" (The feminization of the 2002 World Cup and the female fandom), *Tangdae pip'yŏng* (Contemporary criticism) 20 (2002): 48–61.

See also Chŏng Chin-wung, "Pulkŭn mulkyŏl hyŏnsangŭl t'onghae pon yokmangŭi munhwachŏngch'ihak, kŭ ch'angchowa kusŏng sai" (Cultural politics of desire in the red wave phenomenon), *Tangdae pip'yŏng* (Contemporary criticism) 20 (2002): 8–23; Yi Yun-hŭi, "2002nyŏn wŏldŭk'ŏp kilgŏri ŭngwŏnŭi ch'ukche kongdongch'ejŏk t'ŭksŏng" (Characteristics of street cheering as festival community at the 2002 World Cup and its sociocultural implications), *Sahoewa iron* (Society and theory) 3 (2003): 125–156.

5 Sergeants Nino and Walker were found not guilty of negligent homicide on November 20 and November 22. Kim Chun "Mujoe p'yŏlgyŏl migun 2myŏng kot chŏnyŏk chŏnch'ul" (The two "acquitted" soon to be transferred and discharged), *Chosun Ilbo,* November 26, 2002.

6 Young-sup Kwak, "Court Clears U.S. Soldier of Killing Korean Girls," *Korea Herald,* November 21, 2002.

7 Ch'oe Yun-jung, "Migun changbi kyŏlham ch'isa' mujoerani" (Failure of communication devices? Cannot accept a not-guilty verdict), *Chosun Ilbo,* November 22, 2002; Chŏng Kwang-sup and Suh Chung-min, "Migun pŏpjŏng, hankukin kiman urong, sopa kaejŏng chaep'ankwon iyang

'mokch'ŏng" ("U.S. court deceived Koreans," mounting demand for SOFA Revision), *Hankyoreh,* November 21, 2002.

8 "Sasŏl: Migunmanŭi baesim ppŏnhan p'yŏnggyŏl" (Editorial: A jury of U.S. officials, the verdict was expected), *Chosun Ilbo,* November 22, 2002; "Sasŏl: Migun mujoe hang'ŭirŭl p'okryŏkŭro ŏkaphan kyŏngch'al" (Editorial: Excessive police violence in the protests against the GIs acquittal), *Hankyoreh,* November 23, 2002.

9 Chung-Laden, "Mich'igetneyŏ" (It drives me crazy), *Moim,* November 21, 2002; Torongii, "Urinŭn shingminji paeksŏngi animnida!!" (We are not a colony!!), *Moim,* November 22, 2002; Oasis, "11wŏl 1il paekakkwan saibŏ t'erŏ chakchŏn!!" (Cyber terror on the White House on December 1!!), *Moim,* November 21, 2002.

10 A Life For You, "Han'guk? Sŏnjin'guk? Kaesori hane :P :P :P" (Korea? A developed country? It's a joke :P :P :P), *Moim,* November 24, 2002.

11 Katharine Moon's *Protesting America* offers an excellent comprehensive analysis of South Korean movements against the U.S. military presence. As she describes, a large number of NGOs were established in the 1990s around human rights, women's rights, and the environment, and, simultaneously, crimes by GIs, toxic wastewater from bases, and the terms of land use established in the 1950s drew public attention. Since then, Korean activists protesting the terms of the U.S. military presence have made SOFA a "household word" by campaigning aggressively for its revision. Katharine H. S. Moon, *Protesting America: Democracy and the U.S.–Korea Alliance* (Berkeley: University of California Press, 2013), 125.

12 Robert Hariman and John Louis Lucaites, *No Caption Needed: Iconic Photographs, Public Culture, and Liberal Democracy* (Chicago: University of Chicago Press, 2007), 198.

13 Huhui, "Nach'am ŏiga ŏpsŏsŏri . . . Migundŭl wanjŏn kaesaekkidŭlineyo . . ." (Well, I'm speechless . . . Those GIs are beasts . . .), *Moim,* November 24, 2002; T. T., "Ttibal miguk . . ." (Damn, U.S. . . .), *Moim,* November 24, 2002.

14 "2002 Taehanmin'guk?" (2002 Great Korea?), "Re: Ch'umo mak'ŭ ŏnjebut'ŏ saengkyŏtŏyo? Choesong, chŏngmal kunggŭmhaesŏyo" (Re: Where did the commemoration mark first come from? Sorry, I'm Just Curious), *Moim,* November 30, 2002.

15 Nikneim, "Sarin migugi mujoemyŏn" (If the murderous U.S. was not guilty), *Moim,* November 25, 2002.

16 I Hate My Country, "Hanmadiro . . . urinaranŭn ŏnjekkajina . . . miguge tcholttagu saenghwarŭl halsubagenŭn" (In a nutshell, we're doomed to be subordinate to the U.S.), *Moim,* November 21, 2002.

17 This parody was posted more than once in the wake of the verdicts. For example, LOVEØIS, "Chŏnŭn,,," (I am,,,), *Moim*, November 26, 2002; Kim Wansu, "Kinkŭpsokpo: Osama Bin Laden pŏpjŏngesŏ mujoe sŏngo!!!" (Breaking news: Osama Bin Laden found not guilty at court!!!), *Moim*, November 22, 2002.

18 Robert Hariman, "Political Parody and Public Culture," *Quarterly Journal of Speech* 94, no. 3 (2008): 253, 255.

19 Mikhail Bakhtin, *Problems of Dostoevsky's Poetics*, ed. and trans. Caryl Emerson (Minneapolis: University of Minnesota Press, 1984), 193.

20 A cartoonist using the pen name Kang Full was the author. After his 2003 formal debut he quickly became one of the most popular cartoonists in South Korea, and his distinctive cartoons are now well known among the public. However, in 2002 his style was not widely recognized, and this commemorative cartoon was identified as anonymous.

21 Using a poetic style in commemorative postings is a characteristic of the Internet discourse of the period. It should be mentioned that the Korean custom of online writing includes writing short lines while double-spacing for better readability, and therefore many online posts appear to be a poem.

22 The ellipses are in the original. Nautes, "Yaedŭra, kŭrigo yŏrŏbun choesonghapnida" (Girls, and all of you, I'm sorry), *Moim*, November 22, 2002.

23 Zizi A. Papacharissi, *Affective Publics: Sentiment, Technology, and Politics.* Kindle ed. (New York: Oxford University Press, 2014), 638.

24 buzz, "Chigŭm" (Now), *Moim*, November 27, 2002; Kŭnani, "Hu . . ." (Alas . . .), *Moim*, November 27, 2002; Kim Dŏk-yŏn, "Uriga taehanmin'guk kukmininga?" (Are we Korean people?), *Moim*, November 27, 2002.

25 Kim Chi-ŭn, "Wŏltŭk'ŏp hwanho kwanghwamunsŏ ch'otpul siwi Hyosun Misŏn ch'umo 1mannyŏ myŏng unjip" (10,000 gathered to commemorate Hyo-sun and Mi-sŏn in Kwanghwamun, the epicenter of the World Cup cheering), *Oh My News*, January 5, 2003.

26 Wish You Were Happy, "Ibamjungedo 20myŏngi nŏmŭn saramdŭri chŏpsok'aeinneyo" (More than 20 members are logged on tonight), *Moim*, November 27, 2002; Mr. Sŏninjang, "Kwanghwamunŭro Moipsida !!!!!!!!!!!!!!!!!!!!!!" (Let's Go to Kwanghwamun !!!!!!!!!!!!!!!!!!!!!!), *Moim*, November 26, 2002; Wangch'ik, "12wŏl 1il midaesagwan apesŏ moipsida" (Let's meet in front of the U.S. Embassy on December 1), *Moim*, November 27, 2002.

27 Kim So-yŏn, "Ch'otbulsiwi chean net'ijŭn 'angma' omainyusŭ sŏnjŏng 'olhaeŭi inmul" (Netizen Angma, who proposed the candlelight vigils, is the

"person of the year" chosen by Oh My News), *Oh My News,* December 31, 2002.

28 Hayan Pada, "Sop'a kaejonge kyoljipdoen net'ijun p'awo" (Netizens join forces for SOFA reform), *Moim,* December 7, 2002.

29 Yurich'onsa, "Re: Kŭge paro sopa hyŏkchŏngiyeyo" (Re: That is SOFA), *Moim,* November 30, 2002; prefer, "Kŭdongan migukŭi ŏpjŏk(?)dŭl!!" (The great works(?) by the U.S.!!), *Moim,* November 30, 2002; PureMind, "Chinan 60nyŏngan migugi urinarae chŏjirŭn manhaeng" (What the U.S. has done to us for the last 60 years), *Moim,* December 1, 2002.

30 Kim Dŏk-yŏn, "Uriga taehanmin'guk"; Oogiboogi, "Tae! Han! Min! Kuk! Kwanghwamun midaesagwan apesŏ taegyumo siwihapnida" (Great! Korea! Let's stage a massive protest in front of the U.S. Embassy in Kwanghwamun), *Moim,* November 27, 2002; Noir, "Chŏngukjŏk taegyomo chiphoe--tŏisang sogyumo chiphoeronŭn ssido anmŏphinda" (A massive national protest--small-scale protests don't work anymore), *Moim,* November 27, 2002; Pina, "Choppari miguk hant'e han'gukminŭi himŭl poyŏjupsida" (Let's demonstrate the Korean people's power to the U.S.), *Moim,* November 26, 2002; Wangch'ik, "12wŏl 1il."

31 Rachael Joo similarly argues that the memories of participating in the 2002 World Cup contributed to creating possibilities for large-scale protests. Rachael Miyung Joo, *Transnational Sport: Gender, Media, and Global Korea* (Durham, NC: Duke University Press, 2012), 251.

32 "Sasŏl: Pusi sagwawa apŭroŭi hanmi tongmang" (Editorial: Bush's apology and the future Korea–U.S. Alliance), *Chosun Ilbo,* November 28, 2002.

33 "Sasŏl: 'Panmi' nŏmŏ haebŏp ch'atja" (Editorial: Let's find solution beyond "anti-Americanism"), *Chosun Ilbo,* November 29, 2002.

34 Ibid. See also Chu Yŏng-jung, "Ŏnron, min'gan kigwan panŭng: mi 'han'guk panmi simgak'" (Media and public response: Americans think "Korean Anti-Americanism is a serious problem"), *Chosun Ilbo,* November 29, 2002.

35 Ryu Jae-hun, "Pusi sagwa anp'ak, panmi kamjŏng pulgil uryŏ" (Bush's apology, concerns about rising anti-American sentiment), *Hankyoreh,* November 28, 2002.

36 See, for example, Ch'oe Chŏng-ku, "Chagungmin musihanŭn sop'a wihŏn choyak" (SOFA, an "unconstitutional treaty" that disregards the Korean people), *Hankyoreh,* November 30, 2002; Hong Sŏng-han, "Chaep'anjŏng chubyŏn siwidae-chŏnggyŏng taerip 'wae urikkiri ssauna' hyŏnsil taptap" (Clash between Korean protesters and police, "why are we fighting each other?"), *Hankyoreh,* November 23, 2002.

37 "Sasŏl: Pulpyŏngdŭng sopa chaehyŏpsang sijak hara" (Editorial: Begin the
renegotiation of unfair SOFA), *Hankyoreh,* November 24, 2002.

38 Ch'oe, "Chagungmin musihanŭn sop'a."

39 Ryu, "Pusi sagwa anp'ak."

40 "Sasŏl: Pusi sagwawa apŭroŭi hanmi tongmang."

41 For example, Hong, "Chaep'anjŏng chubyŏn siwidae-chŏngyŏng"; Yi Min-ji
and Pak Tae-yong, "Changgapch'a samang yŏjungsaeng migun mujoe
p'yŏnggyŏlŭl pogo" (Upon the acquittal of the GIs who killed the
schoolgirls), *Hankyoreh,* November 23, 2002.

Chapter 3: The Internet in Mainstream Politics

1 Yeon-Ok Lee, "Internet Election 2.0? Culture, Institutions, and Technology
in the Korean Presidential Elections of 2002 and 2007," *Journal of
Information Technology & Politics* 6, nos. 3–4 (2009): 312. See also Noriko
Hara and Youngmin Jo, "Internet Politics: A Comparative Analysis of U.S.
and South Korea Presidential Campaigns," *First Monday* 12, no. 9 (2007).

2 Scholars have explained Roh's dramatic victory as resulting from the voting
strength of younger segments of the electorate, from the anti-Americanism
educed by the girls' deaths, and from the scandals surrounding Roh's
opponent, Lee Hoi-chang. However, I consider these not as causes but rather
as visible outcomes of the convergence of Internet and mainstream politics.
See, for instance, Byong-Kuen Jhee, "Anti-Americanism and Electoral
Politics in Korea," *Political Science Quarterly* 123, no. 2 (2008): 301–318;
Mary Joyce, "The Citizen Journalism Web Site 'OhmyNews' and the 2002
South Korean Presidential Election," *Berkman Center Research Publication*
No. 2007–15 (December 2007); Mark E. Manyin, *South Korean Politics and
Rising "Anti-Americanism": Implications for US Policy Toward North Korea,*
Report for Congress (2003).

3 Howard W. French and Don Kirk, "American Policies and Presence Are
under Fire in South Korea, Straining an Alliance," *New York Times,*
December 8, 2002, p. 20.

4 Hoon Jaung, "President Roh Moo-Hyun and the New Politics of South
Korea," *Asia Society,* 2003.

5 In the MDP's "people's primaries," an electoral college of seventy
thousand cast votes: 20 percent were members of the National Council, which
traditionally elected presidential candidates; 30 percent were party members.
The MDP also invited any Korean voter to apply to become part of the
electoral college, and these new additions constituted 50 percent of those
voting in the primaries. In the 2002 primaries 1.84 million Koreans applied
for the thirty-five thousand seats available. Chang Hun, "16tae taesŏnŭgwa

hubo sŏnch'ulgwanjŏng: Chŏngdang kaehyŏkŭi kyŏngjaeng" (The sixteenth presidential election and the process of electing candidates: A competition for party reform), in *16tae Taesŏnŭi Sŏngŏ Kwajŏnggwa Ŭiui* (The process and implications of the sixteenth presidential election), ed. Kim Se-gyun (Seoul: Seoul National University Press, 2003), 3–28.

6 Chang Hun, "16tae taesŏnŭgwa hubo."

7 An Pu-kŭn, "16tae taesŏnŭi chijido byŏnhwawa t'up'yo kyŏlgwa" (Changes in the approval rate and the election result in the sixteenth presidential election), in Kim Se-gyun, *16tae Taesŏnŭi Sŏngŏgwajŏnggwa Ŭiŭi*, 81–104.

8 Political scientist Eui Hang Shin found that regionalism, one of the most influential determinants of South Korean elections, had less impact on the 2002 election than on the previous two presidential elections; meanwhile, the younger generation's support for Roh, their anti-Americanism, and the growing sympathy for North Korea certainly contributed to the election result. Eui Hang Shin, "Correlates of the 2002 Presidential Election in South Korea: Regionalism, the Generation Gap, Anti-Americanism, and the North Korea Factor," *East Asia* 21, no. 2 (2004): 18–38. See also Hong Yung Lee, "South Korea in 2002: Multiple Political Dramas," *Asian Survey* 43, no. 1 (2003): 64–77.

9 Jaung, "President Roh Moo-Hyun."

10 Sook-Jong Lee, "The Rise of Korean Youth as a Political Force," *Brookings Northeast Asia Survey 2003–2004* (2004).

11 Victor D. Cha, "America and South Korea: The Ambivalent Alliance?," *Current History* 102 (2003): 279–284; Chaibong Hahm, "South Korea's Miraculous Democracy," *Journal of Democracy* 19, no. 3 (2008): 128–142.

12 Kim Yong-ho, "Int'ŏnet k'ŏmyunit'iwa chŏngch'i: Nosamo sarye yŏn'gu" (Internet community and politics: A study of Rohsamo), in *Proceedings from the 2003 Korean Sociological Association Biannual Conference* (Seoul: Korean Sociological Association, 2003), 519–541; Jae-Yun Moon and Shinkyu Yang, "The Internet as an Agent of Political Change: The Case of 'Rohsamo' in the South Korean Presidential Campaign of 2002," in *International Conference on Information Systems 2003 Proceeding* (Seattle: Association for Information Systems, 2003), 903–908.

13 Chŏn Chong-hwi, "Kijŏkŭl mandŭn 7man siminŭi him" (Seventy thousand citizens who made a miracle), *Hankyoreh,* December 19, 2002.

14 Fifty-eight percent of voters in their fifties and 64 percent of voters in their sixties voted for Lee. An, "16tae Taesŏnŭi Chijido."

15 Yi Mi-ju, "Pusan simindŭl ilgojuseyo" (Pusan citizens, please read this), *Moim,* June 28, 2002; Paekt'ongsin'gibigaksul, "Chŏngmallo . . . chŏngmallo" (Really . . . really), *Moim,* November 25, 2002; Kim Pa-da, "Yŏrŏbun! Uri

modu ch'amyŏhapsida" (Folks! Let's all participate), *Moim,* November 30, 2002.

16 Haebaragi, "Chŏngmal" (Indeed), *Moim,* November 24, 2002.

17 Haegyŏlsa, "Taehanminguki chugwŏngukkanya?" (Is the Republic of Korea a sovereign nation?), *Moim,* December 1, 2002.

18 Media scholars Bruce Hardy, Kathleen Hall Jamieson, and Kenneth Winneg find that mistrust of mainstream U.S. media coverage of elections increases cynicism toward politics and leads to reliance on the Internet. Bruce Hardy, Kathleen Hall Jamieson, and Kenneth Winneg, "Wired to Fact: The Role of the Internet in Identifying Deception during the 2004 U.S. Presidential Campaign," in *Routledge Handbook of Internet Politics,* ed. Andrew Chadwick and Philip N. Howard (New York: Taylor & Francis, 2010), 131–143.

19 "Sasŏl: 'Panmi' nŏmŏ haebŏp ch'atja" (Editorial: Let's find a solution beyond "anti-Americanism"), *Chosun Ilbo,* November 29, 2002, 2.

20 Editorial, *JoongAng Ilbo,* December 3, 2002.

21 Developing Alfred Gell's concept of captivation, Anne D'Alleva explains captivation as a metonymic evocation of the origination process. Like a metonym (an attribute or part that evokes the whole), captivation with an object points to the existence of the invisible yet potent larger forces that brought the object into being. Anne D'Alleva, "Captivation, Representation, and the Limits of Cognition: Interpreting Metaphor and Metonymy in Tahitian Tamau," in *Beyond Aesthetics: Art and the Technologies of Enchantment,* ed. Christopher Pinney and Nicholas Thomas (Oxford: Berg, 2001), 79–96.

22 Hanmanŭnja, "Annyŏng" (Hello), *Moim,* December 1, 2002.

23 Cho Chang-hŭi, "Roh Moo-hyun taesŏn hubokke put'akhago sipsŭpnida" (I would ask this to presidential candidate Roh Moo-hyun), *Moim,* October 7, 2002.

24 SadSpirit, "T'up'yrŭl hago nasŏ" (After casting vote), *Moim,* December 19, 2002.

25 jazu, "Ssŏkŭn chŏnch'iin 1pŏn, hobo 1pŏni sopa gaejŏng sŏmyŏngundong sŏnp'osike kandago hanŭnde" (The no. 1 corrupt politician, candidate no.1 goes to the ceremony launching the petition for SOFA reform), *Moim,* December 19, 2002.

26 Many online postings appear to have the format of a poem because of the online custom of writing short lines and double-spacing for better readability. Chŏngbuyŏ Pukkŭrŏunjul Alla, "Ukyŏk tajim, Lee Hoichang bŏjŏn" (Angry speech, by Lee Hoi-chang), *Moim,* December 6, 2002.

27 In "Epic and Novel," Mikhail Bakhtin notes that laughter as a discursive strategy destroys the "absolute past" by eliminating the distance that keeps

the past incontestable. When a person can laugh at an object that he or she once feared, the laughter shows that person has managed to "demolish fear before an object." Mikhail M. Bakhtin, "Epic and Novel," in *The Dialogic Imagination,* ed. Michael Holquist (Austin: University of Texas Press, 1981), 21–23.

28 Jürgen Habermas, *The Structural Transformation of the Public Sphere,* trans. Thomas Burger and F. Lawrence (1962; Cambridge, MA: MIT Press, 1989); Walter Lippmann, *Public Opinion* (New York: Harcourt, Brace, and Co., 1922); Max Weber, "The Nature of Charismatic Authority and Its Routinization," in *Max Weber: On Charisma and Institution Building* (1922; Chicago: University of Chicago Press, 1968).

29 Habermas, *Structural Transformation,* 195.

30 It was the Frankfurt School scholars who were most troubled by the illusion and false satisfaction offered by modern culture. See Max Horkheimer and Theodor W. Adorno, *Dialectic of Enlightenment: Philosophical Fragments* (1947; Stanford, CA: Stanford University Press, 2002).

31 Habermas, *Structural Transformation,* 160.

32 Clay Shirky, *Here Comes Everybody: The Power of Organizing without Organizations* (New York: Penguin Press, 2008).

33 Cho Gabje, "Sŭt'aensŭrŭl irŭn Lee Hoi-chang" (Lee Hoi-chang lost his stance), *chogabje.com,* December 6, 2002.

34 Clay Shirky, "The Political Power of Social Media," *Foreign Affairs,* January 1, 2011.

35 Hanaa, "Yŏjungsaeng haegyŏlŭl wihae: Taet'ongryŏng huboege sŏyaksŏrŭl ponaeja!!-Ansan" (Let's demand a pledge from the presidential candidates: To solve the issue of the girls!!-Ansan), *Moim,* December 4, 2002.

36 Manuel Castells, *Communication Power* (Oxford: University of Oxford Press, 2009), 286.

37 As I discussed in chapter 1, the activism of South Korea's democratization movement in the 1980s affected mainstream politics through protests that often entailed violent confrontation with police and the sacrifice of young protesters. Scholarship on counterpublics has illustrated how marginalized groups gain visibility in the larger public through strategies that induce shock and through risqué performances that attract attention. Daniel C. Brouwer, "ACT-ing up in Congressional Hearings," in *Counterpublics and the State,* ed. Robert Asen and Daniel Brouwer (Albany: State University of New York Press, 2001), 87–110; John W. Delicath and Kevin Michael DeLuca, "Image Events, the Public Sphere, and Argumentative Practice: The Case of Radical Environmental Groups," *Argumentation* 17, no. 3 (2003): 315–333.

38 yerbenbi!, "Naeil Kwanghwamune Lee Hoi-changi opnida (P'ildok)" (Lee Hoi-chang is coming to Kwanghwamun tomorrow! [Must Read]), *Moim,*

December 7, 2002; (Chu) Hyeyoung, "Ch'otpul siwi cheanhasyŏtton puni ssŭngŭl p'ŏwatsŭpnida. . . . chŏngmal orŭn malipnida" (I copied and pasted the posting by the proposer of the candlelight vigils. . . . I completely agree with him), *Moim,* December 7, 2002.

39 Koindol, "Chŏngch'iin nomdŭliran!!!" (Those politicians are!!!), *Moim,* December 9, 2002.

40 Sarang'aga, "Parŏni . . . chom" (That comment was . . . a little), *Moim,* December 8, 2002.

41 Chŏn-Hong Ki-hye, " 'Sŏdaep'yo, tangsindo pumoipnikka'—hannara sŏch'ŏngwon taep'yo 'poiji annŭn son' parŏn p'amun" ("Representative Sŏ, are you a parent?"—the "invisible hand" statement by Representative Sŏ Chŏng-wŏn of GNP generates a sensation), *PRESSian,* December 10, 2002.

42 Opt'ik Lŏbŭ, "Hannara dang'ŭn misoni wa hyosuniŭi chukŭmŭl hŏktoeke haji malla" (GNP, You should not make the deaths of Hyosun and Misŏn be in vain), *Moim,* December 9, 2002.

43 Ch'ŏnnyŏn sarang, "P'ŏm: Hannaradang Sŏ Chŏng-wŏn taep'yo poiji annŭn son parŏn" (Reposting: GNP Representative Sŏ Chŏng-wŏn's "invisible hand" statement), *Moim,* December 10, 2002.

44 Ibid.

45 Ibid.

46 "Panmiŭi poiji annŭn son ije chom poisijo?" (Do you now see the invisible hand of anti-Americanism?), *Oh My News,* December 15, 2002.

47 Ch'ŏnnyŏn sarang, "P'ŏm: Hannara dang Sŏ Chŏng-wŏn taep'yo."

48 Rhetorical scholar Catherine Squires's concept of oscillation considers this contingent connection and disconnection between an oppositional group and mainstream politics, even though her language evokes entering and withdrawing instead of connecting and disconnecting. Squires argues that a social group in opposition to dominant norms does not merely remain in enclaves outside of mainstream politics; instead, it rises to challenge the dominant society, faces threats, retreats into enclaves, and rises again in critique. Catherine Squires, "The Black Press and the State," in *Counterpublics and the State,* ed. Robert Asen and Daniel C. Brouwer (Albany: State University of New York Press, 2001), 111–126.

49 Kim Chi-ŭn, "Kwanghwamun e simin dŭri moyŏdŭlgo itta" (Citizens are on their way to Kwanghwamun), *Oh My News,* December 19, 2002.

50 Chajugukgarŭl Kkumkkumyŏ, "Re: Uri taehanminguki paljŏnhalsu itnŭn iyu" (Re: Reasons that our Republic of Korea can advance), *Moim,* February 12, 2003.

51 Hŭkmong Taehanminkuk, "Re: K'at'usa sŏngp'okhaeng migun yujeo p'yŏnggyŏl" (Re: U.S. GI found guilty for raping a KATUSA), *Moim,* February 13, 2003.

52 hansamuna, "Ehyu" (Aw), *Moim,* January 16, 2003.

53 Kim Kang-t'ae, "Re: Re: Puranhan maŭm" (Re: Re: Anxious mind), *Moim,* January 17, 2003.

54 Taehanminguk, "Roh Moo-hyun! Chŏngmal chŏngch'irŭl muŏlro anŭn kŏpnikka?" (Roh Moo-hyun! You think politics is nothing?), *Moim,* December 4, 2003.

55 Chajugukgarŭl Kkumkkumyŏ, "Han'gukkun irakŭ p'abyŏngŭl pandaehanda!" (I oppose sending Korean troops to Iraq!), *Moim,* March 18, 2003.

56 Isipyukse Ch'ungnyŏn, "Pyŏnhangŏti ŏpta. pyonhangŏti ŏpnŭnde urinŭn wae chujŏhanŭnga" (Nothing has changed, why do we hesitate when nothing has changed?), *Moim,* January 10, 2003.

57 Hagi99, "1 wŏl 5 il pup'yŏng munhwaŭi kŏri ch'otpul haengsa pogoipnida" (Report on the candlelight ceremony at the Pup'yŏng cultural fair on January 5), *Moim,* January 6, 2003.

58 Joyce, "The Citizen Journalism Web Site 'OhmyNews.'"

59 Kim Yŏng-sun, "Roh Moo-Hyun chŏngbuŭi pokchijŏngch'aek" (The assessment of the social welfare policies in the Roh Moo-Hyun government), *Kyŏngjewa sahoe* (Economy and society) 82 (2009): 161–185.

60 Anthony Faiola, "Court Rejects S. Korean President's Impeachment," *Washington Post,* May 14, 2004.

61 Many studies have found that the Internet is a space for discussing political agendas, spreading information, and motivating citizens to vote. For instance, Byoungkwan Lee, Karen M. Lancendorfer, and Ki Jung Lee, "Agenda-Setting and the Internet: The Intermedia Influence of Internet Bulletin Boards on Newspaper Coverage of the 2000 General Election in South Korea," *Asian Journal of Communication* 15, no. 1 (2005): 57–71; Dick Morris, *Vote.com: Influence, and the Internet Is Giving Power Back to the People* (New York: Macmillan, 2011); Pippa Norris, "Did the Media Matter? Agenda-Setting, Persuasion and Mobilization Effects in the British General Election Campaign," *British Politics* 1, no. 2 (2006): 195–221; Sarah Oates, Diana Owen, and Rachel K. Gibson, *The Internet and Politics: Citizens, Voters and Activists* (London: Routledge, 2006); Andrew Paul Williams and John C. Tedesco, *The Internet Election: Perspectives on the Web in Campaign 2004* (Lanham, MD: Rowman & Littlefield, 2006).

62 Emily Schultheis, "Poll: Millennials Disillusioned with President Obama," *Politico,* December 4, 2013.

Chapter 4: Remembering the Vigils

1   The general election of June 2006, in which the conservative Grand National Party won a landslide victory over Roh Moo-hyun's Millennium Democratic Party, affirms this change. Kim Kwang-dŏk, "Taesŏn 1nyŏnjŏn

kukmin ŭisik chosa . . . chinbo chulgo chungdo nŭlŏtta" (Opinion poll one year before presidential election . . . less progressive more moderate), *Hankook Ilbo,* December 8, 2006.

2   For more details about the collaboration and tensions between participants organized on the Internet and traditional activists during the 2002 candlelight vigils, see Jinsun Lee, "Net Power in Action: Internet Activism in the Contentious Politics of South Korea" (PhD diss., Rutgers University, 2009).

3   The Akira Kurosawa film *Rashomon* was released in 1950, but the term "Rashomon effect" has been used since the late 1970s. For more discussion on the academic adoption of the term, see Karl G. Heider, "The Rashomon Effect: When Ethnographers Disagree," *American Anthropologist* 90, no. 1 (1988): 78.

4   Sidney Tarrow, "Cycles of Collective Action: Between Moments of Madness and the Repertoire of Contention," *Social Science History* 17, no. 2 (1993): 286. See also Charles Tilly, "Contentious Repertoires in Great Britain, 1758–1834," in *Repertoire and Cycles of Collection Action,* ed. Mark Traugott (Durham, NC: Duke University Press, 1995), 15–42; Mark Traugott, "Barricades as Repertoire: Continuities and Discontinuities in the History of French Contention," in Traugott, *Repertoire and Cycles,* 43–56.

5   Danielle S. Allen, *Talking to Strangers: Anxieties of Citizenship since Brown v. Board of Education* (Chicago: University of Chicago Press, 2006), 10.

6   Ŭn-ha, interview by author, Seoul, South Korea, June 14, 2006.

7   W. Lance Bennett and Alexandra Segerberg, *The Logic of Connective Action: Digital Media and the Personalization of Contentious Politics* (Cambridge: Cambridge University Press), 2014.

8   Hye-gŭn, interview by author, Seoul, South Korea, June 19, 2006.

9   Chin-su, Ho-wŏn, and Si-yŏng, group interview by author, Seoul, South Korea, June 13, 2006.

10 Arthur Kleinman and Joan Kleinman, "How Bodies Remember: Social Memory and Bodily Experience of Criticism, Resistance, and Delegitimation Following China's Cultural Revolution," *New Literary History* 25 (2004): 707–723.

11 Edward Casey, *Remembering: A Phenomenological Study*, 2nd ed. (Bloomington: Indiana University Press, 2000), 149.

12 An Sun-dŭk et al., "Haksaeng kyoyukwŏnŭi kyoyukchŏngch'aek punsŏk" (Analysis of educational programs of student training centers) (Seoul: Korean Women's Development Institute, 1991).

13 Myungkoo Kang, "Compressed Modernization and the Formation of the Developmentalist Mentalité," in *Reassessing the Park Chung Hee Era, 1961– 1979: Development, Political Thought, Democracy, and Cultural Influence,*

ed. Hyung-A Kim and Clark W. Sorensen (Seattle: University of Washington Press, 2011), 166–186.

14 Yun-ji, interview by author, Seoul, South Korea, June 8, 2006.

15 Nam-hŭi, Hyo-ju, and Myŏng, group interview by author, Seoul, South Korea, June 17, 2006.

16 Chŏng Yun-su, "Kunsabu ilch'e, ch'eryŏk tallyŏn, ch'otpul ŭisik kŭkki hullyŏn, kŭgŏ kkok pataya halkkayo?" (The unity of leader, teacher, and father, physical trainings, candle ceremonies: Do students need them?), *Oh My News,* April 17, 2007.

17 Ibid.

18 Hwang Byŏng-ju, "Park Chung Hee sidae ch'ukkuk wa minjok juŭi: kukkajuŭijŏk tongwŏn kwa kukmin hyŏngsŏng" (The Park Chung Hee era nationalism: Mobilization by the state and the formation of the people), *Tangdae pip'yŏng* (Contemporary criticism) 19 (2002): 145–187.

19 Kang Su-dol, "Woldŭk'ŏp 4 kang'gwa 'kyŏngje 4 kang' sinhwa" (The World Cup semifinal and the myth of the "semifinal in economic development"), *Tangdae pip'yong* (Contemporary criticism) 20 (2002): 90–110.

20 Paul Connerton, "Cultural Memory," in *Handbook of Material Culture,* ed. Christopher Tilley, et al. (London: Sage, 2006), 315–324.

21 Saba Mahmood, "Feminist Theory, Embodiment, and the Docile Agent: Some Reflections on the Egyptian Islamic Revival," *Cultural Anthropology* 16, no. 2 (2001): 216. See also Timothy Reiss, "Denying the Body? Memory and the Dilemmas of History in Descartes," *The Journal of the History of Ideas* 57, no. 4 (1996): 587–607.

22 Casey, *Remembering,* 192.

23 Anthropologist Heonik Kwon proposes the "decomposition of the Cold War" in lieu of the end of the Cold War to underscore that the post–Cold War transition was not a break but a local participatory process. Heonik Kwon, *The Other Cold War* (New York: Columbia University Press, 2010), 8.

24 Ministry of National Defense, *Kukpang paeksŏ* (Ministry of National Defense white paper), 2012.

25 Hun, Chin-su, Ho-wŏn, and Si-yŏng, group interview by author, Seoul, South Korea, June 17, 2006.

26 "Eighth United States Army (EUSA)," *Global Security,* December 1, 2006.

27 Eighth Army Public Affairs, "KATUSAs Stand as Symbol of ROK-U.S. Alliance," *The United States Army,* November 1, 2011.

28 Yi Hyŏng-sam, "K'at'usa 50nyŏn kkumdo yŏngŏro kkunŭn ellit'ŭ pyŏngsadŭl" (Fifty years of KATUSA: Elite soldiers who even dream in English), *Sindong'a,* May 2001.

29 Wŏn-hŭi, group interview by author, Seoul, South Korea, July 6, 2006.

30 Wŏn-hŭi and Ho-jun, group interview by author, Seoul, South Korea, July 6, 2006.

31 Sŏn-hee, interview by author, Seoul, South Korea, June 8, 2006.

32 Su-min, interview by author, Seoul, South Korea, June 17, 2006.

33 Chu-yŏng, interview by author, Seoul, South Korea, June 8, 2006.

34 Ka-in, interview by author. Seoul, South Korea, June 8, 2006.

35 Tarrow, "Cycles of Collective Action," 282–283.

36 Hyŏn-ho, interview by author, Yangju, South Korea, June 20, 2006.

37 Po-mun, interview by author, Seoul, South Korea, July 21, 2006.

38 Hong-min, interview by author, Seoul, South Korea, July 22, 2006.

39 The 1980s oppositional movement found its roots in the peasant movement of the late nineteenth century that resisted the invasion of Western powers and Japanese colonizers. Korean peasants fought against those colonizers with spears and other simple weapons, and some left their land and went to China or Manchuria to organize against Japanese rule. This peasant movement, in particular the 1894 Tonghak Uprising, symbolized grassroots power, sacrifice, and patriotism, and the 1980s *minjung* movement took it as a historical model. Namhee Lee, *The Making of Minjung: Democracy and the Politics of Representation in South Korea* (Ithaca, NY: Cornell University Press), 2007.

40 Hyŏn-ho, interview by author, Yangju, South Korea, June 20, 2006.

41 Su-min, interview by author, Seoul, South Korea, June 14, 2006.

42 Ibid.

43 Ibid.

44 T'ae-ju, interview by author, Seoul, South Korea, July 11, 2006.

45 Ibid.

46 Ibid.

47 "South Korea Youth Unemployment," *The Global Economy.*

48 Ŭn-ha, interview by author, Seoul, South Korea, June 14, 2006.

49 Yi Ŏ-yŏng, "Chiralt'an, sagwat'anŭl kiŏk hasipnikka?" (Do you remember tear gas bombs?), *JoongAng Ilbo,* June 9, 2007.

50 An Sŏn-hŭi, "Sahŏe chuyŏk tt'ŏorŭn p'i sedae" (Generation P: A new leader of society), *Hankyoreh,* June 9, 2003.

51 Ŭn-ha, interview by author, Seoul, South Korea, June 14, 2006.

52 Myŏng, interview by author, Seoul, South Korea, June 17, 2006.

53 Casey, *Remembering,* 191–192.

Chapter 5: Internet Activism Transforming Street Politics

1 Andante, "1chŏnman sŏmyŏng: Kukhoe e Lee Myung-bak taet'ongryŏng t'anhaekŭl yogu hamnida" (Ten million signatures: We demand the impeachment of Lee Myung-bak), *Agora,* April 6, 2008.

2   On April 29 *PD Journal* broadcast a report titled "American Beef, Is It Safe from Mad Cow Disease?" Video clips from the show were among the most widely circulated in these online discussions. David Brown, "The 'Recipe for Disaster' That Killed 80 and Left a £5bn Bill," *The Telegraph,* April 7, 2008.

3   During this period, health and medical experts appeared both in mass media and on the Internet, claiming that "95% of Koreans have methionin/methionin (M/M), a genetic factor more vulnerable to BSE" and accusing public agencies of defending the government while forsaking the safety of citizens. Sung-gi Hong, "A Look at the Changes in Debate Structure in Korea through the Candlelight Vigils," *Korea Journal* 50, no. 3 (2010): 113.

4   Ch'u Kwang-kyu, "Taet'ongryŏng t'anhaek chean . . . ko 2 haksaeng" (Proposal for impeachment . . . from an eleventh-grader), *Sinmungo,* May 4, 2008; Kang Yun-jae, "Kwangubyŏng wihŏmgwa ch'otpulchip'oe" (The risk of BSE and the candlelight protests), *Kyŏngjewa sahoe* (Economy and society) 89 (2011): 269–297.

5   Hyejong Yoo, "The Candlelight Girls' Playground: Nationalism as Art of Dialogy, the 2008 Candlelight Vigil Protests in South Korea," *Invisible Culture: Spectacle East Asia* 15 (2010): 50.

6   Kim Ung-il, "T'anhaek ch'ŏngwŏnhan Andante poho yŏnki hwaksan" (Move to protect Andante, the proposer of impeachment), *News Town,* May 14, 2008.

7   Agora P'yeindŭl, *Taehanminkuk sangsik sajŏn Agora* (Common sense of the republic of Korea: Agora). Seoul: Yŏu wa Turumi, 2008; Yi Hae-jin, "Ch'ŏtpul chiphoewa 10 tae ch'amyŏja ŭi chuch'e hyŏngsŏng" (Candlelight protests and the subjectivity of the teenage participants), in *Ch'ŏtpul chiphoewa Hankuk sahoe* (Candlelight protests and Korean society), ed. Hong Sŏng-t'ae (Seoul: Munhwa Kwahak, 2009), 164–205.

8   *Seoul Sinmun* reports that members of online fan communities circulated calls for the first May 2 candlelight festivals, inserting the image of their idols onto the poster. The tightly organized hierarchical structure of these communities, with regional chapters, also played a critical role in organizing protests outside of Seoul. In a survey during this period, 71 percent of teenagers reported that it was their own decision to join the candlelight festivals. "Ch'ŏtpul 100 Il: Ch'ŏtpul 10tae 71% chabaljŏk ch'amyŏ" (100 days of candle: 71 percent of teenagers voluntarily joined), *Seoul Sinmun,* July 29, 2008.

9   Ye-jin, interview by author, Seoul, South Korea, June 20, 2012.

10   John Postill, *Localizing the Internet: An Anthropological Account* (New York: Berghahn Books, 2011), 21.

11   Ibid.

12   Stephen Gaukroger, *The Collapse of Mechanism and the Rise of Sensibility: Science and the Shaping of Modernity, 1680–1760* (Oxford: Oxford University Press, 2012), 390.

13   Saba Mahmood, *Politics of Piety: The Islamic Revival and the Feminist Subject* (Princeton, NJ: Princeton University Press, 2012), 137. This also resonates with Raymond Williams's "structure of feeling," which he calls "not feeling against thought but thought as felt and feeling as thought." Raymond Williams, *Marxism and Literature* (Oxford: Oxford University Press, 1977), 131.

14   Kim Sŏng-hwan, "Tallajin ch'otpulchip'oe: 10tae pinjarie 20–40tae, insolchado ŏpshi kŏrihaengjin" (The changing candlelight protests: Participants in their twenties–forties are replacing teenagers and marching without a leader), *Hankyoreh*, May 27, 2008.

15   For women's online communities, see Yeran Kim, "Kamsŏng kongronjang: Yŏsŏng k'ŏmyunit'i, nŭkkigo malhago haengdonghada (Affective public sphere: woman communities feel, speak and act)," *Ŏllon kwa sahoe* (Media and society) 18, no. 3 (2010): 146–191; Young Ok Kim, "Understanding the Candlelight Demonstration and Women's Political Subjectivity through the Perspective of Changing Publicity," *Korea Journal* 50, no. 3 (2010): 38–70.

16   For a description of the various groups and generations at the candlelight festivals, see Chŏn Sang-jin, "2008nyŏn ch'otpul hyŏnsange taehan sedaesahoehakchŏk koch'al" (A generational sociological consideration on "candlelight protest"), *Hyŏndae chŏngch'i yŏn'gu* (Journal of contemporary politics) 2, no. 1 (2009): 5–31; Yi Kap-yun, "Ch'otpul chiphoe ch'amyŏja ŭi inku sahoehakchŏk t'ŭksŏng mit chŏngch'ijŏk chŏnghyqnggwa t'aedo" (Social and demographic characteristics and political orientations of participants in the candlelight protests of 2008), *Hankuk chŏngdang hakhoebo* (Journal of the association for Korean party studies) 9, no. 1 (2010): 95–120.

17   "Kwang'ubyŏng nollan int'ŏnet kwahak k'ŏmyunit'isŏdo kayŏl" (The mad cow disease controversy is heating up in an Internet science community), *SBS*, May 6, 2008.

18   In 2003, South Korean health experts and environmental activists raised concerns about contaminated beef potentially being imported into the Korean market, calling for a halt to importation. Two years later in 2005, when South Korea was about to resume beef import, BSE-suspected cows reappeared in the United States. However, the Roh Moo-hyun government continued negotiations with the U.S., and in 2007 agreed to import American beef but excluded bone and marrow (which were known to have a higher risk of BSE contamination). Public concern continued as news reports occasionally described how pieces of bone had been found in beef

shipments from the U.S. and the entire cargo returned or disposed of. According to an October 2007 survey, 75 percent of South Koreans viewed American beef as unsafe. "Kukmin 10 myŏng chung 7 myŏng ppyŏ soegogi suip pandae (7 out of 10 Koreans are against beef import)," *Hankyoreh,* October 20, 2007.

19 Kim Chŏng-ha, "T'up'yŏyul 62.9% taesŏn sasang ch'oejŏ . . . 16 taewa pigyo hae poni" (62.9%, the lowest voting rate, a comparison to the 16th election), *JoongAng Ilbo,* December 20, 2007.

20 Stuart Hall, Doreen Massey, and Michael Rustin, "After Neoliberalism: Analysing the Present," *Soundings: A Journal of Politics and Culture* 53, no. 1 (2013): 17.

21 Kang Nae-hŭi, "Pyŏnhyŏgundongŭi kŏjŏmesŏ shinjayujuŭi chibaegongganŭro: 1980nyŏndae ihu han'gugŭi taehak" (From the stronghold of a revolutionary movement to a space of neoliberal domination: The university in South Korea since the 1980s), *Yŏksa pip'yŏng* (Critical review of history) 104 (2013): 65–88. See also Seung-Ook Lee, Sook-Jin Kim, and Joel Wainwright, "Mad Cow Militancy: Neoliberal Hegemony and Social Resistance in South Korea," *Political Geography* 29, no. 7 (2010): 359–369.

22 "Ch'ŏtpul chiphoe 2 nyŏn, sangch'ŏ ch'iyu andoen sahoe" (Two years after the candlelight protests, wounds are not healed), *Yonhap News,* May 12, 2010; EAI et al., *EAI Opinion Review: Che 5hoe Chibang Sŏngŏ Chonkuk P'aenŏl 1–2cha Chosa* (The fifth municipal election panel survey 1–2), accessed March 18, 2014.

23 Yoo, "The Candlelight Girls' Playground."

24 No Chin-ch'ŏl, "2008nyŏn ch'otpulchip'oerŭl t'onghae pon kwangubyŏng kongp'owa mujiŭi wihŏmsot'ong" (The communication and risk of ignorance during the 2008 candlelight protests), *Kyŏngjewa sahoe* (Economy and society) 84 (2009): 158–182.

25 Ru-mi, interview by author, Seoul, South Korea, July 3, 2011.

26 Kim Chong-yŏp, "Ch'ŏtpul chiphoe wa 87nyŏn ch'eje" (Candlelight protests and the '87 regime), *Ch'angjak kwa pip'yong* (Creation and criticism) 36, no. 3 (2008): 36–59; Pak Chun-sŏk, "Ŏmma appa chŏ ch'ŏtpul chiphoe nagayo: 386; Pumowa 2.0 chanyŏga mandŭrŏ kanŭn haengbokhan kajŏng" (Mom, dad, I'm off to a candlelight protest: A happy family of Generation 386 parents and 2.0 children), *Mal,* November 2008.

27 Ch'ang-min, interview by Kim Chong-yŏng and Lee Hae-jin, Seoul, South Korea, November 25, 2011. I am grateful to Kim Chul-kyu and Lee Hae-jin for sharing this interview transcript with me.

28 Chi-yun, interview by author, Seoul, South Korea, July 8, 2011.

29 Chi-yun, Interview by author.

30 The impeachment was viewed as an attempt to halt Roh's rapprochement with North Korea. Citizens against the impeachment (70 percent, according to one survey) organized candlelight protests in downtown Seoul, which lasted nightly until the Constitutional Court rejected the charges two months later. Anthony Faiola, "Court Rejects S. Korean President's Impeachment," *Washington Post,* May 14, 2004.

31 Kim Yong-ch'ŏl, "4manbul siedae en pissan soegogi? Soga utkenne" (Expensive beef for an era of $40,000 GDP? Even cows would laugh), *Oh My News,* April 28, 2008.

32 "Sasŏl: Hyŏnsilkwa tongtt'ŏlŏjin taet'ongryŏng ŭi soegogi palŏn" (Editorial: The President's comments on beef are out of touch with reality), *Hankyoreh* April 28, 2008.

33 "Korean Youth Study Longest Hours in OECD," *Chosun Ilbo* (Eng. ed.), August 10, 2009.

34 Ch'u, "Taet'ongryŏng t'anhaek chean . . . ko 2 haksaeng"; "Kwang'ubyŏng t'ujaengŭl pan FTA and Lee Myung-bak t'ujaengŭro" (From protest against mad cow to protest against FTA and Lee Myung-bak), *People's Solidarity for Social Progress,* May 22, 2008.

35 Ch'otpul Chuyŏng, "Ch'otk'o sikkutŭri kaesahan 'Ppoppoppo' sinmune nawakŏyo" ("Ppoppoppo," the song adapted by the Candle Girls' Korea Members, is published in the newspaper), *Candle Girls' Korea,* June 4, 2008.

36 Zizi A. Papacharissi, *A Private Sphere: Democracy in a Digital Age* (Cambridge: Polity, 2010), 149. See also Alice E Marwick, *Status Update: Celebrity, Publicity, and Branding in the Social Media Age* (New Haven, CT: Yale University Press, 2013); Guy Redden, "Changing Times Again: Recent Writing on Globalization, Communications and the New Activism," *Social Movement Studies* 4, no. 1 (2005): 99–103; Barry Wellman, "Changing Connectivity: A Future History of Y2.03K," *Sociological Research Online* 4 (2000).

37 Clay Shirky, "The Political Power of Social Media," *Foreign Affairs,* January 1, 2011.

38 Anthony Giddens, *Modernity and Self-Identity: Self and Society in the Late Modern Age* (Stanford, CA: Stanford University Press, 1991); John Connolly and Andrea Prothero, "Green Consumption Life-Politics, Risk and Contradictions," *Journal of Consumer Culture* 8, no. 1 (2008): 117–145.

39 Kim Ung-il, "T'anhaek ch'ŏngwŏnhan."

40 It is noteworthy that the conservative media had originally been concerned about American beef import and critical of the FTA during the Roh regime. Even though many cite MBC's investigative *PD Journal* episode on April 29, 2008, as a major catalyst for the beef protest, all three major broadcast

channels (MBC, KBS, and SBS) reported on the threat of mad cow disease, including "The Terror of Mad Cow Disease" by KBS in 2006 and "The Rumor of Mad Cow Disease?" by SBS in 2007. During Lee's FTA negotiation earlier in 2008, the conservative newspapers criticized beef import, calling the FTA a "submission to Washington," an "embarrassment," "not a negotiation but tribute to the U.S.," and "a shame to national food security." They also compared the Korean FTA to the terms of the Japan–U.S. FTA (which gives more regulatory power to Japan), drawing on the familiar repertoire of the Korea–Japan rivalry. Kang, "Kwangubyŏng wihŏmgwa."

41 "Sasŏl: Tashi ch'otpulro chaemi poryŏnŭn choapa seryŏk" (Editorial: The leftists are taking advantage of the candle again), *Dong-a Ilbo,* May 5, 2008.

42 Yi Kil-sŏng, "'P'ik'et tŭlcha,' 'andoenda,' tto kallasŏn 'ch'otpulchip'oe'" ("Raise the flag" "No": The candlelight protest is split again), *Chosun Ilbo,* May 7, 2008.

43 Ibid.

44 Hŏ Mun-myŏng, "Int'ŏnet senoe" (Internet brainwashing), *Dong-a Ilbo,* May 5, 2008.

45 Kang Yŏng-su, "Paek Sang-Ch'ang sojang, 'ch'otpul shiwinŭn chugŭm ch'anmiŭi shimri, manyŏsanyang katta'" (Director Paek Sang-Ch'ang says, "The beef protest is out of necrophilia. It is a witch hunt"), *Chosun Ilbo,* May 22, 2008.

46 Kang Pyŏng-han, Pak Su-jŏng, and Yu Chŏng-in, "'Uridŭl chinjihan komin wae p'yŏmhwehago mangnayo'-ch'otpulshiwi chuch'uk 10taedŭl tashi punno" (Why do you insult and block our serious opinions?), *Kyŏnghyang Sinmun,* May 7, 2008.

47 Ch'oe Min-yŏng, "Kŏriŭi chŏngch'i: Shimin'gwa kwŏllyŏk ch'ungdol" (Street politics: Clash between citizens and police), *Kyŏnghyang Sinmun,* May 6, 2008.

48 "Kyoyuk, posuŏnnon pip'an isyu hwaksan: Tŭlburi toen ch'otpul" (Education and conservative media become issues: Candlelight is turning into wildfire), *Kyŏnghyang Sinmun,* May 18, 2008.

49 Chŏng Min-yŏng, "1%rŭl wihan chŏngch'aek, taejŏnhwan p'illyohada" (Policy for 1% has to change), *Hankyoreh,* June 16, 2008.

50 Kang, Pak, and Yu, "Uridŭl chinjihan komin."

51 Ch'oe Hyŏn-jun, "Miguksan soegogi 'sŏngnan minshim': Int'ŏnet 'koedamuro pon sahoehak" (Anger over American beef: The sociology of Internet rumor), *Hankyoreh,* May 7, 2008. See also Yi Ch'ang-ho, "Ch'ŏngsonyŏn'gwa sot'ong chisok'aeya" (Need to communicate with youth), *Kyŏnghyang Sinmun,* June 6, 2008.

52 Agora P'yeindŭl, *Taehanminkuk Sangsik Sajŏn Agora.*

53 Ibid.

54 Naŭi Yuwolŭn, "Chaech'i manjom kuhodŭl! moŭm" (Smart slogans! A list), *Candle Girls' Korea,* June 4, 2008.

55 Ibid.

56 Mabin, "P'ossŭ chaktyŏl Pusan simindŭl" (Pusan citizens are in full force), *Candle Girls' Korea,* June 5, 2008.

57 Agora P'yeindŭl, *Taehanminkuk Sangsik Sajŏn Agora.*

58 Song Chu-min, "Simindŭl chŏnkyŏng'e sugohanda, ch'ungdol ŏpyi mamuri" (Citizens give combat police pat on the back for hard work), *Oh My News,* June 27, 2008.

59 Yi Hyŏn, "Sinnanŭn takchang t'uŏrŭl asimnikka?" (Do you know the exhilarating hencoop tour?), *Ilgan Sports,* May 28, 2008.

60 Ch'a Tae-un, "Takchang T'uŏ yuhaeng 'kongkwŏnryŏk heŭihwa vs pulpukchong undong'" (Mockery of state authority or civil disobedience), *Yonhap News,* May 29, 2008.

61 Vicente L. Rafael, "The Cell Phone and the Crowd: Messianic Politics in the Contemporary Philippines," *Public Culture* 15, no. 3 (2003): 416.

62 Gustave Le Bon, *The Crowd: A Study of the Popular Mind* (New York: Macmillan, 1897; repr. Mineola: Dover Publications, 2001); Jürgen Habermas, *The Structural Transformation of the Public Sphere,* trans. Thomas Burger and F. Lawrence (Cambridge, MA: MIT Press, 1989); Theodor W. Adorno, *The Culture Industry: Selected Essays on Mass Culture* (London: Routledge, 2005).

63 Mikhail Bakhtin, "Epic and Novel," in *The Dialogic Imagination,* ed. Michael Holquist (Austin: University of Texas Press, 1981), 23.

64 Kyung Lee, "Fighting in the Shadow of the Past: The Mobilizing Role of Vernacular Memories of the 1987 Pro-Democracy Movement in the 2008 Candlelight Protests in Korea," *Memory Studies* 7, no. 1 (2014): 61–75; Sim Yang-sŏp, "Hankuk ŭi panmi undong" (The anti-American movement in South Korea), *Sidae Chŏngsin* (Zeitgeist), 2012.

65 91nyŏnsaeng Alice, "Uri appaga chiha ch'wijosil esŏ iruŏnaen minjuhwa yeyo" (This democratization is what my dad has achieved in the basement interrogation room), *Agora,* June 1, 2008; T'ungt'ungyi, "79 hakpŏn igo, 5–18 ch'amyŏ haksaeng iŏtton uriga ijenun chane ege" (We, who entered college in 1979 and participated in the democratization movement of 1980, are now telling you), *Agora,* June 2, 2008.

66 O Tong-kŭn, "Ch'otpulkwa hamsŏng simin jugwŏn sidaerŭl yŏlda" (Candle and scream opens up an era of citizen sovereignty), *Kyŏnghyang Sinmun,* June 4, 2008.

67 Kim Chi-sŏng, "Mi soegogi suip, taeunha pandae 100 in sikuk sŏnŏn" (A one-hundred-person political statement against the American beef import and the grand canal), *SBS News,* June 2, 2008.

68   Chang Chae-wan, "Ch'ŏnjukuy sindodŭl kwangubyŏng soegogi taeunha pandae" (Catholics opposed the American beef import and the grand canal), *Oh My News*, June 9, 2008.

69   It was generally regarded that after June 10 teenagers retreated from the candlelight festival, and new actors, such as conventional social movement organizations, began to dominate the protest. However, sociologist Kim Chul-Kyoo refutes this with a survey reporting that new teenagers continued to gather to "see and participate firsthand" in the protest. These students nevertheless remained unorganized, and their presence was gradually overshadowed by organized activists. Chul-Kyoo Kim, "Teenage Participants of the 2008 Candlelight Vigil: Their Social Characteristics and Changes in Political Views," *Korea Journal* 50, no. 3 (2010): 23.

70   Andant'e Yogul, "Chilmun: Yebiyŏk ch'otpul hwaldong e taehae ŏttŏngke saengkak hasinayo?" (Question: What do you think about the candlelight participation of reservists?), *Candle Girls' Korea*, May 30, 2008; Winterer, "Sŭkŭraep: Kyobok ŭl yipki p'okryŏk ŭl makŭsil pundŭl kuhapnida" (Reposted: I am seeking those who will stand against violence in school uniforms), *Candle Girls' Korea*, June 9, 2008.

71   Han Yun-hyŏng, "Wae urinŭn muryŏkhan ch'otpuri toeŏnna" (How have we become powerless candles?), in *Kŭdaenŭn wae ch'otpurŭl kkŭsyŏnnayo* (Why did you put out the candle?), ed. Tangdae Pip'yŏng (Seoul: Tangdae, 2009), 19–35.Similarly, communication scholar Sang-gil Lee argues that the protesters' obsession with "purity" in the motive and mode of the festivals constrained the political influence of the gatherings. Yi Sang-gil, "Sunsusŏngŭi Moral: Ch'ŏtpul siwie nat'anan 'oyŏm'e taehan tansang" (A moral of purity: A reflection on the idea of "corruption" during the candlelight protests), in *Kŭdaenŭn wae ch'otpurŭl kkŭsyŏnnayo*, 89–108.

72   Ryu Chŏng-min, "Yi taet'ongryŏng t'ŏtbat seoul, kukchŏng chijido 3%" (President Lee's approval rate hits 3% in Seoul), *Media Today*, June 16, 2008.

73   Hong Sŏng-t'ae, "Ch'ŏtpul chiphoewa minjujuŭi" (The candle assembly and democracy), *Economy and Society* 80 (2008): 10–39.

74   Williams, *Marxism and Literature*, 131.

75   Mimi Sheller, "Mobile Publics: Beyond the Network Perspective," *Environment and Planning D: Society and Space* 22, no. 1 (2004): 50.

Chapter 6: Youth at the End of the Candlelight Decade

1   The organization was a small group of twentysomethings and members of the democratization generation working together around ecological and peace issues. In 2008 they noticed the prominent presence of high school students in the streets in the early stages of the beef protests and invited

these youths to listen to them. Later in May they created the iconic "candle girl" image and made posters and banners for the protests.

2 Ta-jŏng, interview by author, Seoul, South Korea, June 20, 2012.

3 For instance, according to a 2011 survey, South Korean teens were the unhappiest among the twenty-three member countries of the Organization of Economic Co-operation and Development (OECD). This was not unique to teens, however: South Koreans in general were the second-unhappiest in the OECD countries. South Korea's suicide rate was the world's highest in 2009 and remained third in 2013. Ha-Joon Chang, "South Korea's Economic Reforms—a Recipe for Unhappiness," *The Guardian*, April 1, 2012.

4 Ta-jŏng, interview by author.

5 Lauren Berlant, *The Female Complaint: The Unfinished Business of Sentimentality in American Culture* (Durham, NC: Duke University Press, 2008), 11. Berlant develops the concept of "intimate public" by reading popular women's literature with a focus on how textual displays of emotion associated with suffering, alienation, and disconnection build a sense of connection. Even though the candlelight festival is not strictly a textual display, images and performances of shared feelings offer similar opportunities to build affective connection.

6 Berlant argues that "disappointment" is a "partner of fulfillment" because it indicates and animates an object of desire. Berlant, *Female Complaint*, 13.

7 Feminist scholar Eva Chen cites popular television shows that offer a variety of characters and stories to satisfy progressive or even radical viewers. She argues that neoliberalism reversed the feminist adage "The personal is the political" such that everything—including the political—is reduced to matters of lifestyle choice. Eva Chen, "Neoliberalism and Popular Women's Culture: Rethinking Choice, Freedom and Agency," *European Journal of Cultural Studies* 16, no. 4 (2013): 445.

8 Berlant, *Female Complaint*, 8.

9 Ta-jŏng, interview by author.

10 Chi-yun, interview by author, Seoul, South Korea, July 8, 2011.

11 Kang Nae-hŭi, "Pyŏnhyŏgundongŭi kŏjŏmesŏ shinjayujuŭi chibaegongganŭro: 1980nyŏndae ihu han'gugŭi taehak" (From the stronghold of a revolutionary movement to a space of neoliberal domination: The university in South Korea since the 1980s), *Yŏksa pip'yŏng* (Critical review of history) 104 (2013): 65–88.

12 Su-rin and Min-ji, interview by author, Seoul, South Korea, June 2011.

13 Ibid.

14 Ibid.

15 Berlant, *Female Complaint*, 2.

16   Ibid.

17   Yi Hae-jin, "Ch'ŏtpul chiphoewa 10 tae ch'amyŏjaŭi chuch'e hyŏngsŏng" (Candlelight pretests and the subjectivity of the teenage participants), in *Ch'ŏtpul chiphoewa Hankuk sahoe* (Candlelight protests and Korean society), ed. Hong Sŏng-t'ae (Seoul: Munhwa Kwahak, 2009), 164–205.

18   Kŏn-ho, interview by author, Seoul, South Korea, June 2012.

19   Bin-na, interview by author, Seoul, South Korea, June 2011.

20   Ch'an-ki, interview by author, Seoul, South Korea, June 21 2012.

21   Joseph Sung-Yul Park, "The Promise of English: Linguistic Capital and the Neoliberal Worker in the South Korean Job Market," *International Journal of Bilingual Education and Bilingualism* 14, no. 4 (2011): 443–455; So Jin Park and Nancy Abelmann, "Class and Cosmopolitan Striving: Mothers' Management of English Education in South Korea," *Anthropological Quarterly* 77, no. 4 (2004): 645–672.

22   Ch'an-ki, interview by author.

23   "Ollain p'ulppu-ri' sesangŭl pakkunda" (Online grassroots power changes the world: Generation Web 2.0), *Hankyoreh,* June 3, 2008; "Saeroun minjujuŭi shirhŏm: Ch'otpulgwa hamsŏng shiminjugwŏn shidaerŭl yŏlda" (Experimenting with new democracy: Candles and screams open new era for people power), *Kyŏnghyang Sinmun,* June 5, 2008; Song Kyŏng-hwa and Kim Sŏng-hwan, "Miguksan soegogi 'sŏngnan minshim'" (American beef "angry crowds"), *Hankyoreh,* May 5, 2008; "Ttŏorŭnŭn 'int'ŏnet kongnonjang' chumok: Chŏhangŭi mek'a 'taŭm" (Rising Internet public sphere: Daum is the mecca of resistance), *Kyŏnghyang Sinmun,* May 27, 2008

24   Kim Chong-yŏp, "Ch'otpul tŭn yŏhaksaengdŭrŭi paehu?" (Seeking mobilizers of candle girls?), *Hankyoreh,* May 12, 2008.

Conclusion: The Ignition of the Internet and Its Aftermath

1   Heonik Kwon, *The Other Cold War* (New York: Columbia University Press, 2010), 8.

2   Raymond Williams, *Marxism and Literature* (Oxford: Oxford University Press, 1977), 131.

3   Kurt Andersen, "Person of the Year 2011: The Protester," *Time,* December 14, 2011.

4   Anne D'Alleva, "Captivation, Representation, and the Limits of Cognition: Interpreting Metaphor and Metonymy in Tahitian Tamau," in *Beyond Aesthetics: Art and the Technologies of Enchantment,* ed. Christopher Pinney and Nicholas Thomas (Oxford: Berg, 2001), 89.

5   Williams, *Marxism and Literature,* 121.

6   "Witnesses Report Rioting in Tunisian Town," *Reuters Africa,* December 19, 2010.

7   Christine Harold, "Pranking Rhetoric: 'Culture Jamming' as Media Activism," *Critical Studies in Media Communication* 21, no. 3 (2004): 189–211.

8   "Culture Jamming (tm): Brought to You by Adbusters," *Stay Free*.

9   Stephen Zunes, "Occupy Fizzled, but Made 99% a Force," *CNN*, September 17, 2012.

10 Christopher Hayes, *Twilight of the Elites: America after Meritocracy* (New York: Broadway Books, 2013).

11 Kent A. Ono and John M. Sloop, *Shifting Borders: Rhetoric, Immigration, and California's Proposition 187* (Philadelphia: Temple University Press, 2002), 12–13.

12 Michael Hardt and Antonio Negri, "The Fight for 'Real Democracy' at the Heart of Occupy Wall Street," *Foreign Affairs*, October 11, 2011; Sarah van Gelder, "Introduction: How Occupy Wall Street Changes Everything," in *This Changes Everything: Occupy Wall Street and the 99% Movement*, ed. Sarah van Gelder (San Francisco: Berrett-Koehler Publishers, 2011), 1–13.

13 Clay Shirky, *Here Comes Everybody: The Power of Organizing without Organizations* (New York: Penguin Press, 2008), 205.

14 Kristina Boréus and Tobias Hübinette, "Hate Speech and Violent Right Wing Extremism in Scandinavia," *OpenDemocracy*, July 16, 2012; Kirstin Hausen, "Italy's Extreme Right-Wing on the Rise," *Deutsche Welle*, November 9, 2013.

15 For more critical reflection on these notions, see Jodi Dean, "Cybersalons and Civil Society: Rethinking the Public Sphere in Transnational Technoculture," *Public Culture* 13, no. 2 (2001): 243–266; Zizi Papacharissi, "The Virtual Sphere: The Internet as the Public Sphere," *New Media & Society* 4 (2002): 5–23.

16 For instance, Brian Leiter, "Cleaning Cyber-Cesspools: Google and Free Speech," in *The Offensive Internet*, ed. Saul Levmore and Martha Craven Nussbaum (Cambridge, MA: Harvard University Press, 2010), 155–173.

17 Larissa Hjorth and Michael Arnold, *Online@Asia Pacific: Mobile, Social and Locative Media in the Asia-Pacific* (Oxon, UK: Routledge, 2013), 135.

18 Mimi Sheller, "Mobile Publics: Beyond the Network Perspective," *Environment and Planning D: Society and Space* 22, no. 1 (2004): 50.

19 Brian T. Edwards, "Tahrir: Ends of Circulation," *Public Culture* 23, no. 3 (2011): 499. Similarly, in her study of social media during the 2010–2011 Egyptian popular uprising, Linda Herrera argues that a broader social change (including video games, mobile phones, and alternative media) led to a "cultural spring" in which use of the Internet helped to "break boundaries and shatter taboos." Herrera, *Revolution in the Age of Social Media: The Egyptian Popular Insurrection and the Internet* (London: Verso, 2014), 12.

20 Stephen Gaukroger, *The Collapse of Mechanism and the Rise of Sensibility: Science and the Shaping of Modernity, 1680–1760* (Oxford: Oxford University Press, 2012), 390.

21 Sung-gi Hong, "A Look at the Changes in Debate Structure in Korea through the Candlelight Vigils," *Korea Journal* 50, no. 3 (2010): 100.

22 Chang May Choon, "Thousands Rally in Seoul to Protest Against Govt," *The Straits Times*, November 15, 2015; Michael Schuman, "Fallout of Ex South Korea President's Suicide," *Time*, May 25, 2009; "South Koreans Hold Candlelight Vigil to Protest against Alleged Election Meddling," *Reuters*, August 3, 2013.

23 "Annyŏngdŭl hasipnikka? Kodae taejabo ŏttŏn naeyong?" (Are you doing all right? What's in the letter posted at Korea University?), *Crossroads*, December 12, 2013.

24 "Annyŏngdŭl hasipnikka?" (Are you doing all right?), *Facebook*.

25 "South Korea's Spreading Poster Protests," *BBC News*, December 19, 2013.

26 Ho-kyun Song, Dae-ha Jung, and Jin-sik Jeon, "'How Are You?' Student Movement Becomes Nationwide Phenomenon," *Hankyoreh International*, December 17, 2014.

Bibliography

Primary Sources

2002 Taehanmin'guk? "Re: I ch'umo makŭ ŏnjebut'ŏ saengkyŏtŏyo? choesong chŏngmal kunggŭmhaesŏyo" (Re: Where did the commemoration mark first come from? Sorry I'm just curious). *Moim,* November 30, 2002. http://cafe.daum.net/dlrtn44.

91nyŏnsaeng Alice. "Uri appaga chiha ch'wijosil esŏ iruŏnaen minjuhwa yeyo" (This democratization is what my dad has achieved in the basement interrogation room). *Agora,* June 1, 2008. http://bbs1.agora.media.daum.net /gaia/do/debate/read?bbsId=D101&articleId=1713785.

A Life For You. "Han'guk? Sŏnjin'guk? Kaesori hane" (Korea? A developed country? It's a joke :P :P :P). *Moim,* November 24, 2002. http://cafe.daum .net/dlrtn44.

Andant'e Yogul. "Chilmun: Yebiyŏk ch'otpul hwaldong e taehae ŏttŏngke saengkak hasinayo?" (Question: What do you think about the candlelight participation of reservists?). *Candle Girls' Korea,* May 30, 2008. http://cafe .daum.net/candlegirls/2iKU/143.

Andante. "1chŏnman sŏmyŏng: Kukhoe e Lee Myung-Bak taet'ongryŏng t'anhaek ŭl yogu hamnida" (Ten million signatures: We demand the impeachment of Lee Myung-Bak). *Agora,* April 6, 2008. http://bbs3.agora .media.daum.net/gaia/do/petition/read?bbsId=P001&articleId=40221.

buzz. "Chigŭm" (Now). Moim, November 27, 2002. http://cafe.daum.net /dlrtn44.

Chajugukgarŭl Kkumkkumyŏ. "Han'gukkun irakŭ p'abyŏngŭl pandaehanda!" (I oppose sending Korean troops to Iraq!). *Moim,* March 18, 2003. http:// cafe.daum.net/dlrtn44.

———. "Re: Uri taehanminguki paljŏnhalsu itnŭn iyu" (Re: Reasons that our Republic of Korea can advance). *Moim,* February 12, 2003. http://cafe.daum .net/dlrtn44.

Cho Chang-hŭi. "Roh Moo-Hyun taesŏn hubokke put'akhago sipsŭpnida" (I would ask this to presidential candidate Roh Moo-Hyun). *Moim,* October 7, 2002. http://cafe.daum.net/dlrtn44.

Chŏngbuyŏ Pukkŭrŏunjul Alla. "Ukyŏk tajim, Lee Hoi-chang bŏjŏn" (Angry speech, by Lee Hoi-chang). *Moim,* December 6, 2002. http://cafe.daum.net /dlrtn44.

Ch'ŏnnyŏn sarang. "P'ŏm: Hannaradang Seo Chungwon taep'yo poiji annŭn son parŏn" (Reposting: GNP Representative Seo Chungwon's "invisible hand" statement). *Moim,* December 10, 2002.

Ch'otpul Chuyŏng. "Ch'otk'o sikkutŭl e kaesahan 'Ppoppoppo' sinmun e nawakŏyo" ("Ppoppoppo," the song adapted by the Candle Girls' Korea members, is in newspaper). *Candle Girls' Korea,* June 4, 2008. http://cafe .daum.net/candlegirls/2iKU/253.

(Chu) Hyeyoung. "Ch'otpul Siwi cheanhasyŏtton puni ssŭngŭl p'ŏwatsŭpnida . . . chŏngmal orŭn malipnida" (I copied and pasted the posting by the proposer of the candlelight vigils . . . I completely agree with him). *Moim,* December 7, 2002. http://cafe.daum.net/dlrtn44.

Chung-Laden. "Mich'igetneyŏ" (It drives me crazy). *Moim,* November 21, 2002. http://cafe.daum.net/dlrtn44.

Haebaragi. "Chŏngmal" (Indeed). *Moim,* June 28, 2002. http://cafe.daum.net /dlrtn44.

Haegyŏlsa. "Taehanminguki chugwŏngukkanya?" (Is the Republic of Korea a sovereign nation?). *Moim,* June 28, 2002. http://cafe.daum.net/dlrtn44.

Hagi99. "1 wŏl 5 il pup'yŏng munhwaŭi kŏri ch'otpul haengsa pogoipnida" (Report on the candlelight ceremony at the Pup'yŏng cultural fair on January 5). *Moim,* January 6, 2003. http://cafe.daum.net/dlrtn44.

Hanaa. "Yŏjungsaeng haegyŏlŭl wihae: Taet'ongryŏng huboege sŏyaksŏrŭl ponaeja!!-Ansan"(Let's demand a pledge from the presidential candidates: To solve the issue of the girls!!-Ansan). *Moim,* December 4, 2002. http:// cafe.daum.net/dlrtn44.

Hanmanŭnja. "Annyŏng" (Hello). *Moim,* December 1, 2002. http://cafe.daum .net/dlrtn44.

hansamuna. "Ehyŭ" (Aw). *Moim,* January 16, 2003. http://cafe.daum.net /dlrtn44.

Hayan Pada. "Sop'a kaejonge kyoljipdoen net'ijun p'awo" (Netizens join forces for SOFA reform). *Moim,* December 7, 2002. http://cafe.daum.net /dlrtn44.

Huhui. "Nach'am ŏiga ŏpsŏsŏri . . . migundŭl wanjŏn kaesaekkidŭlineyo" (Well, I'm speechless . . . those G.I.'s are beasts)." *Moim,* November 24, 2002. http://cafe.daum.net/dlrtn44.

Hŭkmong Taehanminkuk. "Re: K'at'usa sŏngp'okhaeng migun yujeo p'yŏnggyŏl" (Re: U.S. GI found guilty for raping a KATUSA). *Moim,* February 13, 2003.

I Hate My Country. "Hanmadiro . . . urinaranŭn ŏnjekkajina . . . miguge tcholttagu saenghwarŭl halsubagenŭn" (In a nutshell, we're doomed to be subordinate to the U.S.). *Moim,* November 21, 2002. http://cafe.daum.net /dlrtn44.

Isipyukse Ch'ungnyŏn. "Pyŏnhangŏti ŏpta. Pyonhangŏti ŏpnŭnde urinŭn wae chujŏhanŭnga" (Nothing has changed, why do we hesitate when nothing has changed?). *Moim,* January 10, 2003.

————. "Re: Uri Taehanminguki paljŏnhalsu itnŭn iyu" (Re: Reasons that our Republic of Korea can advance). *Moim,* February 12, 2003. http://cafe.daum .net/dlrtn44.

jazu. "Ssŏkŭn chŏnch'iin 1pŏn, hobo 1pŏni sopa gaejŏng sŏmyŏngundong sŏnp'osike kandago hanŭnde" (The no. 1 corrupt politician, candidate no.1 goes to the ceremony launching the petition for SOFA reform). *Moim,* December 19, 2002. http://cafe.daum.net/dlrtn44.

Kim Dŏk-yŏn. "Uriga taehanmin'guk kukmininga?" (Are we Korean people?). *Moim,* November 27, 2002. http://cafe.daum.net/dlrtn44. http://cafe.daum .net/dlrtn44.

Kim Kang-t'ae. "Re: Re: Puranhan maŭm" (Re: Re: Anxious mind). *Moim,* January 17, 2003. http://cafe.daum.net/dlrtn44.

Kim Pa-da. "Yŏrŏbun! Uri modu ch'amyŏhapsida" (Folks! Let's all participate). *Moim,* November 30, 2002. http://cafe.daum.net/dlrtn44.

Kim, Wansu. "Kinkŭpsokpo: Osama Bin Laden pŏpjŏngesŏ mujoe sŏngo!!!" (Breaking news: Osama Bin Laden found not guilty at court!!!). *Moim,* November 22, 2002. http://cafe.daum.net/dlrtn44.

Koindol. "Chŏngch'iin nomdŭliran!!!" (Those politicians are!!!). *Moim,* December 9, 2002. http://cafe.daum.net/dlrtn44.

Kŭnani. "Hu . . ." (Alas . . .). *Moim,* November 27, 2002. http://cafe.daum.net /dlrtn44.

LOVEØIS. "Chŏnŭn" (I am). *Moim,* November 26, 2002. http://cafe.daum.net /dlrtn44.

Mabin. "P'ossŭ chaktyŏl Pusan simindŭl" (Pusan citizens are in full force). *Candle Girls' Korea,* June 5, 2008. http://cafe.daum.net/candlegirls/2iKU/276.

Mr. Sŏninjang. "Kwanghwamunŭro moipsida !!!!!!!!!!!!!!!!!!!!!!!" (Let's go to Kwanghwamun !!!!!!!!!!!!!!!!!!!!!!!). *Moim,* November 26, 2002. http://cafe.daum .net/dlrtn44.

Naŭi Yuwolŭn. "Chaech'i manjom kuhodŭl! Moŭm" (Smart slogans! A list). *Candle Girls' Korea,* June 4, 2008. http://cafe.daum.net/candlegirls/2iKU /246.

Nautes. "Yaedŭra, kŭrigo yŏrŏbun choesonghapnida" (Girls, and all of you, I'm sorry). *Moim,* November 22, 2002. http://cafe.daum.net/dlrtn44.

Nikneim. "Sarin migugi mujoemyŏn" (If the murderous U.S. was not guilty). *Moim,* November 25, 2002. http://cafe.daum.net/dlrtn44.

Noir. "Chŏngukjŏk taegyomo chiphoe--tŏisang sogyumo chiphoeronŭn ssido anmŏphinda" (A massive national protest--small-scale protests don't work anymore). *Moim,* November 27, 2002. http://cafe.daum.net/dlrtn44.

Oasis. "11wŏl 1il paekakkwan saibŏ t'erŏ chakchŏn!!" (Cyber terror on the White House on December 1!!). *Moim,* November 21, 2002. http://cafe.daum.net /dlrtn44.

Oogiboogi. "Tae! Han! Min! Kuk! Kwanghwamun midaesagwan apesŏ taegyumo siwihapnida" (Great! Korea! Let's stage a massive protest in front of the U.S. Embassy in Kwanghwamun). *Moim,* November 27, 2002. http:// cafe.daum.net/dlrtn44.

Opt'ik Lŏbŭ. "Hannara dang'ŭn mi-sŏniwa hyo-suni ŭi chukŭmŭl hŏktoeke haji malla" (GNP, You should not make the deaths of Hyo-sun and Mi-sŏn be in vain). *Moim,* December 9, 2002. http://cafe.daum.net/dlrtn44.

Paekt'ongsin'gibigaksul. "Chŏngmallo . . . chŏngmallo" (Really . . . really.). *Moim,* November 25, 2002. http://cafe.daum.net/dlrtn44.

Pina. "Choppari miguk hant'e han'gukminŭi himŭl poyŏjupsida" (Let's demonstrate the Korean people's power to the U.S.). *Moim,* November 26, 2002. http://cafe.daum.net/dlrtn44.

prefer. "Kŭdongan migukŭi ŏpjŏk(?)dŭl!!" (The great works (?) by the U.S.!!). *Moim,* November 30, 2002. http://cafe.daum.net/dlrtn44.

PureMind. "Chinan 60nyŏngan migugi urinarae chŏjirŭn manhaeng" (What the U.S. has done to us for the last sixty years). *Moim,* December 1, 2002. http://cafe.daum.net/dlrtn44.

SadSpirit. "T'up'yrŭl hago nasŏ" (After casting vote). *Moim,* December 19, 2002. http://cafe.daum.net/dlrtn44.

Sarang'aga. "Parŏni . . . chom" (That comment was . . . a little). *Moim,* December 8, 2002. http://cafe.daum.net/dlrtn44.

T'ungt'ungyi. "79 hakpŏn igo, 5–18 ch'amyŏ haksaeng iŏtton uriga ijenun chane ege" (We, who entered college in 1979 and participated in the democratization movement of 1980, are now telling you). *Agora,* June 2, 2008. http://bbs1 .agora.media.daum.net/gaia/do/debate/read?bbsId=D101&articleId =1718056.

Taehanminguk. "Roh Moo-Hyun! Chŏngmal chŏngch'irŭl muŏlro anŭn kŏpnikka?" (Roh Moo-Hyun! You think politics is nothing?). *Moim,* December 4, 2003. http://cafe.daum.net/dlrtn44.

Torongii. "Urinŭn shingminji paeksŏngi animnida!!" (We are not a colony!!) *Moim,* November 22, 2002. http://cafe.daum.net/dlrtn44.

T. T. "Ttibal miguk" (Damn, U.S.). *Moim,* November 24, 2002. http://cafe .daum.net/dlrtn44.

Wangch'ik. "12wŏl 1il midaesagwan apesŏ moipsida" (Let's meet in front of the U.S. Embassy on December 1). *Moim,* November 27, 2002. http://cafe .daum.net/dlrtn44.

Winterer. "Sŭkŭraep: Kyobok ŭl yipki p'okryŏk ŭl makŭsil pundŭl kuhapnida" (Reposted: I am seeking those who will stand against violence in school

uniforms). *Candle Girls' Korea,* June 9, 2008. http://cafe.daum.net
/candlegirls/2iKU/347.

Wish You Were Happy. "Ibamjungedo 20myŏngi nŏmŭn saramdŭri
chŏpsok'aeinneyo" (More than twenty members are logged on tonight).
Moim, November 27, 2002. http://cafe.daum.net/dlrtn44.

yerbenbi! "Naeil Kwanghwamune Lee Hoi-changi opnida (P'ildok)" (Lee Hoi-
chang is coming to Kwanghwamun tomorrow! [Must Read]). *Moim,*
December 7, 2002. http://cafe.daum.net/dlrtn44.

Yi Mi-ju. "Pusan simindŭl ilgojuseyo" (Pusan citizens, please read this). *Moim,*
June 28, 2002. http://cafe.daum.net/dlrtn44.

Yurich'onsa. "Re: Kŭge paro sopa hyŏkchŏngiyeyo" (Re: That is SOFA). *Moim,*
November 30, 2002. http://cafe.daum.net/dlrtn44.

Secondary Sources

Abelmann, Nancy. "Minjung Movement and the Minjung." In *South Korea's
Minjung Movement: The Culture and Politics of Dissidence,* edited by
Kenneth M. Wells, 119–153. Honolulu: University of Hawai'i Press,
1995.

Abelmann, Nancy, Jung-Ah Choi, and So Jin Park, eds. *No Alternative?:
Experiments in South Korean Education.* Berkeley: University of California
Press, 2012.

Abelmann, Nancy, So Jin Park, and Hyunhee Kim. "College Rank and Neoliberal Subjectivity in South Korea: The Burden of Self-development."
Inter-Asia Cultural Studies 10, no. 2 (2009): 229–247.

Adorno, Theodor W. *The Culture Industry: Selected Essays on Mass Culture.*
London: Routledge, 2005. Originally published 1944.

Agora P'yeindŭl. *Taehanmin'guk sangsik sajŏn Agora* (Common sense of the
republic of Korea: Agora). Seoul: Yŏu wa Turumi, 2008.

Allen, Danielle S. *Talking to Strangers: Anxieties of Citizenship since Brown v.
Board of Education.* Chicago: University of Chicago Press, 2006.

Alterman, Jon B. "The Revolution Will Not Be Tweeted." *Washington Quarterly*
34, no. 4 (2011): 103–116.

An Pu-kŭn. "16tae taesŏnŭi chijido byŏnhwawa t'up'yo kyŏlgwa" (Changes
in the approval rate and the election result in the sixteenth presidential
election)." In *16tae Taesŏnŭi Sŏngŏgwajŏnggwa Ŭiŭi* (The process and
implications of the sixteenth presidential election), edited by Kim Se-gyun,
81–104. Seoul: Seoul National University Press, 2003.

An Sŏn-hŭi. "Sahŏe chuyŏk tt'ŏorŭn p'i sedae" (Generation P: A new leader of
society). *Hankyoreh,* June 9, 2003. Kinds.or.kr database.

An Sun-dŭk, Kim Chae-in, Chŏng Hae-suk, and Kim Myŏng-suk. "Haksaeng
kyoyukwŏnŭi kyoyukchŏngch'aek punsŏk" (Analysis of educational

programs of student training centers). Seoul: Korean Women's Development Institute, 1991.

Andersen, Kurt. "Person of the Year 2011: The Protester." *Time,* December 14, 2011. Accessed May 25, 2014. http://content.time.com/time/specials /packages/article/0,28804,2101745_2102132,00.html.

Anderson, Benedict. *Imagined Communities: Reflections on the Origin and Spread of Nationalism.* London: Verso, 1983.

"Annyŏngdŭl hasipnikka?" (Are you doing all right?). *Facebook.* Accessed June 26, 2014. https://www.facebook.com/cantbeokay.

"Annyŏngdŭl hasipnikka? Kodae taejabo ŏttŏn naeyong?" (Are you doing all right? What's in the letter posted at Korea University?). *Crossroads,* December 12, 2013. Accessed June 26, 2014. http://tvshowdictionary.tistory .com/1288.

Ash, James. "Technologies of Captivation: Videogames and the Attunement of Affect." *Body & Society* 19, no. 1 (2013): 27–51.

Bae Myŏng-jae. "Ch'ŏngsonyŏn 41 myŏng dŭng hangjaeng chung 165 myŏng samang" (165 died during the uprising including 41 teenagers). *Kyŏnghyang Sinmun,* May 15, 2005. Accessed May 3, 2014. http://news.khan.co.kr/kh _news/khan_art_view.html?artid=200505151749001&code=210000&s _code=af016.

Bakhtin, Mikhail. "Epic and Novel." In *The Dialogic Imagination,* edited by Michael Holquist, 21–23. Austin: University of Texas Press, 1981.

———. *Problems of Dostoevsky's Poetics.* Edited and translated by Caryl Emerson. Minneapolis: University of Minnesota Press, 1984.

Barkun, Michael. *A Culture of Conspiracy: Apocalyptic Visions in Contemporary America.* Berkeley: University of California Press, 2003.

Bauman, Richard, and Charles Briggs. "Poetics and Performance as Critical Perspectives on Language and Social Life." *Annual Review of Anthropology* 19 (1990): 59–88.

Bennett, W. Lance. "Review of *The Language of Contention: Revolutions in Words, 1688–2012.*" *Perspectives on Politics* 12, no. 2 (June 2014): 471–472.

Bennett, W. Lance, and Alexandra Segerberg. *The Logic of Connective Action: Digital Media and the Personalization of Contentious Politics.* Cambridge: Cambridge University Press, 2014.

Berlant, Lauren. *The Female Complaint: The Unfinished Business of Sentimentality in American Culture.* Durham, NC: Duke University Press, 2008.

Bolter, Jay David. *Writing Space.* Hillsdale, NJ: Lawrence Erlbaum, 1991.

Boréus, Kristina, and Tobias Hübinette. "Hate Speech and Violent Right Wing Extremism in Scandinavia." *OpenDemocracy,* July 16, 2012. http://www .opendemocracy.net/opensecurity/kristina-bor%C3%A9us-tobias-h%C3% BCbinette/hate-speech-and-violent-right-wing-extremism-in-scandi.

Brouwer, Daniel C. "ACT-ing up in Congressional Hearings." In *Counterpublics and the State,* edited by Robert Asen and Daniel Brouwer, 87–110. Albany: State University of New York Press, 2001.

Brouwer, Daniel C., and Robert Asen. Introduction to *Public Modalities: Rhetoric, Culture, Media, and the Shape of Public Life,* edited by Daniel C. Brouwer and Robert Asen, 1–32. Tuscaloosa: University of Alabama Press, 2010.

Brown, David. "The 'Recipe for Disaster' That Killed 80 and Left a £5bn Bill." *The Telegraph,* April 7, 2008. Accessed March 29, 2014. http://www.telegraph.co.uk/news/uknews/1371964/The-recipe-for-disaster-that-killed-80-and-left-a-5bn-bill.html.

Capaccio, Anthony, and Nicole Gaouette. "U.S. Adding 800 Troops for South Korea Citing Rebalance." *Bloomberg Business.* January 7, 2014. Accessed April 8, 2015. http://www.bloomberg.com/news/articles/2014–01–07/u-s-adding-800-troops-for-south-korea-citing-rebalance.

Carty, Victoria, and Jake Onyett. "Protest, Cyberactivism and New Social Movements: The Reemergence of the Peace Movement Post 9/11." *Social Movement Studies* 5 (2006): 229–249.

Casey, Edward. *Remembering: A Phenomenological Study.* 2nd ed. Bloomington: Indiana University Press, 2000.

Castells, Manuel. *Communication Power.* Oxford: Oxford University Press, 2009.

———. *The Information Age: Economy, Society and Culture, The Power of Identity.* Vol. 2. Oxford: Blackwell, 1997.

Ch'a Tae-un. "Takchang t'uŏ yuhaeng "kongkwŏnryŏk heŭihwa vs pulpukchong undong'" (Mockery of state authority or civil disobedience). *Yonhap News,* May 29, 2008. Accessed March 18, 2014. http://news.hankooki.com/lpage/society/200805/h2008052907074021950.htm.

Cha, Victor D. "America and South Korea: The Ambivalent Alliance?" *Current History* 102 (2003): 279–284.

Chang Chae-wan. "Ch'ŏnjukuy sindodŭl kwangubyŏng soegogi taeunha pandae" (Catholics opposed the American beef import and the grand canal). *Oh My News,* June 9, 2008. Accessed March 10, 2014. http://www.ohmynews.com/nws_web/view/at_pg.aspx?CNTN_CD=A0000922630.

Chang, Ha-Joon. "South Korea's Economic Reforms—a Recipe for Unhappiness." *The Guardian,* April 1, 2012. Accessed April 12, 2014. http://www.theguardian.com/commentisfree/2012/apr/01/south-korea-recipe-for-unhappiness.

Chang Hun. "16tae taesŏnŭgwa hubo sŏnch'ulgwanjŏng: Chŏngdang kaehyŏkŭi kyŏngjaeng" (The sixteenth presidential election and the process of electing candidates: A competition for party reform). In *16tae Taesŏnŭi Sŏngŏgwajŏnggwa Ŭiui* (The process and implications of the sixteenth presidential election), edited by Kim Se-gyun, 3–28. Seoul: Seoul National University Press, 2003.

Chang Sun-wŏn. "Ch'ŏngnyŏn sirŏptyul ŏttŏke kyesan halkka?" (How is the youth unemployment rate calculated?). *E Daily*, March 21, 2012. Accessed June 5, 2014. http://edaily.co.kr/news/NewsRead.edy?SCD=JA61&newsid =01128326599465616&DCD=A00106&OutLnkChk=Y.

Chen, Eva. "Neoliberalism and Popular Women's Culture: Rethinking Choice, Freedom and Agency." *European Journal of Cultural Studies* 16, no. 4 (2013): 440–452.

Cho Gabje. "Sŭt'aensŭrŭl irŭn Lee Hoi-Chang" (Lee Hoi-Chang lost his stance). *Chogabje.com*, December 6, 2002. Accessed June 13, 2014. http://www .chogabje.com

Cho, Ki-suk. "The Ideological Orientation of 2008 Candlelight Vigil Participants : Anti-American, Pro-North Korean Left or Anti-Neoliberalism?" *Korean Journal of Politics* 43, no. 3 (2009): 125–148.

Cho Han, Hae-joang. "Beyond the FIFA's World Cup: An Ethnography of the 'Local' in South Korea around the 2002 World Cup." *Inter-Asia Cultural Studies* 5, no. 1 (2004): 8–26.

Ch'oe Chŏng-ku. "Chagungmin musihanŭn sop'a wihŏn choyak" (SOFA, an "unconstitutional treaty" that disregards the Korean people). *Hankyoreh*, November 30, 2002. Kinds.or.kr database.

Ch'oe Hyŏn-jun. "Miguksan soegogi 'sŏngnan minshim': Int'ŏnet 'koedamuro pon sahoehak" (Anger over American beef: Sociology of Internet rumor). *Hankyoreh*, May 7, 2008. Kinds.or.kr database.

Ch'oe Hyŏng-ik. "Hankukŭi sahoe kujowa ch'ŏngnyŏn chuch'eŭi wigi" (The Korean social structure and the crisis of youth subjectivity). *Munhwa/ Kwahak* (Culture/Science) 37 (2004): 69–85.

Ch'oe Min-yŏng. "Kŏriŭi chŏngch'i: Shimin'gwa kwŏllyŏk ch'ungdol" (Street politics: Clash between citizens and police). *Kyŏnghyang Sinmun*, May 6, 2008.

Ch'oe Wŏn-sik, Kim Hong-jun, and Kim Chong-yŏp. "Chŏngdam: Wŏldŭk'ŏp ihu han'gukŭi punhwawa munhwa undong" (Interview: Korean culture and cultural movement after the World Cup). *Ch'angjakkwa pip'yŏng* (Creation and criticism) 117 (2002): 14–54.

Ch'oe Yun-jung. "Migun changbi kyŏlham ch'isa' mujoerani" (Failure of communication devices? Cannot accept a not-guilty verdict). *Chosun Ilbo*, November 22, 2002. Kinds.or.kr database.

Choi, Chungmoo. "The Minjung Culture Movement and the Construction of Popular Culture in Korea." In *South Korea's Minjung Movement: The Culture and Politics of Dissidence*, edited by Kenneth M. Wells, 105–118. Honolulu: University of Hawai'i Press, 1995.

Choi Jang-jip. "Ch'otpul chiphoewa han'guk minjujuŭi ott'ŏkk'e polgŏsin'ga" (How to view the candlelight protest and Korean democracy). In *Proceedings of ch'otpul chiphoewa han'guk minjujuŭi* (The candlelight protest and Korean democracy). Seoul, 2008. http://www.dibrary.net/jsp/download.jsp?file_id =FILE-00005607962.

————. "Political Cleavages in South Korea." In *State and Society in Contemporary Korea,* edited by Hagen Koo, 13–51. Ithaca, NY: Cornell University Press, 1993.

Choi, Kang-shik. "The Rising Supply of College Graduates and Declining Returns for Young Cohort: The Case of Korea." *Global Economic Review* 34 (2005): 167–180.

Chŏn Chong-hwi. "Kijŏkŭl mandun 7man siminŭi him" (Seventy thousand citizens who made a miracle). *Hankyoreh,* December 19, 2002. http://legacy .www.hani.co.kr/section-003300000/2002/12/0033000002002121922567 99.html.

Chŏn Sang-bong. *Han'guk kŭnhyŏndae ch'ŏngnyŏn undongsa* (A history of the contemporary Korean youth movement). Seoul: Duri media, 2004.

Chŏn-Hong Ki-hye. "'Sŏdaep'yo, tangsindo pumoipnikka'—hannara Sŏch'ŏngwon taep'yo 'poiji annŭn son' parŏn p'amun" (Representative Sŏ, are you a parent?: The "invisible hand" statement by Representative Sŏ Ch'ŏng-wŏn of GNP generates a sensation). *PRESSian,* December 10, 2002. Accessed July 10, 2007. http://www.pressian.com/news/article.html?no=70675.

Chŏn Sang-jin. "2008nyŏn ch'otpul hyŏnsange taehan sedaesahoehakchŏk koch'al" (A generational sociological consideration on "candlelight protest'"). *Hyŏndae chŏngch'i yŏn'gu* (Journal of contemporary politics) 2, no. 1 (2009): 5–31.

Chŏng Chin-wung. "Pulkŭn mulkyŏl hyŏnsangŭl t'onghae pon yokmangŭi munhwachŏngch'ihak, kŭ ch'angchowa kusŏng sai" (Cultural politics of desire in the red wave phenomenon). *Tangdae pip'yŏng* (Contemporary criticism) 20 (2002): 8–23.

Chŏng In-hwan. "Pusi panghan pandae kisŭp siwi" (Flash protest against Bush's visit). *Hankyoreh,* February 15, 2002. Accessed September 26, 2012. http:// legacy.www.hani.co.kr/section-009000777/2002/02/00900077720020215 1418001.html.

Chŏng Jin-sŏng, ed. *Wihŏm sahoe, wihŏm chŏngch'i* (Risk society, risk politics). Seoul: Seoul National University Press, 2010.

Chŏng Kwang-sup and Suh Chung-min. "Migun pŏpjŏng, hankukin kiman urong, sopa kaejŏng chaep'ankwon iyang 'mokch'ŏng" ("U.S. court deceived Koreans," mounting demand for SOFA revision). *Hankyoreh,* November 21, 2002.

Chŏng Min-yŏng. "1%rŭl wihan chŏngch'aek, taejŏnhwan p'illyohada" (Policy for 1% has to change). *Hankyoreh,* June 16, 2008. Kinds.or.kr database.

Chŏng Yun-su. "Kunsabu ilch'e, ch'eryŏk tallyŏn, ch'otpul ŭisik kŭkki hullyŏn, kŭgŏ kkok pataya halkkayo?" (The unity of leader, teacher, and father, physical trainings, candle ceremonies: Do student need them?). *Oh My News*, April 17, 2007. Accessed October 7, 2013. http://www.ohmynews.com /NWS_Web/view/at_pg.aspx?CNTN_CD=A0000404892.

"Ch'ŏtpul 100 Il: Ch'ŏtpul 10tae 71 % chabaljŏk ch'amyŏ" (100 days of candle: 71 percent of teenagers voluntarily joined). *Seoul Sinmun*, July 29, 2008. Accessed March 18, 2014. http://www.seoul.co.kr/news/newsView.php?id =20080729001008.

"Ch'ŏtpul chiphoe 2 nyŏn, sangch'ŏ ch'iyu andoen sahoe" (Two years after the candlelight protests, wounds are not healed). *Yonhap News*, May 12, 2010. Accessed March 18, 2014. http://news.naver.com/main/read.nhn?mode =LSD&mid=sec&oid=001&aid=0003272745&sid1=001.

Choon, Chang May. "Thousands rally in Seoul to protest against govt." *The Straits Times*, November 15, 2015. Accessed November 29, 2015. http://www .straitstimes.com/asia/east-asia/thousands-rally-in-seoul-to-protest-against -govt.

Ch'u Kwang-kyu. "Taet'ongryŏng t'anhaek chean . . . ko 2 haksaeng" (Proposal for impeachment . . . from an eleventh grader). *Sinmungo*, May 4, 2008. Accessed May 3, 2014. http://www.shinmoongo.net/sub_read.html?uid=3675.

Chu Ŭn-wu. "Chayuwa sobiŭi shidae, kŭrigo naengsojuŭiŭi shijak" (A decade of freedom and consumption, and the onset of cynicism: The Republic of Korea, its conditions of everyday life in the 1990s). *Sahoewa Yŏksa* (Society and history) 88 (2010): 307–344.

———. "4.19 sidae ch'ŏngnyŏnkwa onŭlŭi ch'ŏngnyŏn" (Youth in the April Revolution and youth today). *Munhwa/Kwahak* (Culture/Science) 37 (2004): 86–117.

Chu Yŏng-jung. "Ŏnron, min'gan kigwan panŭng: mi 'han'guk panmi simgak'" (Media and public response: Americans think "Korean Anti-Americanism is a serious problem"). *Chosun Ilbo*, November 29, 2002. Kinds.or.kr database.

Cohen, Margaret. "Walter Benjamin's Phantasmagoria." *New German Critique*, no. 48 (1989): 87–107.

Connerton, Paul. "Cultural Memory." In *Handbook of Material Culture*, edited by Christopher Tilley, Webb Keane, Susanne Kochler, Michael Rowlands, and Patricia Spyer, 315–324. London: Sage, 2006.

Connolly, John, and Andrea Prothero. "Green Consumption Life-Politics, Risk and Contradictions." *Journal of Consumer Culture* 8, no. 1 (2008): 117–145.

Couldry, Nick. "Actor Network Theory and Media: Do They Connect and on What Terms?" In *Cultures of Connectivity*, edited by Andreas Hepp, Friedrich Krotz, Shaun Moores, and Carsten Winter, 93–110. Creskill, NJ: Hampton Press, 2008.

"Culture Jamming (tm): Brought to You by Adbusters." *Stay Free*. Accessed June 4, 2014. http://www.stayfreemagazine.org/9/adbusters.htm.

Cumings, Bruce. "Anti-Americanism in the Republic of Korea." *Joint U.S.-Korea Academic Studies* 14 (2004): 205–229.

———. "The Asian Crisis, Democracy, and the End of 'Late' Development." In *The Politics of the Asian Economic Crisis*, edited by T. J. Pempel, 17–44. Ithaca, NY: Cornell University Press, 1999.

D'Alleva, Anne. "Captivation, Representation, and the Limits of Cognition: Interpreting Metaphor and Metonymy in Tahitian Tamau." In *Beyond Aesthetics: Art and the Technologies of Enchantment*, edited by Christopher Pinney and Nicholas Thomas, 79–96. Oxford: Berg, 2001.

Davenport, Thomas H., and John C. Beck. *The Attention Economy: Understanding the New Currency of Business*. Boston: Harvard Business Review Press, 2002.

Dawkins, Richard. *The Selfish Gene*. 2nd ed. Oxford: Oxford University Press, 1990.

———. "Viruses of the Mind." In *Dennett and His Critics: Demystifying Mind*, edited by Bo Dahlbom, 13–27. Oxford: Wiley-Blackwell, 1993.

Dean, Jodi. "Cybersalons and Civil Society: Rethinking the Public Sphere in Transnational Technoculture." *Public Culture* 13, no. 2 (2001): 243–266.

Debord, Guy. *The Society of the Spectacle*. Translated by Donald Nicholson-Smith. New York: Zone Books, 1995. Originally published 1967.

Delanty, Gerard, and Patrick O'Mahony. *Nationalism and Social Theory: Modernity and the Recalcitrance of the Nation*. Thousand Oaks: Sage Publications, 2002.

Delicath, John W., and Kevin Michael DeLuca. "Image Events, the Public Sphere, and Argumentative Practice: The Case of Radical Environmental Groups." *Argumentation* 17, no. 3 (2003): 315–333.

EAI, SBS, Chungang Ilbo, and Korea Research. *EAI Opinion Review: Che 5hoe Chibang Sŏngŏ Chonkuk P'aenŏl 1–2cha Chosa* (The fifth municipal election panel survey 1–2). Accessed March 18, 2014. http://www.eai.or.kr/inc/view ContentPanel.asp?catcode=&code=kor_report&idx=9273&gubun=E&table _wid=697.

Eckert, Carter J. "Epilogue: Exorcising Hegel's Ghosts: Toward a Postnationalist Historiography of Korea." In *Colonial Modernity in Korea*, edited by Gi-wook Shin and Michael Robinson, 363–378. Cambridge, MA: Harvard University Press, 1999.

"Editorial." *JoongAng Ilbo*, December 3, 2002.

Ediciones El País. "1,000 Euros a Month? Dream On . . ." *El País*, March 12, 2012. Accessed July 19, 2013. http://elpais.com/elpais/2012/03/12/inenglish /1331575980_208983.html.

Edwards, Brian T. "Tahrir: Ends of Circulation." *Public Culture* 23, no. 3 (2011): 493–504.

Eighth Army Public Affairs. "KATUSAs Stand as Symbol of ROK-U.S. Alliance." *The United States Army,* November 1, 2011. Accessed June 10, 2014. http://www.army.mil/article/68409/.

"Eighth United States Army (EUSA)." *Global Security,* December 1, 2006. Accessed October 7, 2013. http://www.globalsecurity.org/military/agency /army/8army.htm.

Else, Liz. "The Revolution Will Be Tweeted." *New Scientist,* February 6, 2012. Accessed May 30, 2014. http://www.newscientist.com/article/mg21328500 .400-the-revolution-will-be-tweeted.html#.U4jZ5pRdV0E.

Ess, Charles, and Fay Sudweeks. *Culture, Technology, Communication: Towards an Intercultural Global Village.* Albany: State University of New York Press, 2001.

Faiola, Anthony. "Court Rejects S. Korean President's Impeachment." *Washington Post,* May 14, 2004. Accessed February 19, 2014. http://www .washingtonpost.com/wp-dyn/articles/A25441–2004May13.html.

Feinerman, James V. "The U.S.-Korea Status of Forces Agreement as a Source of Continuing Korean Anti-American Attitudes." In *Korean Attitudes toward the United States: Changing Dynamics,* edited by David I. Steinberg, 196– 219. Armonk, NY: M. E. Sharpe, 2005.

Finnegan, Cara A. "Recognizing Lincoln: Image Vernaculars in Nineteenth-Century Visual Culture." *Rhetoric & Public Affairs* 8, no. 1 (2005): 31–57.

Finnegan, Cara A., and Jiyeon Kang. " 'Sighting' the Public: Iconoclasm and Public Sphere Theory." *Quarterly Journal of Speech* 90, no. 4 (2004): 377–402.

French, Howard W., and Don Kirk. "American Policies and Presence Are under Fire in South Korea, Straining an Alliance." *New York Times.* December 8, 2002.

Gaonkar, Dilip Parameshwar, and Elizabeth A. Povinelli. "Technologies of Public Forms: Circulation, Transfiguration, Recognition." *Public Culture* 15, no. 3 (2003): 385–397.

Gaukroger, Stephen. *The Collapse of Mechanism and the Rise of Sensibility: Science and the Shaping of Modernity, 1680–1760.* Oxford: Oxford University Press, 2012.

Gell, Alfred. *Art and Agency: An Anthropological Theory.* Oxford: Oxford University Press, 1998.

Ghedin, Guido. "Social Media in South Korea: How Facebook Won Cyworld." *Digital in the Round.* April 4, 2013. Accessed July 10, 2013. http://www .digitalintheround.com/south-korea-cyworld-facebook/.

Giddens, Anthony. *Modernity and Self-Identity: Self and Society in the Late Modern Age.* Stanford, CA: Stanford University Press, 1991.

Gladwell, Malcolm. "Why the Revolution Will Not Be Tweeted." *New Yorker,* October 4, 2010. Accessed February 26, 2014. http://www.newyorker.com /reporting/2010/10/04/101004fa_fact_gladwell?currentPage=all.

Glasius, Marlies, and Geoffrey Pleyers. "The Global Moment of 2011: Democracy, Social Justice and Dignity." *Development and Change* 44, no. 3 (2013): 547–567.

"Greece's Lost Generation." *Now Public News.* May 22, 2008. Accessed July 19, 2013. http://www.nowpublic.com/world/greeces-lost-generation.

Habermas, Jürgen. *The Structural Transformation of the Public Sphere.* Translated by Thomas Burger and F. Lawrence. Cambridge, MA: MIT Press, 1989. Originally published 1962.

Hadzantonis, Michael. *English Language Pedagogies for the Northeast Asian Learner: Developing and Contextually Framing the Transition Theory.* New York: Routledge, 2013.

Hahm, Chaibong. "Anti-Americanism, Korean Style." *Issues and Insights* 3, no. 5 (2003): 9–22. Accessed September 17, 2013. http://www.csis.org/pacfor /issues/v03n05_chap02.cfm.

———. "South Korea's Miraculous Democracy." *Journal of Democracy* 19, no. 3 (2008): 128–142.

Hall, Stuart, Doreen Massey, and Michael Rustin. "After Neoliberalism: Analysing the Present." *Soundings: A Journal of Politics and Culture* 53, no. 1 (2013): 8–22.

Han, Do-Hyun. "Contemporary Korean Society Viewed through the Lens of the Candlelight Vigils." *Korea Journal* 50, no. 3 (2010): 14–37.

Han Hong-ku. "Han Hong-Ku ŭi yŏksa iyagi: 10 man nyŏn ŏchi kamok sarirŭl pŏrŏtta" (History by Han Hong-ku: We saved jail time worth 100,000 years). *Hankyoreh* 21, December 20, 2002. Accessed October 7, 2013. http://www.hani.lco.kr/h21.

Han Yun-hyŏng. "Wae urinŭn muryŏkhan ch'otpuri toeŏnna" (How have we become powerless candles?). In *Kŭdaenŭn wae ch'otpurŭl kkŭsyŏnnayo* (Why did you put out the candle?), edited by Tangdae Pip'yŏng, 19–35. Seoul: Tangdae, 2009.

Hara, Noriko, and Youngmin Jo. "Internet Politics: A Comparative Analysis of U.S. and South Korean Presidential Campaigns." *First Monday* 12, no. 9 (2007). Accessed December 31, 2014. http://firstmonday.org/ojs/index.php /fm/article/view/2005.

Hardt, Michael, and Antonio Negri. "The Fight for 'Real Democracy' at the Heart of Occupy Wall Street." *Foreign Affairs,* October 11, 2011. Accessed January 29, 2014. http://www.foreignaffairs.com/articles/136399/michael -hardt-and-antonio-negri/the-fight-for-real-democracy-at-the-heart-of -occupy-wall-street.

Hardy, Bruce, Kathleen Hall Jamieson, and Kenneth Winneg. "Wired to Fact: The Role of the Internet in Identifying Deception during the 2004 U.S. Presidential Campaign." In *Routledge Handbook of Internet Politics*, edited by Andrew Chadwick and Philip N. Howard, 131–143. New York: Taylor & Francis, 2010.

Hariman, Robert. "Political Parody and Public Culture." *Quarterly Journal of Speech* 94, no. 3 (2008): 247–272.

Hariman, Robert, and John Louis Lucaites. *No Caption Needed: Iconic Photographs, Public Culture, and Liberal Democracy*. Chicago: University of Chicago Press, 2007.

Harold, Christine. "Pranking Rhetoric: 'Culture Jamming' as Media Activism." *Critical Studies in Media Communication* 21, no. 3 (2004): 189–211.

Hart-Landsberg, Martin, and Paul Burkett. "Economic Crisis and Restructuring in South Korea: Beyond the Free Market-Statist Debate." *Critical Asian Studies* 33, no. 3 (2001): 403–430.

Hausen, Kirstin. "Italy's Extreme Right-Wing on the Rise." *Deutsche Welle*, November 9, 2013. Accessed June 27, 2014. http://www.dw.de/italys -extreme-right-wing-on-the-rise/a-17216239.

Hauser, Gerald. *Vernacular Voices*. Columbia: University of South Carolina Press, 1999.

Hayashi, Yuka. "Japan's Nationalist Movement Strengthens." *Wall Street Journal*, August 14, 2012. Accessed July 9, 2013. http://online.wsj.com/article/SB100 00872396390444130304577558364214636398.html.

Hayes, Christopher. *Twilight of the Elites: America after Meritocracy*. New York: Broadway Books, 2013.

Heider, Karl G. "The Rashomon Effect: When Ethnographers Disagree." *American Anthropologist* 90, no. 1 (1988): 73–81.

Herrera, Linda. *Revolution in the Age of Social Media: The Egyptian Popular Insurrection and the Internet*. London: Verso, 2014.

Hjorth, Larissa, and Michael Arnold. *Online@Asia Pacific: Mobile, Social and Locative Media in the Asia-Pacific*. Oxon, UK: Routledge, 2013.

Hŏ Mun-myŏng. "Int'ŏnet senoe" (Internet brainwashing). *Dong-a Ilbo*, May 5, 2008. Kinds.or.kr database.

Hong, Seoung-tae. "The World Cup, the Red Devils, and Related Arguments in Korea." *Inter-Asia Cultural Studies* 5, no. 1 (2004): 89–105.

Hong Sŏng-han. "Chaep'anjŏng chubyŏn siwidae-chŏnggyŏng taerip 'wae urikkiri ssauna' hyŏnsil taptap" (Clash between Korean protesters and police, "Why are we fighting each other?'"). *Hankyoreh*, November 23, 2002.

Hong Sŏng-t'ae. "Ch'otpul chiphoewa minjujuŭi" (The candle assembly and democracy). *Kyŏngjewa Sahoe* (Economy and society) 80 (2008): 10–39.

————. "Kŭndaehwa kwajŏngesŏ ŏrininŭn ŏttŏk'e charawannŭn'ga: Han'guk sahoeesŏŭi ŏrini tamnonŭi pyŏnhwa" (How children grew up in the modernization process: Changes in the discourse on children in Korean society). *Tangdae pip'yŏng* (Contemporary criticism) 25 (2004): 245–255.

Hong, Sung-gi. "A Look at the Changes in Debate Structure in Korea through the Candlelight Vigils." *Korea Journal* 50, no. 3 (2010): 100–127.

Hong Yŏng-rim. "Yŏron chosa: Miguk hogamdo" (Opinion poll: Koreans' image of the United States). *Chosun Ilbo,* March 4, 2002. Kinds.or.kr database.

Horkheimer, Max, and Theodor W. Adorno. *Dialectic of Enlightenment: Philosophical Fragments.* Stanford: Stanford University Press, 2002. Originally published in 1947.

Hounshell, Blake. "The Revolution Will Be Tweeted." *Foreign Policy,* June 20, 2011. http://www.foreignpolicy.com/articles/2011/06/20/the_revolution _will_be_tweeted.

Hughes, Theodore. *Literature and Film in Cold War South Korea: Freedom's Frontier.* New York: Columbia University Press, 2012.

Hwang Byŏng-ju. "Park Chung Hee sidae ch'ukkuk wa minjok juŭi: Kukkajuŭijŏk tongwŏn kwa kukmin hyŏngsŏng" (The Park Chung Hee era nationalism: Mobilization by the state and the formation of the people). *Tangdae pip'yŏng* (Contemporary criticism) 19 (2002): 145–187.

Hwang Ho-t'aek. "Kamsangjŏk panmi juŭi" (Sentimental anti-Americanism). *Dong-a Ilbo,* March 25, 2002. Accessed July 23, 2013. http://news.naver.com /main/read.nhn?mode=LSD&mid=sec&oid=020&aid=0000120373&sid1 =001.

Incorvaia, Antonio, and Alessandro Rimassa. *Generazione Mille Euro.* Milan: BUR, 2006.

Jaung, Hoon. "President Roh Moo-Hyun and the New Politics of South Korea." *Asia Society,* February 2003, 10–11.

Jenkins, Henry, Sam Ford, and Joshua Green. *Spreadable Media: Creating Value and Meaning in a Networked Culture.* New York: New York University Press, 2013.

Jeon, Gyuchan, and Tae-jin Yoon. "Cultural Politics of the Red Devils: The Desiring Multitude versus the State, Capital and Media." *Inter-Asia Cultural Studies* 5, no. 1 (2004): 77–88.

Jhee, Byong-Kuen. "Anti-Americanism and Electoral Politics in Korea." *Political Science Quarterly* 123, no. 2 (2008): 301–318.

Jin, Dal Yong. *Korea's Online Gaming Empire.* Cambridge: MIT Press, 2010.

Johnson, Chalmers A. *The Sorrows of Empire: Militarism, Secrecy, and the End of the Republic.* New York: Metropolitan Books, 2004.

Jones, Gill. *Youth.* London: Polity, 2009.

Joo, Rachael Miyung. *Transnational Sport: Gender, Media, and Global Korea.* Durham, NC: Duke University Press, 2012.

Joyce, Mary. "The Citizen Journalism Web Site 'OhmyNews' and the 2002 South Korean Presidential Election." *Berkman Center Research Publication* No. 2007–15 (December 2007). Accessed September 7, 2013. Available at http://papers.ssrn.com/sol3/papers.cfm?abstract_id=1077920.

Kang, C. S. Eliot. "Restructuring the U.S.–South Korea Alliance to Deal with the Second Korean Nuclear Crisis." *Australian Journal of International Affairs* 57, no. 2 (2003): 309–324.

Kang Chŏng-ku. *Hyŏndae hankuk sahoeŭi ihaewa chŏnmang (Understanding contemporary Korean society).* Seoul: Hanul, 2000.

Kang, Jiyeon. "A Volatile Public: The 2009 Whole Foods Boycott on Facebook." *Journal of Broadcasting & Electronic Media* 56, no. 4 (2012): 562–577.

Kang, Jiyeon, and Nancy Abelmann. "The Domestication of South Korean Pre-College Study Abroad in the First Decade of the Millennium." *Journal of Korean Studies* 16, no. 1 (2011): 89–118.

Kang, Man-gil. "Contemporary Nationalist Movement and the *Minjung*." In *South Korea's Minjung Movement: The Culture and Politics of Dissidence,* edited by Kenneth M. Wells, 31–38. Honolulu: University of Hawai'i Press, 1995.

Kang, Myungkoo. "Compressed Modernization and the Formation of the Developmentalist Mentalité." In *Reassessing the Park Chung Hee Era, 1961– 1979: Development, Political Thought, Democracy, and Cultural Influence,* edited by Hyung-A Kim and Clark W. Sorensen, 166–186. Seattle: University of Washington Press, 2011.

Kang Nae-hŭi. "Pyŏnhyŏgundongŭi kŏjŏmesŏ shinjayujuŭi chibaegongganŭro: 1980nyŏndae ihu han'gugŭi taehak" (From the stronghold of a revolutionary movement to a space of neoliberal domination: The university in South Korea since the 1980s). *Yŏksa pip'yŏng* (Critical review of history) 104 (2013): 65–88.

Kang Pyŏng-han, Pak Su-jŏng, and Yu Chŏng-in. "'Uridŭl chinjihan komin wae p'yŏmhwehago mangnayo'-ch'otpulshiwi chuch'uk 10taedŭl tashi punno" (Why do you insult and block our serious opinions?). *Kyŏnghyang Sinmun,* May 7, 2008.

Kang Su-dol. "Woldŭk'ŏp 4 kang'gwa 'kyŏngje 4 kang' sinhwa" (The World Cup semifinal and the myth of the "semifinal in economic development"). *Tangdae pip'yŏng* (Contemporary criticism) 20 (2002): 90–110.

Kang, Yŏng-su. "Paek Sang-Ch'ang sojang, 'ch'otpul shiwinŭn chugŭm ch'anmiŭi shimri, manyŏsanyang katta'" ("Director Paek Sang-Ch'ang says, 'The beef protest is out of necrophilia. It is a witch hunt'"). *Chosun Ilbo,*

May 22, 2008. Accessed May 15, 2015. http://news.chosun.com/site/data
/html_dir/2008/05/22/2008052200975.html.

Kang Yun-jae. "Kwangubyŏng wihŏmgwa ch'otpulchip'oe" (The risk of BSE and
the candlelight protests). *Kyŏngjewa sahoe* (Economy and society) 89 (2011):
269–297.

Kant, Immanuel. *The Critique of Judgment.* Translated by J. H. Bernard. 2nd ed.
London: Macmillan, 1914.

Keane, John. "Monitory Democracy and Media-Saturated Societies." *Griffith
Review* 24 (2009): 1–23.

Kelly, Tim, Vanessa Gray, and Michael Minge. *Broadband Korea: Internet Case
Study.* International Telecommunication Union, March 2003. Accessed
December 7, 2015. http://www.itu.int/itudoc/gs/promo/bdt/cast_int/85867.pdf.

Kim, Andrew Eungi. "Civic Activism and Korean Democracy: The Impact of
Blacklisting Campaigns in the 2000 and 2004 General Elections." *The
Pacific Review* 19, no. 4 (2006): 519–542.

Kim, Byung-Kook. "The Politics of Crisis and a Crisis of Politics: The Presidency
of Kim Dae Jung." In *Korea Briefing, 1997–1999: Challenges and Change at
the Turn of the Century,* edited by Kongdan Oh, 35–74. Armonk: M. E.
Sharpe, 2000.

Kim Chi-ŭn. "Wŏltŭk'ŏp hwanho kwanghwamunsŏ ch'otpul siwi Hyo-sun Mi-sŏn
ch'umo 1mannyŏ myŏng unjip" (Ten thousand gathered to commemorate
Hyo-sun and Mi-sŏn in Kwanghwamun, the epicenter of the World Cup
cheering). *Oh My News,* January 5, 2003. Accessed June 9, 2014. http://www
.ohmynews.com/nws_web/view/at_pg.aspx?CNTN_CD=A0000096428.

Kim Chŏng-ha. "T'up'yŏyul 62.9% taesŏn sasang ch'oejŏ . . . 16 taewa pigyo hae
poni" (62.9%, the lowest voting rate, a comparison to the 16th election).
JoongAng Ilbo, December 20, 2007. Accessed November 11, 2013. http://
article.joins.com/news/article/article.asp?Total_ID=2985323.

Kim, Chul-Kyoo. "Teenage Participants of the 2008 Candlelight Vigil: Their
Social Characteristics and Changes in Political Views." *Korea Journal* 50, no.
3 (2010): 14–37.

Kim Hyŏn-mi. "2002nyŏn wŏldŭk'ŏpŭi yŏsŏnghwawa yŏsŏng p'aentŏm" (The
feminization of the 2002 World Cup and the female fandom)."*Tangdae
pip'yŏng* (Contemporary criticism) 20 (2002): 48–61.

Kim, Hyuk-Rae. "The State and Civil Society in Transition: The Role of Non-
Governmental Organizations in South Korea." *The Pacific Review* 13, no. 4
(2000): 595–613.

Kim, Jeong-ho. "The Internet and the Public in South Korea: Online Political
Talk and Culture." PhD diss. University of Illinois, Urbana–Champaign,
2012.

Kim Chi-sŏng. "Mi Soegogi suip, taeunha pandae 100 in sikuk sŏnŏn" (A one-hundred-person political statement against the American beef import and the grand canal). *SBS News*, June 2, 2008. Accessed March 10, 2014. http://news.sbs.co.kr/section_news/news_read.jsp?news_id=N1000424433.

Kim Chi-ŭn. "Kwanghwamun e simin dŭri moyŏdŭlgo itta" (Citizens are on their way to Kwanghwamun). *Oh My News,* December 19, 2002. Accessed June 6, 2014. http://www.ohmynews.com/NWS_Web/View/at_pg.aspx?cntn_cd=A0000099497.

Kim Chong-yŏp. "Ch'ŏtpul chiphoewa 87nyŏn ch'eje" (Candlelight protests and the 87 regime). *Ch'angjak kwa pip'yŏng* (Creation and criticism) 36, no. 3 (2008): 36–59.

———. "Ch'otpul tŭn yŏhaksaengdŭrŭi paehu?" (Seeking mobilizers of candle girls?). *Hankyoreh,* May 12, 2008. Kinds.or.kr database.

———. *Sahŏejŏk chouljŭng kwa naengsojuŭi* (Social manic depression and cynicism). Seoul: Munhak Tongne, 2001.

Kim Chun. "Mujoe p'yŏlgyŏl migun 2myŏng kot chŏnyŏk chŏnch'ul" (The two "acquitted" soon to be transferred and discharged). *Chosun Ilbo,* November 26, 2002.

Kim Kwang-dŏk. "Taesŏn 1nyŏnjŏn kukmin ŭisik chosa . . . chinbo chulgo chungdo nŭlŏtta" (Opinion poll one year before Presidential Election . . . less progressive more moderate). *Hankook Ilbo,* December 8, 2006.

Kim Min-sik. "1980 nyŏn 5 wol kwangju, p'oktong kwa minjuhwa undongŭi ch'ai" (Kwangju in May 1980, the difference between a riot and a democratization movement), *Oh My News,* May 18, 2007. Accessed May 3, 2014. http://www.ohmynews.com/nws_web/view/at_pg.aspx?CNTN_CD =A0000411232.

Kim Sa-kwa, Chŏng Da-hae, Han Yun-hyŏng, and Chŏng So-hyŏng. "20 tae yaegi, tŭrŏnŭn poassŏ?" (Have you ever listened to twentysomethings?). *Ch'angjak kwa pip'yŏng* (Creation and criticism) 38, no. 1 (2010): 269–299.

Kim Se-gyun. "Han'gukŭi chŏngch'i chihyŏnggwa ch'otpul sedae" (Korea's political terrain and the candle generation). *Munhwa/Kwahak* (Culture/Science) 63 (2010): 47–65.

Kim, Seung-Hwan. "Anti-Americanism in Korea." *The Washington Quarterly* 26, no. 1 (2002–2003): 109–22.

———. "Yankee Go Home? A Historical View of South Korean Sentiment toward the United States, 2001–2004." In *Strategy and Sentiment: South Korean Views of the United States and the U.S.-ROK Alliance,* edited by Derek J. Mitchell, 24–35. Washington, DC: Center of Strategic and International Studies, 2004.

Kim Sŏng-hwan. "Tallajin ch'otpulchip'oe: 10tae pinjarie 20–40tae, insolchado ŏpshi kŏrihaengjin" (The changing candlelight protests: Participants in their twenties–forties are replacing teenagers and marching without a leader). *Hankyoreh,* May 27, 2008.

Kim So-yŏn. "Ch'otbulsiwi chean net'ijŭn 'angma' omainyusŭ sŏnjŏng 'olhaeŭi inmul'" (Netizen Angma, who proposed the candlelight vigils, is the "person of the year" chosen by Oh My News). *Oh My News,* December 31, 2002. Accessed October 7, 2013. http://www.ohmynews.com/nws_web/view /at_pg.aspx?CNTN_CD=A0000100917.

Kim Ung-il. "T'anhaek ch'ŏngwŏnhan Andante poho yŏnki hwaksan" (Move to protect Andante, the proposer of impeachment). *News Town,* May 14, 2008. Accessed January 16, 2014. http://www.newstown.co.kr/news/articleView .html?idxno=55874.

Kim, Yeran. ""Kamsŏng kongronjang: Yŏsŏng k'ŏmyunit'i, nŭkkigo malhago haengdonghada (Affective public sphere: woman communities feel, speak and act)." *Ŏllon kwa sahoe* (Media and society) 18, no. 3 (2010): 146–191.

Kim, Yong Cheol, and June Woo Kim. "South Korean Democracy in the Digital Age: The Candlelight Protests and the Internet." *Korea Observer* 40, no. 1 (2009): 53–83.

Kim Yong-ch'ŏl. "4manbul siedae en pissan soegogi? soga utkenne" (Expensive beef for an era of $40,000 GDP? Even cows would laugh). *Oh My News,* April 28, 2008. Accessed February 10, 2014. http://www.ohmynews.com /nws_web/view/at_pg.aspx?CNTN_CD=A0000888088.

Kim Yong-ho. "Int'ŏnet k'ŏmyunit'iwa chŏngch'i: Nosamo sarye yŏn'gu" (Internet community and politics: A study of Nosamo). In *Proceedings from the 2003 Korean Sociological Association Biannual Conference,* 519–541. Seoul: Korean Sociological Association, 2003.

Kim Yŏng-kyŏng. "Han'gugŭi chŏngch'isedaee kwanhan kyŏnghŏmjŏk yŏn'gu: 'Minjuhwa sedae' wa 'sinsedae' ŭi pigyorŭl chungshimŭro" (An empirical study of Korean political generations: The "democratization generation" and the "new generation"). *Tonghyang kwa chŏnmang* (Journal of Korean social trends and perspectives) 41 (1999): 119–133.

Kim Yong-min. "Nŏhŭinŭn hŭimang'i ŏptt'a" (You're hopeless). *Kim Yong-Min's Blog,* June 14, 2009. Accessed November 24, 2014. http://newstice.tistory .com/224.

Kim, Young Ok. "Understanding the Candlelight Demonstration and Women's Political Subjectivity through the Perspective of Changing Publicity." *Korea Journal* 50, no. 3 (2010): 38–70.

Kim Yŏng-ok. "Yŏsŏngjuŭiŭi kwanjŏmesŏ pon ch'otpul chiphoewa yŏsŏngŭi chŏngch'ijŏk juch'esŏng (The candlelight protest and political subjectivity of women from the feminist perspective)." *Asia yŏsŏng yŏn'gu* (Journal of Asian women) 48, no. 2 (2009): 7–34.

Kim Yŏng-sun. "Roh Moo-Hyun chŏngbuŭi pokchijŏngch'aek" (The assessment of the social welfare policies in the Roh Moo-Hyun government). *Kyŏngjewa sahoe* (Economy and society) 82 (2009): 161–185.

Kirk, Don. "America on Thin Ice in South Korea." *New York Times,* March 1, 2002. Accessed May 19, 2014. http://www.nytimes.com/2002/03/01/news /01iht-t1_2.html.

"Kirok ŭro ponŭn o mai nyus 10 nyŏn" (Ten years of Oh My News). *Oh My News,* 2010. Accessed May 3, 2014. http://www.ohmynews.com/nws_web /event/10th_lst01.aspx?page_gb=00.

Kleinman, Arthur, and Joan Kleinman. "How Bodies Remember: Social Memory and Bodily Experience of Criticism, Resistance, and Delegitimation Following China's Cultural Revolution." *New Literary History* 25 (2004): 707–723.

Ko Kil-sŏp. "Ch'ŏngnyŏn munhwa, hokŭn sosu munhwaronjŏk yŏn'gu e taehayŏ" (On the study of youth culture or subculture). *Munhwa/Kwahak* (Culture/Science) 20 (1999): 145–172.

Ko Yŏng-bok. "4wŏl hyŏkmyŏngŭi ŭisik kujo" (The structure of consciousness in the April Revolution). In *4wol hyŏkmyŏngron* (On the April revolution), edited by Man-gil Kang, 85–129. Seoul: Han'gilsa, 1983.

Kong, Pyung-won. "Change in the Political System of Republic of Korea (ROK) and the United States (U.S.)-ROK Relationship." PhD diss., West Virginia University, 2005.

Koo, Hagen. "Civil Society and Democracy in South Korea." *Good Society* 11, no. 2 (2002): 40–45.

———. "The Changing Faces of Inequality in South Korea in the Age of Globalization." *Korean Studies* 31, no. 1 (2007): 1–18.

"Korean Anger as US Soldiers Cleared." *BBC,* November 22, 2002, sec. Asia-Pacific. Accessed September 9, 2013. http://news.bbc.co.uk/2/hi/asia-pacific /2497947.stm.

"Korean Youth Study Longest Hours in OECD." *Chosun Ilbo* (English Edition), August 10, 2009. Accessed March 17, 2014. http://english.chosun.com/site /data/html_dir/2009/08/10/2009081000200.html.

"Kukmin 10 myŏng chung 7 myŏng ppyŏ soegogi suip pandae" (Seven out of ten Koreans are against beef import). *Hankyoreh,* October 20, 2007.

Kwak, Young-sup. "Court Clears U.S. Soldier of Killing Korean Girls." *Korea Herald,* November 21, 2002.

"Kwang'ubyŏng nollan int'ŏnet kwahak k'ŏmyunit'isŏdo kayŏl" (The mad cow disease controversy is heating up in an Internet science community). *SBS,* May 6, 2008. Accessed March 31, 2014. http://news.sbs.co.kr/news/endPage .do?news_id=N1000413043.

"Kwang'ubyŏng t'ujaengŭl pan FTA and Lee Myung-bak t'ujaengŭro" (From protest against mad cow to protest against FTA and Lee Myung-bak). *People's Solidarity for Social Progress,* May 22, 2008. Accessed March 31, 2014. http://www.pssp.org/bbs/view.php?board=sola&nid=4909.

Kwon, Heonik. *The Other Cold War.* New York: Columbia University Press, 2010.

Kwon Hyŏk-pŏm. "Wŏltŭk'ŏp 'kungmin ch'ukche' 'pŭllaekhol ppallyŏ tŭrŏgan taehanmin'guk-tongnipchŏk chisŏngŭn ŏdie innŭn'ga?" (The Republic of Korea subsumed under the "national festival" of the World Cup—where are independent intellectuals?). *Tangdae pip'yŏng* (Contemporary criticism) 20 (2002): 62–89.

Kwon, Yong-rip. "Ch'inmiwa panmi, kŭ saiesŏ sumŭn kŭrim ch'atki" (Pro-Americanism and anti-Americanism, finding the middle ground between them). *Tangdae pip'yŏng* (Contemporary criticism) 21 (2003): 169–186.

"Kyoyuk, posuŏnnon pip'an isyu hwaksan: Tŭlburi toen ch'otpul" (Education and conservative media became issues: Candlelight is turning into wildfire). *Kyŏnghyang Sinmun,* May 18, 2008.

Labov, William. *Language in the Inner City: Studies in the Black English Vernacular.* Philadelphia: University of Pennsylvania Press, 1972.

Landow, George P. *Hypertext 2.0: The Convergence of Contemporary Critical Theory and Technology.* 2nd ed. Baltimore: Johns Hopkins University Press, 1997.

Lanham, Richard A. *The Economics of Attention: Style and Substance in the Age of Information.* Chicago: University of Chicago Press, 2006.

Latour, Bruno. *Reassembling the Social: An Introduction to Actor-Network-Theory.* Oxford: Oxford University Press, 2007.

Lau, T. Y., Si Wook Kim, and David Atkin. "An Examination of Factors Contributing to South Korea's Global Leadership in Broadband Adoption." *Telematics and Informatics,* WSIS Special Issue: The World Summit on the Information Society (WSIS) from an Asian-Pacific Region Perspective, 22, no. 4 (2005): 349–359.

Law, John. "Notes on the Theory of Actor-Network: Ordering, Strategy and Heterogeneity." *Systems Practice* 5 (1992): 379–393.

Le Bon, Gustave. *The Crowd: A Study of the Popular Mind.* New York: Macmillan, 1897. Reprint, Mineola: Dover Publications, 2001.

Lee, Byoungkwan, Karen M. Lancendorfer, and Ki Jung Lee. "Agenda-Setting and the Internet: The Intermedia Influence of Internet Bulletin Boards on Newspaper Coverage of the 2000 General Election in South Korea." *Asian Journal of Communication* 15, no. 1 (2005): 57–71.

Lee, Hong Yung. "South Korea in 2002: Multiple Political Dramas." *Asian Survey* 43, no. 1 (2003): 64–77.

Lee, Ho-young. "The Configuration of the Korean Cyberspace: A Tentative Study on Cultural Traits of Korean Internet Users." *Sahoe kwahak nonch'ong* (The journal of social sciences) 12 (2010): 123–153.

Lee, Jinsun. "Net Power in Action: Internet Activism in the Contentious Politics of South Korea." PhD diss., Rutgers University, 2009.

Lee, Kyung. "Fighting in the Shadow of the Past: The Mobilizing Role of Vernacular Memories of the 1987 pro-Democracy Movement in the 2008 Candlelight Protests in Korea." *Memory Studies* 7, no. 1 (2014): 61–75.

Lee, Namhee. *The Making of Minjung: Democracy and the Politics of Representation in South Korea.* Ithaca, NY: Cornell University Press, 2007.

Lee, Seung-Ook, Sook-Jin Kim, and Joel Wainwright. "Mad Cow Militancy: Neoliberal Hegemony and Social Resistance in South Korea." *Political Geography* 29, no. 7 (2010): 359–369.

Lee, Sook-Jong. "Anti-Americanism in Korean Society: A Survey-Based Analysis." *Joint U.S.-Korea Academic Studies* 14 (2004): 183–204.

———. "The Rise of Korean Youth as a Political Force." *Brookings Northeast Asia Survey 2003–2004,* 2004. Accessed September 17, 2013. http://www.brook .edu/fp/cnaps/papers/survey2004/2korea2.pdf.

Lee, Yeon-Ok. "Internet Election 2.0? Culture, Institutions, and Technology in the Korean Presidential Elections of 2002 and 2007." *Journal of Information Technology & Politics* 6, nos. 3–4 (2009): 312–325.

Lee, Yoonkyung. "Democracy without Parties? Political Parties and Social Movements for Democratic Representation in Korea." *Korea Observer* 40, no. 1 (2009): 27–52.

Leiter, Brian. "Cleaning Cyber-Cesspools: Google and Free Speech." In *The Offensive Internet,* edited by Saul Levmore and Martha Craven Nussbaum, 155–173. Cambridge, MA: Harvard University Press, 2010.

Lenzo, Brian. "Will the Revolution Be Tweeted?" *International Socialist Review,* July 2013. Accessed May 30, 2014. http://isreview.org/issue/90/will -revolution-be-tweeted.

Lippmann, Walter. *Public Opinion.* New York: Harcourt, Brace, and Co., 1922.

Mahmood, Saba. "Feminist Theory, Embodiment, and the Docile Agent: Some Reflections on the Egyptian Islamic Revival." *Cultural Anthropology* 16, no. 2 (2001): 202–236.

———. *Politics of Piety: The Islamic Revival and the Feminist Subject.* Princeton, NJ: Princeton University Press, 2012.

Malinowski, Bronisław K. "The Primitive Economics of the Trobriand Islanders." *The Economic Journal* 31, no. 121 (1921): 1–16.

Manyin, Mark E. *South Korean Politics and Rising "Anti-Americanism": Implications for US Policy Toward North Korea.* Report for Congress, 2003.

Accessed September 17, 2013. http://www.nautilus.org/wp-content/uploads /2011/12/CRS-RL31906ROKAntiAmericanism.pdf.

Marwick, Alice E. *Status Update: Celebrity, Publicity, and Branding in the Social Media Age.* New Haven, CT: Yale University Press, 2013.

Marwick, Alice E., and danah boyd. "I Tweet Honestly, I Tweet Passionately: Twitter Users, Context Collapse, and the Imagined Audience." *New Media & Society* 13, no. 1 (2011): 114–133.

Mauss, Marcel, and W. D. Halls. *The Gift: Forms and Functions of Exchange in Archaic Societies.* New York: W. W. Norton & Company, 1954. Originally published 1925.

Miller, Daniel. "The Fame of Trinis: Websites as Traps." In *Beyond Aesthetics: Art and the Technologies of Enchantment,* edited by Christopher Pinney and Nicholas Thomas, 137–155. New York: Bloomsbury Academic, 2001.

Ministry of National Defense. *Kukpang paeksŏ* (Ministry of National Defense white paper), 2012. Accessed May 3, 2014. http://www.mnd.go.kr/user/mnd /upload/pblictn/PBLICTNEBOOK_201308060946041630.pdf.

Mirae Hankuk. "Chŏnkyojo, sahoe isyu tt'aemada kyeki suŏp charyo ollyŏ" (KTU publishes curriculum for every social issue). *Mirae Hankuk* (Future Korea), November 11, 2005. Accessed May 3, 2014. http://www.futurekorea .co.kr/news/articleView.html?idxno=8991.

Moon, Jae-Yun, and Shinkyu Yang. "The Internet as an Agent of Political Change: The Case of 'Rohsamo' in the South Korean Presidential Campaign of 2002." In *International Conference on Information Systems 2003 Proceeding,* 903–908. Seattle: Association for Information Systems, 2003. Available at: http://aisel.aisnet.org/cgi/viewcontent.cgi?article=1189&context =icis2003.

Moon, Katharine. *Protesting America: Democracy and the U.S.–Korea Alliance.* Berkeley: University of California Press, 2013.

Moon, Seungsook. "Carving Out Space: Civil Society and the Women's Movement in South Korea." *Journal of Asian Studies* 61, no. 2 (2002): 473–500.

Moran, Andrew. "OECD: South Korea High-Speed Internet Penetration Rate Tops 100%." *Digital Journal.* Accessed July 11, 2013. http://www.digital journal.com/article/329199.

"More Signs That American Youth Are a Lost Generation." *The Atlantic Wire.* September 22, 2011. Accessed July 19, 2013. http://www.theatlanticwire .com/national/2011/09/american-youth-lost-generation/42814/.

Morozov, Evgeny. "The Brave New World of Slacktivism." *Foreign Policy,* May 19, 2009. Accessed August 20, 2013. http://neteffect.foreignpolicy.com /posts/2009/05/19/the_brave_new_world_of_slacktivism.

Morris, Dick. *Vote.com: Influence, and the Internet Is Giving Power Back to the People.* New York: Macmillan, 2011.

No Chin-ch'ŏl. "2008nyŏn ch'otpulchip'oerŭl t'onghae pon kwangubyŏng kongp'owa mujiŭi wihŏmsot'ong" (The communication and risk of ignorance during the 2008 candlelight protests). *Kyŏngjewa sahoe* (Economy and society) 84 (2009): 158–182.

Norris, Pippa. "Did the Media Matter? Agenda-Setting, Persuasion and Mobilization Effects in the British General Election Campaign." *British Politics* 1, no. 2 (2006): 195–221.

O Myŏng-ho. *Han'guk chongch'isaŭi ihae* (Understanding Korea's political history). Seoul: Orum, 2006.

O Tong-kŭn. "Ch'otpulkwa hamsŏng simin jugwŏn sidaerŭl yŏlda" (Candle and scream opens up an era of citizen sovereignty). *Kyŏnghyang Sinmun*, June 4, 2008. Accessed March 10, 2014. http://news.khan.co.kr/kh_news/khan_art _view.html?artid=200806041754265&code=940707.

O Yŏn-ho. *Taehanmin'guk t'ŭksanp'um Omainyusŭ* (Oh My News, a Korean specialty). Seoul: Humanist, 2004.

Oates, Sarah, Diana Owen, and Rachel K. Gibson. *The Internet and Politics: Citizens, Voters and Activists.* London: Routledge, 2006.

Organization for Economic Cooperation and Development (OECD). "OECD Broadband Statistics Update." *OECD.* Accessed July 10, 2013. http://www .oecd.org/sti/broadband/broadband-statistics-update.htm.

"Ollain p'ulppu-ri' sesangŭl pakkunda" (Online grassroots power changes the world: Generation Web 2.0). *Hankyoreh,* June 3, 2008.

Ono, Kent A., and John M. Sloop. *Shifting Borders: Rhetoric, Immigration, and California's Proposition 187.* Philadelphia: Temple University Press, 2002.

Pai, Hyung Il, and Timothy R. Tangherlini. Introduction to *Nationalism and the Construction of Korean Identity,* 1–12. Berkeley: University of California Press, 1998.

Paik Wuk-in. "Saengsanjŏk p'aerŏdi rŭl wihayŏ: Ttanji ilbo rŭl pogo" (Toward productive parody: The case of Ttanji Ilbo). *Tangdae pip'yŏng* (Contemporary criticism) 6, no. 3 (1999): 486–489.

Pak Chi-in. " 'Kwang'upyŏng' Agora t'oronbang chohoe 5200 man kŏn" ("Mad cow disease" Agora page view reached 52 million). *Consumer News,* May 9, 2008. Accessed August 8, 2013. http://consumernews.co.kr/news/view.html ?pid=90134&cate=&page=6536.

Pak Chi-hwan. "Simin kija 7man yŏ myŏng, kijon ŏllonkwa ch'abyŏlhwa" (Seventy thousand citizen reporters, a big distinction from the existing press). *Sinmun kwa pangsong* (Press and broadcasting), December 2011, 68–73.

Pak Chun-sŏk. "Ŏmma appa chŏ ch'ŏtpul chiphoe nagayo: 386 pumowa 2.0 chanyŏga mandŭro kanŭn haengbokhan kajŏng" (Mom, dad, I'm off to a candlelight protest: Generation 386 parents and 2.0 children). *Mal,*

November 2008. Accessed March 31, 2014. http://www.dbpia.co.kr/Journal
/ArticleDetail/913758.

Palczewski, Catherine Helen. "Cyber-Movements, New Social Movements, and
Counterpublics." In *Counterpublics and the State,* edited by Robert Asen and
Daniel Brouwer, 161–186. Albany: State University of New York Press, 2001.

"Panmiŭi poiji annŭn son ije chom poisijo?" (Do you now see the invisible hand
of anti-Americanism?). *Oh My News,* December 15, 2002. Accessed June 14,
2014. http://www.ohmynews.com/NWS_Web/view/at_pg.aspx?cntn_cd
=A0000098856.

Papacharissi, Zizi A. *Affective Publics: Sentiment, Technology, and Politics.* Kindle
ed. New York: Oxford University Press, 2014.

———. *A Private Sphere: Democracy in a Digital Age.* Cambridge: Polity, 2010.

———. "The Virtual Sphere: The Internet as the Public Sphere." *New Media &
Society* 4 (2002): 5–23.

Park, Joseph Sung-Yul. "The Promise of English: Linguistic Capital and the
Neoliberal Worker in the South Korean Job Market." *International Journal
of Bilingual Education and Bilingualism* 14, no. 4 (2011): 443–455.

Park, Mi. "South Korea: Passion, Patriotism, and Student Radicalism." In
Student Activism in Asia, edited by Meredith Leigh Weiss and Edward
Aspinall, 125–151. Minneapolis: University of Minnesota Press, 2012.

Park, So Jin, and Nancy Abelmann. "Class and Cosmopolitan Striving: Mothers'
Management of English Education in South Korea." *Anthropological
Quarterly* 77, no. 4 (2004): 645–672.

Park, Young-a. *Unexpected Alliances: Independent Filmmakers, the State, and the
Film Industry in Postauthoritarian South Korea.* Stanford, CA: Stanford
University Press, 2014.

Prensky, Marc. "Digital Natives, Digital Immigrants Part 1." *On the Horizon* 9,
no. 5 (2001): 1–6.

Pew Research Center. *Millennials: Confident. Connected. Open to Change.* 2010.
Accessed July 19, 2013. http://www.pewresearch.org/millennials.

Pirie, Iain. *The Korean Developmental State: From Dirigisme to Neo-Liberalism.*
New York: Routledge, 2007.

Plato. *Gorgias.* Baltimore: Agora Publications, Inc., 1994.

"Police Go on Nationwide Alert to Prepare for Massive Crowds." *Korea Times,*
June 9, 2002.

Poster, Mark. "Cyber Democracy: Internet and the Public Sphere." In *Information
Subject,* 95–116. London: Routledge, 2013. Originally published 1995.

Postill, John. *Localizing the Internet: An Anthropological Account.* New York:
Berghahn Books, 2011.

Prensky, Marc. "Digital Natives, Digital Immigrants Part 1." *On the Horizon* 9,
no. 5 (2001): 1–6.

"Pulgŭn angmawa wŏldŭk'ŏp sedae" (The Red Devils and the World Cup generation). *National Archive.* Accessed July 17, 2013. http://theme.archives .go.kr/next/worldCup2009/redDevils.do.

Rafael, Vicente L. "The Cell Phone and the Crowd: Messianic Politics in the Contemporary Philippines." *Public Culture* 15, no. 3 (2003): 399–425.

Redden, Guy. "Changing Times Again: Recent Writing on Globalization, Communications and the New Activism." *Social Movement Studies* 4, no. 1 (2005): 99–103.

Reiss, Timothy. "Denying the Body? Memory and the Dilemmas of History in Descartes." *The Journal of the History of Ideas* 57, no. 4 (1996): 587–607.

Rheingold, Howard. *Smart Mobs: The Next Social Revolution.* Cambridge: Perseus, 2002.

Robertson, Jeffrey. "The Anti-American Blowback from Bush's Korea Policy." *Foreign Policy in Focus,* January 2003. Accessed October 7, 2013. http://fpif .org/the_anti-american_blowback_from_bushs_korea_policy.

Ryu Chŏng-min. "Yi taet'ongryŏng t'ŏtbat seoul, kukchŏng chijido 3%" (President Lee's approval rate hits 3% in Seoul). *Media Today,* June 16, 2008. Accessed January 9, 2014. http://www.mediatoday.co.kr/news /articleView.html?idxno=69462.

Ryu Jae-hun. "Pusi sagwa anp'ak, panmi kamjŏng pulgil uryŏ" (Bush's apology, concerns about rising anti-American sentiment). *Hankyoreh,* November 28, 2002.

"Saeroun minjujuŭi shirhŏm: Ch'otpulgwa hamsŏng shiminjugwŏn shidaerŭl yŏlda" (Experimenting with new democracy: Candles and screams open new era for people power). *Kyŏnghyang Sinmun,* June 5, 2008.

Salazar, Juan Francisco. "Articulating an Activist Imaginary: Internet as Counter Public Sphere in the Mapuche Movement, 1997/2002." *Media International Australia, Incorporating Culture & Policy* 107 (2003): 19–30.

"Sasŏl: Hyŏnsilkwa tongtt'ŏlŏjin taet'ongryŏng ŭi soegogi palŏn" (Editorial: The president's comments on beef are out of touch with reality). *Hankyoreh,* April 28, 2008.

"Sasŏl: Migun mujoe hang'ŭirŭl p'okryŏkŭro ŏkaphan kyŏngch'al" (Editorial: Excessive police violence in the protests against the G.I's acquittal). *Hankyoreh,* November 23, 2002.

"Sasŏl: Migunmanŭi baesim ppŏnhan p'yŏnggyŏl" (Editorial: A jury of U.S. officials, the verdict was expected). *Chosun Ilbo,* November 22, 2002.

"Sasŏl: 'Panmi' nŏmŏ haebŏp ch'atja" (Editorial: Let's find solution beyond "anti-Americanism"). *Chosun Ilbo,* November 29, 2002.

"Sasŏl: Pulpyŏngdŭng sopa chaehyŏpsang sijak hara" (Editorial: Begin the renegotiation of unfair SOFA). *Hankyoreh,* November 24, 2002.

"Sasŏl: Pusi sagwawa apŭroŭi hanmi tongmang" (Editorial: Bush's apology and the future Korea–U.S. alliance). *Chosun Ilbo,* November 28, 2002.

"Sasŏl: Tashi ch'otpulro chaemi poryŏnŭn choapa seryŏk" (Editorial: The leftists are taking advantage of the candle again). *Dong-a Ilbo,* May 5, 2008.

Schultheis, Emily. "Poll: Millennials Disillusioned with President Obama." *Politico,* December 4, 2013. Accessed June 9, 2014. http://www.politico.com /story/2013/12/young-voters-obama-approval-rating-100647.html.

Schuman, Michael. "Fallout of Ex South Korea President's Suicide." *Time,* May 25, 2009. Accessed June 24, 2014. http://content.time.com/time/world /article/0,8599,1900808,00.html.

Sheller, Mimi. "Mobile Publics: Beyond the Network Perspective." *Environment and Planning D: Society and Space* 22, no. 1 (2004): 39–52.

Shifman, Limor. "An Anatomy of a YouTube Meme." *New Media & Society* 14, no. 2 (2011): 187–203.

Shin, Eui Hang. "Correlates of the 2002 Presidential Election in South Korea: Regionalism, the Generation Gap, Anti-Americanism, and the North Korea Factor." *East Asia* 21, no. 2 (2004): 18–38.

Shin, Gi-wook. "Nation, History, and Politics: South Korea." In *Nationalism and the Construction of Korean Identity,* edited by Hyung Il Pai and Timothy R. Tangherlini, 148–165. Berkeley: University of California Press, 1999.

Shirky, Clay. *Here Comes Everybody: The Power of Organizing without Organizations.* New York: Penguin Press, 2008.

———. "The Political Power of Social Media." *Foreign Affairs,* January 1, 2011. Accessed July 14, 2013. http://www.foreignaffairs.com/articles/67038/clay -shirky/the-political-power-of-social-media.

Sim Kwang-hyŏn. "Chabonjuŭi apch'uk sŏngjang kwa sedaeŭi chŏngch'i pip'an" (A critique of the capitalist compressed development and the political economy of generation). *Munhwa/Kwahak* (Culture/Science) 63 (2010): 15–46.

———. "Sedaeŭi chŏngch'ihakkwa hankuk hyŏndaesaŭi chaehaesŏk" (Generation politics and the reinterpretation of contemporary Korean history). *Munhwa/Kwahak* (Culture/Science) 62 (2010): 17–71.

Sim Yang-sŏp. "Hankuk ŭi panmi undong" (Anti-American movement in South Korea). *Sidae chŏngsin* (Zeitgeist), 2012. Accessed March 31, 2014. http:// www.sdjs.co.kr/read.php?quarterId=SD201202&num=586.

Simon, Herbert A. "Designing Organizations for an Information-Rich World." In *Computers, Communication, and the Public Interest,* edited by Martin Greenberger, 40–41. Baltimore: Johns Hopkins University Press, 1971.

Smith, Mark A., and Peter Kollock. *Communities in Cyberspace.* New York: Routledge, 1999.

So Yŏng-hyŏn. "Pullyang chŏngnyŏn taemangron" (Hope for mischievous youth). *Naeilŭl yŏnŭn yŏksa* (History for tomorrow) 40 (2010): 20–45.

Song Chu-min. "Simindŭl chŏnkyŏng'e sugohanda, ch'ungdol ŏpyi mamuri" (Citizens give combat police pat on the back for hard work). *Oh My News,* June 27, 2008. Accessed February 7, 2014. http://www.ohmynews.com/nws _web/view/at_pg.aspx?CNTN_CD=A0000935772.

Song Ho-geun. *Hankuk, musŭn iri ilŏnago itna?: Sedae kaldŭnggwa chohwaŭi mihak* (Korea, what is happening: The aesthetics of generational conflict and concord). Seoul: Samsung Economic Research Institute, 2003.

Song, Ho-kyun, Dae-ha Jung, and Jin-sik Jeon. " 'How Are You?' Student Movement Becomes Nationwide Phenomenon." *Hankyoreh International,* December 17, 2013. Accessed May 30, 2014. http://english.hani.co.kr/arti /english_edition/e_national/615717.html.

Song, Jesook. *Living on Your Own: Single Women, Rental Housing, and Post-Revolutionary Affect in Contemporary South Korea.* Albany: State University of New York Press, 2014.

———, ed. *New Millennium South Korea: Neoliberal Capitalism and Transnational Movements.* New York: Routledge, 2010.

———. *South Koreans in the Debt Crisis: The Creation of a Neoliberal Welfare Society.* Durham, NC: Duke University Press, 2009.

Song Kyŏng-hwa, and Kim Sŏng-hwan. "Miguksan soegogi 'sŏngnan minshim' " (American beef "angry crowds"). *Hankyoreh,* May 5, 2008.

"South Korean Hold Candlelight Vigil to Protest against Alleged Election Meddling." *Reuters,* August 3, 2013. Accessed November 30, 2015. http:// www.reuters.com/video/2013/08/03/south-korean-hold-candlelight-vigil-to -p?videoId=244552784&videoChannel=13421.

"South Korea Youth Unemployment." *The Global Economy.* Accessed June 20, 2014. http://www.theglobaleconomy.com/South-Korea/Youth _unemployment.

"South Korea's Spreading Poster Protests." *BBC News,* December 19, 2013. Accessed May 13, 2014. http://www.bbc.com/news/blogs-news-from -clscwhere-25450218.

Sparks, Colin. "The Internet and the Global Public Sphere." In *Mediated Politics: Communication in the Future of Democracy,* edited by W. Lance Bennett and Robert M. Entman, 75–95. Cambridge: Cambridge University Press, 2001.

Squires, Catherine. "The Black Press and the State." In *Counterpublics and the State,* edited by Robert Asen and Daniel C. Brouwer, 111–126. Albany: State University of New York Press, 2001.

Statistics Korea. *2009 Han'guk ŭi sahoe jip'yo chuyo kyŏlkwa* (2009 major social indices in Korea). Statistics Korea, 2009. Accessed July 25, 2013. http://

kostat.go.kr/portal/korea/kor_nw/2/1/index.board?bmode=read&aSeq
=69876.

Steinmetz, Katy. "And Oxford's Word of the Year Is . . ." *Time,* November 18, 2013. Accessed December 29, 2014. http://newsfeed.time.com/2013/11/18 /and-oxfords-word-of-the-year-is/.

Sunstein, Cass. *Republic.com.* Princeton, NJ: Princeton University Press, 2001.

Synott, John P. *Teacher Unions, Social Movements and the Politics of Education in Asia: South Korea, Taiwan and the Philippines.* Burlington, VT: Ashgate, 2002.

Tangdae Pip'yŏng, ed. *Kŭdaenŭn wae ch'otpurŭl kkŭsyŏnnayo* (Why did you put out the candle?). Seoul: Tangdae, 2009.

Tarrow, Sidney. "Cycles of Collective Action: Between Moments of Madness and the Repertoire of Contention." *Social Science History* 17, no. 2 (1993): 281–307.

———. "Review of the Logic of Connective Action: Digital Media and the Personalization of Contentious Politics." *Perspectives on Politics* 12, no. 2 (2014): 468–470.

Tilly, Charles. "Contentious Repertoires in Great Britain, 1758–1834." In *Repertoire and Cycles of Collection Action,* edited by Mark Traugott, 15–42. Durham, NC: Duke University Press, 1995.

Traugott, Mark. "Barricades as Repertoire: Continuities and Discontinuities in the History of French Contention." In *Repertoire and Cycles of Collection Action,* edited by Mark Traugott, 43–56. Durham, NC: Duke University Press, 1995.

"Ttŏorŭnŭn 'int'ŏnet kongnonjang' chumok: Chŏhangŭi mek'a 'taŭm" (Rising Internet public sphere: Daum is the mecca of resistance). *Kyŏnghyang Sinmun,* May 27, 2008.

van Gelder, Sarah. "Introduction: How Occupy Wall Street Changes Every-thing." In *This Changes Everything: Occupy Wall Street and the 99% Movement,* edited by Sarah van Gelder, 1–13. San Francisco: Berrett-Koehler Publishers, 2011.

Vinocur, Nicholas. "Charlie Hebdo, Satirical Weekly, Publishes Cartoons of the Prophet Mohammad." *Huffington Post,* September 19, 2012. Accessed July 14, 2013. http://www.huffingtonpost.com/2012/09/19/charlie -Achebdo-publishes-cartoons-of-the-prophet-mohammad_n_1895780 .html.

Warner, Michael. *Publics and Counterpublics.* New York: Zone Books, 2002.

Weber, Max. "The Nature of Charismatic Authority and Its Routinization." In *Max Weber: On Charisma and Institution Building,* edited by S. N. Eisenstadt, 48–65. Chicago: University of Chicago Press, 1968. Originally published 1922.

Wellman, Barry. "Changing Connectivity: A Future History of Y2.03K." *Sociological Research Online* 4 (2000). Accessed October 16, 2013. http://www .socresonline.org.uk/4/4/wellman.html.

Wi, Hyeongseok, and Wonjae Lee. "The Norm of Normlessness: Structural Correlates of a Trolling Community." In *Proceedings of the 2014 ACM Conference on Web Science,* 275–276. New York: ACM, 2014.

Williams, Andrew Paul, and John C. Tedesco. *The Internet Election: Perspectives on the Web in Campaign 2004.* Lanham, MD: Rowman & Littlefield, 2006.

Williams, Raymond. *Marxism and Literature.* Oxford: Oxford University Press, 1977.

"Witnesses Report Rioting in Tunisian Town." *Reuters Africa,* December 19, 2010. Accessed June 30, 2014. http://af.reuters.com/article/topNews /idAFJOE6BI06U20101219.

Wojcieszak, Magdalena. "'Don't Talk to Me': Effects of Ideologically Homogeneous Online Groups and Politically Dissimilar Offline Ties on Extremism." *New Media & Society* 12 (2010): 637–655.

Woo-Cumings, Meredith. "South Korean Anti-Americanism." *Japan Policy Research Institute Working Paper* 93 (2003). Accessed October 7, 2013. http:// www.jpri.org/publications/workingpapers/wp93.html.

Wortham, Stanton. *Narratives in Action.* New York: Teachers College Press, 2001.

Wu Sŏk-hun and Pak Kwŏn-il. *88 manwon sedae* (Generation 880-thousand won). Seoul: Redian, 2007.

Yi Ch'ang-ho. "Ch'ŏngsonyŏn'gwa sot'ong chisok'aeya" (Need to communicate with youth). *Kyŏnghyang Sinmun,* June 6, 2008.

Yi Chong-wŏn and Yu Sŏng-ho. *Ch'ŏngsonyŏn dul'ŭi onlain keim iyong silt'ae yŏn'gu* (Study on youth online game use). Seoul: Korean Youth Development institute, 2003.

Yi Hae-jin. "Ch'ŏtpul chiphoewa 10 tae ch'amyŏjaŭi chuch'e hyŏngsŏng" (Candlelight protests and the subjectivity of the teenage participants). In *Ch'ŏtpul chiphoewa Hankuk sahoe* (Candlelight protests and Korean society), edited by Hong Sŏng-t'ae, 164–205. Seoul: Munhwa Kwahak, 2009.

Yi Hyŏn. "Sinnanŭn takchang t'uŏrŭl asimnikka?" (Do you know the exhilarating hencoop tour?). *Ilgan Sports,* May 28, 2008. Accessed February 7, 2014. http://article.joins.com/news/article/article.asp?ctg=-1&total_id =3163722.

Yi Hyŏn-hŭi. *Saeroun Han'guksa* (New history of Korea). Paju: Jimmundang, 2005.

Yi Hyŏng-sam. "K'at'usa 50nyŏn kkumdo yŏngŏro kkunŭn ellit'ŭ pyŏngsadŭl" (Fifty years of KATUSA: Elite soldiers who even dream in English).

Sindong'a, May 2001. Accessed July 20, 2015. http://www.donga.com/docs /magazine/new_donga/200105/nd2001050360.html.

Yi, Jeong Duk. "Globalization and Recent Changes to Daily Life in the Republic of Korea." In *Korea and Globalization: Politics, Economics and Culture,* edited by James B. Lewis and Amadu Sesay, 10–35. London: Routledge, 2002.

Yi Kap-yun. "Ch'otpul chiphoe ch'amyŏja ŭi inku sahoehakchŏk t'ŭksŏng mit chŏngch'ijŏk chŏnghyqnggwa t'aedo" (Social and demographic characteristics and political orientations of participants in the candlelight protests of 2008). *Hankuk chŏngdang hakhoebo* (Journal of the association for Korean party studies) 9, no. 1 (2010): 95–120.

Yi Kil-ho. *Urinŭn DC* (We are DC). Seoul: Imagine, 2012.

Yi Kil-sŏng. "'P'ik'et tŭlcha,' 'andoenda,' tto kallasŏn 'ch'otpulchip'oe'" ("Raise the flag," "No": The candlelight protest is split again). *Chosun Ilbo,* May 7, 2008. Accessed May 15, 2015. http://news.chosun.com/site/data/html_dir /2008/05/07/2008050700001.html.

Yi Min-ji and Pak Tae-yong. "Changgapch'a samang yŏjungsaeng migun mujoe p'yŏnggyŏlŭl pogo" (Upon the acquittal of the GIs who killed the schoolgirls). *Hankyoreh,* November 23, 2002.

Yi Mun-jae, and Ch'a Hyŏng-sŏk. "02nyŏn olhaeŭi inmul haengdonghanŭn netijŭn" (02 'person of the year' is the activist-netizen). *Sisa Journal,* December 23, 2002. Accessed September 11, 2013. http://www.sisapress .com/news/read.php?idxno=1609.

Yi Ŏ-yŏng. "Chiralt'an, sakwat'anŭl kiŏk hasipnikka?" (Do you remember tear gas bombs?). *JoongAng Ilbo,* June 9, 2007. Accessed July 19, 2013. http:// article.joins.com/news/article/article.asp?Total_Id=2754975.

Yi Sang-gil. "Sunsusŏngŭi moral: Ch'ŏtpul siwie nat'anan 'oyŏm'e taehan tansang" (A moral of purity: A reflection on the idea of 'corruption' during the candlelight protests). In *Kŭdaenŭn wae ch'otpurŭl kkŭsyŏnnayo* (Why did you put out the candle?), edited by Tangdae Pip'yŏng, 89–108. Seoul: Tangdae, 2009.

Yi Yun-hŭi. "2002nyŏn wŏldŭk'ŏp kilgŏri ŭngwŏnŭi ch'ukche kongdongch'ejŏk t'ŭksŏng" (Characteristics of street cheering as festival community at the 2002 World Cup and its socio-cultural implications). *Sahoewa iron* (Society and theory) 3 (2003): 125–156.

Yoo, Hyejong. "The Candlelight Girls' Playground: Nationalism as Art of Dialogy, the 2008 Candlelight Vigil Protests in South Korea." *Invisible Culture: Spectacle East Asia* 15 (2010). Available at: https://www.rochester .edu/in_visible_culture/Issue_15/articles/yoo/yoo.html.

Zielenziger, Michael. *Shutting Out the Sun: How Japan Created Its Own Lost Generation.* New York: Random House, 2006.

Zunes, Stephen. "Occupy Fizzled, but Made 99% a Force." *CNN,* September 17, 2012. Accessed June 4, 2014. http://www.cnn.com/2012/09/17/opinion /zunes-occupy-movement/index.html.

Zur, Dafna. "The Construction of the Child in Korean Children's Magazines, 1908–1950." PhD diss., University of British Columbia, 2011.

Index

Abelmann, Nancy, 172n13, 174n38
activism: as career, 149. *See also*
   activist identity; candlelight
   protests; democratization
   movement; Internet-born youth
   activism; oppositional movement;
   social movement tradition; student
   movement tradition
activist identity, 87, 97, 103, 136,
   157
actor-network theory (ANT), 168n55
Adbusters (magazine), 6, 155
Afreeca TV, 18
Agora (discussion board), 18, 37, 38,
   110, 113
Allen, Danielle, 170n71
alternative news sources, 17, 37–38
Anderson, Benedict: *Imagined*
   Communities, 11
ANT (actor-network theory),
   168n55
anti-Americanism: among Internet
   communities, 39–40; and bin
   Laden, 53; candlelight vigils viewed
   as, 61–62, 69; and postauthoritarian
   youth, 92–93, 94–95, 96, 101
April Revolution (1960), 25–26
Arab Spring, 6, 7, 155, 156, 199n19
"Are you doing alright?" mass
   gatherings, 161
Asen, Robert, 164n14, 164n15,
   166n26, 184n37
Ash, James, 163n6
Asian financial crisis (1997), 31–32
attention economy, 8, 164n18

Bakhtin, Mikhail, 126, 183n27
Bauman, Richard, 19
beef importation, *see* U.S. beef
   importation
Bennett, Lance, 13
Berlant, Lauren, 134, 141, 197nn5–6
bin Laden, Osama, 53
Bin-na (interviewee), 36, 143,
   145–147, 149–150, 151, 160
Bolter, Jay, 165n19
bovine spongiform encephalopathy
   (BSE), *see* U.S. beef importation
boyd, danah, 12
Brouwer, Daniel, 164n14, 164n15,
   184n37
Briggs, Charles, 19
BSE (bovine spongiform
   encephalopathy), *see* U.S. beef
   importation
Bush, George W., 32, 39, 59–60

Callon, Michel, 168n55
candle girls, 4, 111, 132, 196n1
Candle Girls' Korea, 17–18, 113
candlelight generation, 15
candlelight protests: as alternative
   political space, 59, 61, 76–77, 78;
   changing nature of protest through,
   152–153; commentators on, 14–15;
   critiques of, 151, 160; on education,
   3, 106, 119–120, 124, 147, 148; and
   nonparticipants, 18–19; overview of,
   3–4, 160; participants in, 15–16; as
   protest repertoire, 4, 85, 106, 152,
   160; and Roh Moo-hyun, 3, 79–81,

reactions to, 110, 117–119; and Lee
Myung-bak, 114; media coverage
of, 193n40; media on mad cow
disease, 190n3; overview of,
109–110, 191n18. *See also* candlelight
protests (beef importation) (2008)
user-created forums, 18
U.S. military, 2, 16, 178n11
U.S. military vehicular incident
(2002): approach to, 20, 45–46,
63–64; acquittal of defendants,
2, 48–49, 177n5; alternative
newspapers and Web sites on, 17;
and bin Laden, 53; Bush's apology
for, 59–60, 62; captivation with,
10–11; description of incident, 1;
images circulated on, 50–52; initial
protests after, 45, 50–51, 61;
Internet users' reactions to, 48,
49–50, 57, 59–60; mainstream
media on reactions to, 49; parodies
in reaction to, 12, 53–54; *PD
Journal* on, 57; personal and
commemorative messages on,
54–57; and 2002 presidential
election, 65, 67, 68–69; symbols
and user names in reaction to, 52;
user-created forums on, 18. *See also*
candlelight protests (U.S. military
vehicular incident) (2002)

Variant Creutzfeldt-Jakob disease
(vCJD), 110
vernacular discourse, 10, 78, 82,
155–156
viral phenomenon, 9

Voice of the People (online news site),
17

Walker, Mark, 2, 48–49, 53, 177n5.
See also U.S. military vehicular
incident (2002)
Warner, Michael, 11
WikiLeaks, 14
Wikipedia, 12
Williams, Raymond, 10, 129, 152,
191n13
Winter Olympics (2002) skating
scandal, 39–40
women: in World Cup gatherings,
47–48
Wŏn-hŭi (interviewee), 87, 93–94,
94–96
World Cup soccer tournament
(2002): and candlelight vigils, 47,
60, 88–89, 163n5, 180n31; national
impact of, 1–2, 46–47, 58, 90–91;
and women and teenagers, 47–48
Wortham, Stanton, 19

Ye-jin (interviewee), 112, 130, 136
Yi Kil-ho, 13, 38
Yi Ŏ-yŏng, 28
youth, *see* college students; high
school students; Internet-born youth
activism; millennials; South Korean
youth
youth discipline centers (*kŭkki
hullyŏn*), 89–90
Yun-ji (interviewee), 89–90

Zur, Dafna, 24

ABOUT THE AUTHOR

Jiyeon Kang is assistant professor of communication studies and Korean studies at the University of Iowa. Her research has appeared in *Communication and Critical/Cultural Studies, Journal of Broadcasting and Electronic Media, Quarterly Journal of Speech Communication, Journal of Korean Studies,* and *Global Networks.*